THE EARLY WORKS
OF FELIX MENDELSSOHN

WITHDRAWN

MUSICOLOGY: A BOOK SERIES
Edited by F. Joseph Smith and Ralph P. Locke

This book is part of a series. The publisher will accept continuation orders which may be cancelled at any time and which provide for automatic billing and shipping of each title in the series upon publication. Please write for details.

The Early Works of Felix Mendelssohn

A Study in the Romantic Sonata Style

Greg Vitercik

*Middlebury College
Vermont, USA*

Gordon and Breach

Philadelphia   Reading   Paris   Montreux   Tokyo   Melbourne

Gordon and Breach Science Publishers

5301 Tacony Street, Drawer 330
Philadelphia, Pennsylvania 19137
United States of America

Post Office Box 90
Reading, Berkshire RG1 8JL
United Kingdom

58, rue Lhomond
75005 Paris
France

Post Office Box 161
1820 Montreux 2
Switzerland

3-14-9, Okubo
Shinjuku-ku, Tokyo 169
Japan

Private Bag 8
Camberwell, Victoria 3124
Australia

Library of Congress Cataloging-in-Publication Data

Vitercik, Gregory John.
  The early works of Felix Mendelssohn : a study in the romantic
sonata style / Greg Vitercik.
    p.   cm. -- (Musicology ; 12)
  Includes bibliographical references and index.
  ISBN 2-88124-536-6
  1. Mendelssohn-Bartholdy, Felix, 1809-1847. Instrumental music.
2. Sonata form.   I. Title.   II. Series: Musicology ; v. 12.
NL410.M5V6   1992
784'.092--dc20   91-43062
                                                                CIP

CONTENTS

INTRODUCTION TO THE SERIES

The Gordon and Breach Musicology series, a companion to the *Journal of Musicological Research*, covers a creative range of musical topics, from historical and theoretical subjects to social and philosophical studies. Volumes thus far published show the extent of this broad spectrum, from *Music and Its Social Meanings, Music from the Middle Ages through the Twentieth Century: Essays in Honor of Gwynn S. McPeek* and *Witnesses and Scholars: Studies in Musical Biography* to *From Vivaldi to Viotti: A History of the Early Classical Violin Concerto*. The editors also welcome interdisciplinary studies, ethnomusicological works and performances analyses. With this series, it is our aim to expand the field and definition of musical exploration and research.

ACKNOWLEDGEMENTS

It is a ritual of the writing process to observe that a few words of thanks cannot begin to convey the gratitude of the writer to the various people who have been involved in that process; I find that I can only repeat this truism, observing that, like all rituals, its truth only becomes clear in the performance. This study is based closely on my dissertation at the State University of New York at Stony Brook; the extraordinary musical intelligence, patience, good humor and common sense of my advisor, Professor Leo Treitler, and the members of my committee, Professors Richard Kramer and Charles Rosen at Stony Brook and Professor Douglas Johnson at Rutgers University, sustained and inspired me through a long and often baffling task. I would also like to thank Professors Sarah Fuller at Stony Brook and Jane Bowers at the University of Wisconsin–Milwaukee for their encouragement and advice. For its present form I am particularly grateful to the series editors, F. Joseph Smith and Ralph P. Locke, for their encouragement and suggestions; to Mary Frandsen for her careful reading of the manuscript and preparation of the index; and to Robert and Ellen Eliason of Toad Hill Music Engraving, Lyme, New Hampshire, for their imaginative and patient preparation of the analytical examples.

Research for this study and the invaluable opportunity to observe the work of Professor Carl Dahlhaus at the Technische Universität in Berlin were supported by a fellowship from the Fulbright Commission. Much of the writing was accomplished with the help of a dissertation fellowship from the Graduate School of the State University of New York at Stony Brook. The preparation of the manuscript for publication was in part underwritten by a grant from the Teaching Resources Committee at Middlebury College. Again, my gratitude far exceeds my ability to express it.

Finally, it has always seemed to me that the organization of this part of a book was backwards. The person who played the most demanding and unrewarding role in supporting this process was, of course, my wife, Carol Murray, who revealed seemingly limitless reserves of patience and forbearing. It is with affection and delight that this study is dedicated to her.

ix

CHAPTER 1

THE MENDELSSOHN PROBLEM

If those compositions (including single movements from larger works) which have the qualities of the *Hebrides* Overture were set apart and regarded as the only authentic works of Mendelssohn, there would be no disputing his claim to rank among the great composers. Perhaps when scholars of a thousand years hence decipher European music of the five hundred years between 1450 and 1950, they will conclude that the pseudo-Mendelssohn of early Victorian idolatry was not the same person as the master of the *Midsummer-Night's Dream*, or the *Hebrides*, and many single movements ranging from the tragic scherzo of the F minor Quartet, to those *Songs Without Words* of which the reckless prettiness achieves real beauty. Even to us Mendelssohn is one of the strangest problems in musical history.[1]

—Donald Francis Tovey

That abominable platitude for the trombones with which the thing begins and which is never dropped until you are bored and worried out of your senses by it, will be cited in times to come as conclusive proof that there must have been a pseudo-Mendelssohn: they will not believe that the composer of Fingal and the Midsummer Night's Dream music could possibly have perpetuated the Lobgesang.[2]

—George Bernard Shaw

Every composer is capable of surprising inequalities in his output, but no one has achieved more baffling extremes than Mendelssohn, and in no other instance does the reputation of one group of works cast so forbidding a shadow over our assessment of the others. The tremendous prestige of Beethoven's late works is in no way threatened by the disconcerting fact that they were written by the composer of *Christus am Oelberge*, and Schubert's early quartets and sonatas do not arouse suspicions about the stature of his *Winterreise* or the C-major Symphony. But Paul, Elijah, Athalie, and a host of companions from Mendelssohns's later years lurk menacingly along the approaches to the Octet, the *Hebrides* Overture, the *Midsummer Night's Dream* Overture, and a number of less well known early works. Understandably, but unfortunately, the platitudinous busywork and emotional poverty of these monuments to early Victorian seriousness seem to represent an almost insurmountable barrier to the study of the remarkable series of works Mendelssohn composed in the latter half of the 1820s: if the composer's "mature" works are so distressingly weak, what could anyone expect to find in his youthful creations?

In a majority of cases, ignoring a composer's less successful works can be justified through an appeal to that helpful coincidence of historical method, chronology: after the defects of the offending pieces have been identified as symptoms of immaturity, the music can be isolated in the category "early works" and treated as a benign parasite on the body of the acceptable canon. In the rare case like Schumann's, the situation is reversed, and the most troublesome pieces turn out to be late works which prove to be lamentable evidence of the composer's tragic decline.

Considerations of genre often fulfill a similar function to that of chronology, isolating certain relatively unsuccessful or uncharacteristic works as attempts—often early attempts—to deal with uncongenial stylistic traditions. The irrelevance of Weber's sonatas and chamber music to an estimation of his position in the history of nineteenth-century music is a clear example of this. Beethoven himself invoked both of these considerations is an attempt to protect his *Christus am Oelberge* from hostile criticism when it was published, eight years after the first performance:

> Arrange for the oratorio, and in general everything else, to be reviewed by whomever you like . . . . The only point to consider in connection with my oratorio is that it was my first work in that style and, moreover, an early work, and that it was written in a fortnight and during all kinds of disturbances and other unpleasant and distressing events in my life (my brother happened to be suffering from a mortal disease) . . . . What is quite certain is that now I should compose an absolutely different oratorio from what I composed then.[3]

With Mendelssohn, however, the application of chronology is not quite so straightforward, since the finest of his works—those compositions Shaw and even Wagner admired—are all early; we do not usually think of a composer slipping into his tragic decline at the age of twenty-five. In any event, this does not address the annoying fact that most of the works written after 1834 enjoyed almost universal contemporary renown. It was, after all, in 1840, not in the 1820s, and in a review of the D-minor Piano Trio, not of the *Midsum-*

mer Night's Dream Overture or the A-major String Quintet, that Schumann hailed Mendelssohn as "the Mozart of the nineteenth century, the most brilliant musician, the one who most clearly sees through the contradictions of the age and for the first time reconciles them."[4]

The discovery of pseudo-Mendelssohn by Tovey and Shaw would seem to facilitate a reappraisal of the composer's achievement by offering a correction for both the failure of chronology to provide a workable ordering of the music and for our complete lack of sympathy with the tenets of mid-nineteenth-century taste. In light of this discovery, the works of unquestioned excellence would be held to represent the output of the immensely talented, vigorously original member of the early romantic generation we know as Mendelssohn, while the uniformly unpalatable works could be isolated as forgeries from a later date written by a facile, derivative, classicist imitator now unmasked as pseudo-Mendelssohn. The method is extreme, but the problem is unique. A rational appreciation of Mendelssohn's early works is simply not possible unless some way is found to free them from the ghastly stigma of having been written by the composer of the *Lobgesang*.

Unfortunately, even so radical a strategy does not seem to have opened the way to a completely unbiased assessment of Mendelssohn's early works. One of the most difficult barriers—and one unwittingly reinforced by the discovery of pseudo-Mendelssohn—is biographical. The "real" Mendelssohn, the one on whose works critical attention might be focused without embarrassment, turns out to have been little more than a child, and it simply goes against the critical grain to devote serious effort to the explication of the works of a sixteen-year-old composer, no matter how fine those works might be.

All too often, the perhaps unspoken reaction has been to ascribe the most characteristic, Mendelssohnian features of these works to a mysteriously rare quality best characterized as "youthful spontaneity." This is, in fact, so rare a quality that Mendelssohn appears to have been one of only two undoubted possessors of it; the juvenilia of no other composer—with the obvious exception of Mozart—shows more than very occasional evidence of it.

Of course, youthful spontaneity might seem to be a highly commendable trait for a composer to possess. But in critical practice, its discovery seems to have resulted in the notion that Mendelssohn's achievement in these works is fundamentally unanalyzable. Although the craftsmanship exhibited by these works is invariably mentioned, attention is usually focused on generalities of scoring and part-writing as evidence of the prodigy's astonishing talents. Those talents are indeed astonishing and worthy of comment, but these observations rarely lead to a consideration of more fundamental compositional strategies.

Even Tovey fell under the influence of this biographical curiosity, and as a result he often seems to have found it almost impossible to take Mendelssohn seriously as a composer, even when he was favorably disposed toward the work at hand. Having declared, for example, that the Octet is "unmistakably a work of genius," he can only bring himself to observe that the finale is "very boyish, but so amusing that it wears a good deal better than many a more responsible utterance."[5] Similarly, although he could hope that "some day, when current criticism knows a little more about form, we may come to recognize that the best works of Mendelssohn are not more remarkable for their scoring than for the Haydnesque freedom of their form,"[6] in the course of the essay on the *Hebrides* Overture from which the quotation at the head of this chapter is taken, he lamented, with the condescension of a sympathetic but disapproving headmaster, that

> form really meant little to his artistic consciousness: he judged of forms as schoolboys judge of 'good form'; and instead of developing classical forms on vital evolutionary lines as Beethoven developed them he practiced each form only to demolish it by easy short cuts to effect.[7]

This is a typical—if uniquely Toveyesque—expression of the complex of presuppositions that have shaped much of the critical consideration of Mendelssohn's early works. As a result of these presuppositions, the works, although generally admired, have attracted little analytical attention: there is small scope for critical explication of a style that treats form in the manner Tovey describes. Furthermore, in Tovey's formulation Mendelssohn is simply excluded from a place in the history of the development of sonata forms: his works, fluent but shallow, can offer no evidence concerning the attempt to accommodate sonata-form procedures to the characteristics of the romantic musical language.

It is the purpose of this study to suggest that such an assessment is incorrect; that a close examination of Mendelssohn's early works, unencumbered by either the unfathomable mysteries of biography or the prejudice aroused by the badly tarnished prestige of the later works, will reveal an extensive and carefully worked out complex of strategies reflecting an attempt to create a specifically romantic sonata style—an attempt that, to judge by the esteem in which these works are held, was unusually successful.

Another obstacle to an understanding of Mendelssohn's style grows out of the peculiar status of sonata forms in the nineteenth century. In spite of an often expressly stated impatience with the restrictions of tradition on the part of composers of the nineteenth—and for that matter, the twentieth—century, the tremendous prestige Beethoven's works had bestowed upon the sonata-form genres made it impossible for any composer of serious ambition to avoid writing symphonies, quartets, trios, or sonatas; sonata form had become, as Rosen has put it, the "vehicle of the sublime."[8] Or, as the author of the entry "Scherzo" for the first edition of Grove's wrote in a wonderful amalgam of jargon and sensibility, "either the bold and masculine first movement form, or its sister the weaker and more feminine rondo form, must be the backbone of every piece of music with any pretension to the name."[9]

Unfortunately, neither the elements of the romantic musical language—the harmonic vocabulary and sense of phrase-structure, texture, and rhythm—nor the articulative processes in which these elements are unfolded are particularly suited to the sonata style. As a result, the sonata-form literature of the nineteenth century often seems to consist of a body of extremely problematic works in which moments of great beauty are strung together with apparently unmotivated formal gestures. For the most part, we simply overlook the problems these works pose in return for the delights they offer, and do not probe too deeply into the formal presuppositions they embody. If, in studying the classical sonata style we are becoming gradually more sensitive to the complexly reciprocal interrelations between formal articulations and the musical processes unfolded within a particular movement, in approaching the romantic sonata it often seems appropriate—in many cases absolutely essential—to consider form and content as unrelated aspects of the musical design.

At the same time, it seems clear that to at least a certain extent our tolerance for the formal incongruities of the romantic sonata derives from an inversion of the nineteenth-century scale of values. In approaching the music of this period we tend to relegate sonata-form works to a subsidiary position in their composer's output. The formal aspects of Chopin's sonatas, for example, are not subjected to intense critical scrutiny because we hold these works to be stylistic aberrations that do not accurately reflect his conception of musical coherence. And this attitude is not unfounded: we learn less about Chopin's style from his sonatas, beautiful though they often are, than we do from his Mazurkas—a situation paralleled in the study of almost every important composer of the nineteenth century, with the obvious exception of Brahms.

With Mendelssohn the situation is once again more complicated, since he is the only figure of the early romantic period whose most successful and most characteristic works are all in sonata form. Since the framework of our historical-critical expectations places sonata-form genres at the periphery of the romantic repertory, the relative tameness of Mendelssohn's more recognizably "romantic" works—the *Songs Without Words* (or the songs with words), for example—again seems to place the significance of the early works in doubt: if Mendelssohn apparently could not solve the less rigorous, but more immediately revealing problems of the typical romantic small forms, can we hope to discover anything of interest in his treatment of the tremendously more difficult sonata forms?

Here again, I would suggest that an otherwise often serviceable criterion has severely hampered out understanding of Mendelssohn's early works by imposing presuppositions that are simply irrelevant to the works themselves: the structural principles at work in the Octet or the *Hebrides* Overture have been left uninvestigated in part because of attitudes formulated in response to the *Songs Without Words* on the one hand and to the somewhat inscrutable exercises in classical forms typified by Schumann's String Quartets on the other.

The present study is intended as a preliminary contribution to the reconsideration of these received conceptions of Mendelssohn's achievement, offering an examination of the structural principles that animate the astonishing series of works written between 1825 and, roughly, 1834. The purpose of this examination is to question both the notion that the generally acknowledged excellence of these early works can be explained only in terms of the vague and essentially unanalyzable traits that constitute youthful spontaneity, and that the sureness of form they exhibit simply reflects the historically irrelevant adoption of foolproof formal patterns to a blandly malleable harmonic and melodic dialect: it is precisely in the coordination of surface detail and formal process that the most remarkable elements of that achievement shall be found.

The primary goal of this study, then, is to provide the kind of "accurate, sharp, loving description of the appearance of a work of art" that Susan Sontag has called the most valuable act of criticism.[10] The kind of description that is called for is clearly not that of the train-schedule style of writing that too often passes for critical analysis. It is, similarly, not provided in the tune-detective style of historical inquiry that leaves the page littered with specious comparisons of two measures by Mendelssohn with two measures by Bach (J. S. or C. P. E.), Pleyel, Mozart, Haydn, or Beethoven.

A truly accurate description can only arise from a study that identifies the events of the musical surface as functional elements within a coherent structural process. It is not enough, for example, to point out that the last movement of Mendelssohn's E♭-major String Quartet, Op. 12, ends with a return of the coda from the first movement and claim that in itself this provides (or perhaps fails to provide) a satisfactory rounding-off of the whole. A cyclic return breaks open the self-generated formal integrity of the individual movements of the work—an integrity that is central to the coherence of the sonata style. If this breach is not simply the result of inattention on the composer's part, the structural principles and interactions that motivate it and the network of surface articulations through which these are expressed must be revealed before the significance of the thematic return—which in itself is hardly a secret requiring comment—can be understood.

Mendelssohn's works stand particularly in need of such careful study. The elegance of his method has almost completely obscured the fact that it is a method at all, and neither the subtle delicacy of his sense of musical processes nor the techniques he developed to integrate these processes into larger formal designs have attracted sufficiently sympathetic attention: as we have seen, even Tovey mistook the luminous clarity of Mendelssohn's textures for superficiality.

In order to appreciate the range of Mendelssohn's compositional strategies, it is necessary to have a clear idea of the problems sonata style posed to composers of the nineteenth century. Chapter 2 of this study consists of an outline of some of these problems and their origins in the techniques of the classical style, as well as an examination of Mendelssohn's earliest works— works which, in spite of the astonishing sureness of technique they exhibit, illustrate the frictions inherent in the classicist-romantic sonata style. Chapter 3 is an examination of Mendelssohn's approaches to these problems in his first unquestionable masterpiece, the Octet, Op. 20, a work in which each of the four movements reveals a radically different realization of sonata-form principles. Chapters 4 and 5 are studies of two compositional problems that are of particular importance for the romantic style—the coordination of the thematic pattern to the underlying structural processes of a sonata-form movement, and principles of cyclic form—while Chapter 6 is a brief consideration of the problems posed by Mendelssohn's later sonata-form works. (It should perhaps be noted that the analyses in these later chapters are not meant to encompass every salient, or even interesting, aspect of the works examined.)

Since scores for most of the works to be discussed are readily available, musical examples—which can often distort the meaning of a passage by isolating it from its context—are provided only where the danger of misrepresentation is small and the convenience for the discussion is great.11

CHAPTER 2

THE CLASSICIST HERITAGE

Since its emergence as the preeminent vehicle of musical expression in the latter part of the eighteenth century, sonata form has been the subject of intense and multifarious analytical scrutiny. In the twentieth century, a particularly fruitful line of inquiry has been concerned with the central role of a clearly articulated harmonic structure in the generation of sonata-form movements. The advantages of this conception over the view of sonata form as a melodically organized structure generated by a dialectic opposition of two principle themes are now generally acknowledged. In approaching the sonata-form works of Mendelssohn, it is not my purpose to attempt a reformulation of the fundamental analytical presuppositions of this conception—presuppositions worked out by such diverse figures as Tovey, Schenker, Rosen, and Ratner. But in order to better understand the problems Mendelssohn was addressing in these works, it will be useful to consider these presuppositions from a somewhat unaccustomed vantage point—one that places greater emphasis on the process of closure within the formal design than is normally the case.

The fundamental principles of closure as they relate to artistic forms have been described by Barbara Herrnstein Smith in the following way:

> We tend to speak of conclusions when a sequence of events has a relatively high degree of structure, when, in other words, we can perceive these events as related to one another by some principle of organization or design that implies the existence of a definite termination point. Under these circumstances, the occurrence of the terminal event is a confirmation of expectations that have been established by the structure of the sequence, and is usually distinctly gratifying.[1]

The significance of formal closure obviously does not possess equally wide-ranging explanatory power for all musical styles. But the fundamental role of an expansive and explicit process of harmonic resolution in the classical sonata style is clear evidence that a broadly laid-out area of concluding stability, organized in an immediately discernible pattern, is of central importance for the effectiveness of the style.

The perception of a principle of organization that controls the interrelation of events within a movement requires that the identity of these events as functional elements in the structure of the movement be established with absolute clarity. In the classical sonata style, this is accomplished through the coordination of a distinctive and memorable thematic pattern with a large-scale harmonic design that generates the structure of the entire movement: striking changes in the surface texture—the introduction of a new theme or the reappearance of an already familiar one, for example—mark significant moments in the unfolding harmonic structure. This coordination of surface events and underlying structure—the dramatization of the structure through a specific sequence of surface articulations—is one of the most distinctive characteristics of the classical sonata style. It will be useful for the present study to consider in some detail the role of this fundamental principle of the sonata style within the large-scale process of closure.

A useful tool for examining the nature of the process is provided in Tovey's distinction between works generated by the elaboration of a single musical texture and works in which the form is defined by the shape in which a variety of contrasting textures are arranged.[2] A brief consideration of the fundamental differences between the techniques of the later baroque and of the classical sonata style—the most highly developed examples of these two organizational principles—should help place the significance of closural processes for the classical style in clearer focus.

In many of the typical musical forms of the baroque—fugue, concerto, or fantasy, for example—the maintenance of a uniform texture or the consistent alternation of a limited number of contrasting textures rather than the deployment of a considerable variety of textures in a striking or memorable pattern is a fundamental generating principle of a movement. These forms are, therefore, essentially paratactic in structure, since the generating principle governing them does not, a priori, establish a pattern of events that will be followed over the course of the movement. Since closure is dependent on our ability to identify a principle of organization relating events to one another as elements of a sequence, paratactic structures do not, in themselves, establish the conditions necessary to determine a concluding point. Discussing the effect of paratactic structure in poetry, Smith observes that "the reader will have no idea from the poem's structure how or when it will conclude" because "the coherence of the poem will not be dependent on the sequential arrangement of its major thematic units."[3] Tovey makes such the same point when he observes that a sufficiently long extract, taken at random from a sonata-form movement, offers enough information to allow its place within the movement to be predicted with relative confidence, while the same confidence is not possible in dealing with an extract from a texture-generated work—a fugue from *The Well-Tempered Clavier*, for example.[4] In the former, the generating principle of the movement posits a structural relation between events that allows us to predict, in a general way, a sequence of types of events that will be followed in the course of the movement and, conversely, to predict the location of any specific kind of event within that sequence. In the latter, the generating principle only posits a kind of texture that will be maintained until the piece comes to an end. Since the relation between events in such a piece is not determined by the generating principle, both the succession of events and in particular the nature—and location—of the terminal event are unpredictable.

A paratactic formal structure, then, apparently would require special measures to achieve a stable and convincing close—measures Smith identifies as "terminal modifications."[5] In the music of the baroque, these modifications serve to neutralize the generating principle of the movement, bringing the kaleidoscopic succession of events to a halt and justifying "the absence of further development."[6]

In the ritornello concerto, for example, a complete statement of the opening ritornello in the tonic normally serves to close off a movement. The reappearance of this stable structural unit—stable both because it remains in the tonic throughout and because its initial presentation has established it as a self-contained formal gesture shaped by striking thematic and textural characteristics—is a signal that the alternation of solo and tutti passages which is the fundamental generating principle of a concerto movement is to be understood as no longer being in effect. As Smith points out, a return to the opening element of a paratactic structure implies that the work is about to end simply because it suggests that there is nowhere left to go—that the circle is closed.[7]

Similarly, in fugal writing the avoidance of clearly articulated cadences that results from the continual overlapping of seemingly independent melodic lines is a fundamental characteristic of the style—a natural outgrowth of the obbligato part-writing that defines fugal texture. Some sort of terminal modification of the texture, some break in the almost seamless flow, is necessary if this generating principle is to be disengaged and the piece is to come to an end. This modification therefore normally involves a clear break in the contrapuntal fabric: a long-held pedal; a sudden shift to a more or less homophonic texture; or the introduction of a particularly dense stretto. But nothing in the nature of fugue stipulates a sequence of events which must occur before this terminal modification can take place: each paratactic structure sets its own course, and its conclusion is, if not arbitrary, unpredictable.

In light of this, the tendency typified by Cherubini's attempt in his *Cours de contrepoint et de fugue* to establish a sequential arrangement for the deployment of stretto in fugue—beginning with the most widely spaced entrances and proceeding to the closest strettos at the end of the piece—can be understood as an attempt, in an age acutely concerned with the shape a musical form presented, to impose an organizational principle derived from a fixed succession of textural events onto a paratactic, texture-defined structure.[8] In Cherubini's scheme, a terminal modification is transformed into a shape-defining generating principle. The unnatural stiffness that is the outstanding characteristic of the scholastic fugue is a measure of the violence this kind of transformation does to the fundamental principles of the style.

Even in baroque forms which are organized, to a greater or lesser extent, on the basis of shape, formally defined closural processes do not necessarily play a particularly strong role in the organization of the piece. Binary dance forms, for example, normally display an overall symmetry that is usually rendered in the following way:

A B : A B (melodic pattern)

a b : b a (harmonic pattern)

In such a form, closure would seem to be a function of the interlocking, reinforcing symmetries of the harmonic and melodic patterns. Indeed, these symmetries are emphasized by an approximate balance of proportions between the two halves of the movement that is itself emphasized by the obligatory repetition of each of them.[9]

Often, however, this thematic symmetry is reduced to a parallelism between the opening and closing measures of each half, so that a more accurate rendering of the melodic pattern would be A–x–B : A–y–B in which A and B are each perhaps between two and four measures long, and x an y—representing the bulk of each half of the movement—are related only insofar as almost any material that a baroque composer could spin out from a motivic cell will bear a resemblance to any other material developed from that cell. Similarly, the harmonic symmetry is often only a correspondence between the initial and terminal harmonic events of each half, while the internal harmonic structures of the two sections may bear no particularly strong relation to one another.[10]

In cases like these, the sense of overall form is less the product of an interactive pattern of melodic and harmonic events than of a certain equilibrium of proportions, and the finality of the closing cadence of the second half results less from its position within a sequence of events than from the similarity of that final cadence to the cadence at the end of the first half of the piece—a similarity that functions something like a rhyme.

The da capo aria, on the other hand, would seem to represent a clear example of a shape-organized form, with closure established by the repetition of the entire first part of the aria after the introduction of contrasting material, resulting in the familiar ABA pattern. But again, nothing in the generating principles of the aria form, which like the ritornello concerto is pieced together through the alternation of solo and tutti passages, suggests the necessity of this return, and the result is a formalized balance of parts that Tovey dismissed as "foolproof symmetry."[11] Like the return of the opening ritornello in a concerto movement, the restatement in a da capo aria closes off the generative alternation of textures, but the return is no longer a terminal modification in any normal sense. It has expanded to cover nearly one half of the entire design, and the pattern of events it reveals is so rigidly defined and immediately self-evident that the active anticipation of the achievement of repose that is essential to the process of closure is reduced to little more than the passive observation of a decorously unfolding foregone conclusion.

Although the largest outlines of the thematic pattern of a work in sonata form—which for Tovey represented the only significant example of a shape-organized music—might appear to be identical to the ABA structure of the da capo aria, the mechanism of closure operates in a completely different way, growing out of the fundamentally different role of texture in the organization of the form. In sonata style, sharply differentiated changes of texture are deployed in a pattern that articulates a relatively straightforward harmonic structure—a large-scale motion from tonic stability through harmonic tension and eventually to resolution. As a result of this shift from texture as the generating principle of a movement to texture as an articulative agent, the changes of texture within a movement take on a special formal significance rooted in the identification of various textures with particular events in the harmonic structure. This structural significance is manifested in the relation of the textures to one another established by their position within a comprehensible and memorable shape.

The most striking textural events in a sonata-form movement serve to mark the central events of the harmonic design: the establishment of the tonic key at the beginning of the movement; the initiation of the move away from the tonic; and the establishment of a secondary key as an opposition to the tonic.[12] This opposition is prolonged in the central section of the movement,

which is characterized by motivic fragmentation and rapid tonal disloca-
tions, and is resolved in the closing section, which recapitulates the thematic
pattern of the first section but remains in the tonic throughout. In preparing
an approach to the study of Mendelssohn's treatment of sonata form, it will
be useful to consider the care with which these formal elements were treated
in the classical style.

The first three events—the establishment of the tonic, the move away from
the tonic, and the establishment of the secondary key area—are normally
marked by specific, and strongly marked, contrasts of texture—thematic
statements, transitional passages of rapid harmonic motion and motivic fragmentation, and passages of cadential stability—that weld the first section of
the movement, the exposition, into a large, self-contained structural unit. The
clearly defined textural articulation of these harmonic incidents dramatizes
them, establishing their identity as formal events. The repetition of the entire
exposition, common in the classical period and occasionally found even in
works written at the end of the nineteenth century, serves both to reinforce
the memorability of the pattern these events form and to establish the exposition as a single structural unit within the movement by unambiguously marking off its boundaries.

The striking memorability of the structure of the exposition—both in its
largest contours and in the internal arrangement of its elements—is essential
to the closural process of the form. This process is based on the reinterpretation of the structure of the exposition and is rendered dramatic by the sense of
anticipation the reworking of a familiar pattern engenders: if the course of
events established in the exposition were not memorable, the process of recapitulation would be irrelevant.

Within the exposition, the establishment of the secondary key area represents one of the most significant defining characteristics of the classical sonata style. In the typical baroque forms, a variety of key areas are touched
upon in the course of the movement, but none are established with such solidity that, in Tovey's words, "the starting-point disappears below the horizon."[13] Consequently, the harmonic action of the movement "produces
neither the means nor necessity for emphasis on returns to the tonic"[14]—emphasis that lies at the heart of the sonata style.

In the classical sonata, the sharp break in texture at the arrival in the secondary key—usually marked by a striking thematic statement—identifies the
arrival as a significant structural event and stabilizes the new key, creating a
context in which the tonic does, in fact, temporarily drop below the horizon,
thereby establishing the function of the new key as a polar opposition to the
tonic. It is this dramatization of the harmonic events of the exposition that
identifies the secondary key area as what Rosen has called "a dissonance

raised to a higher power, that of the total structure"—a dissonance requiring a clearly defined resolution explicitly carried out within the processive design of that structure.[15] But this articulative use of texture engenders a problem that was to prove particularly troublesome for the composers of the romantic period. Simply put, the problem is a negative one: to avoid a premature cessation of action when the modulatory impulse is realized in the establishment of the secondary key, and, of course, at the parallel spot in the recapitulation, where the theme that originally articulated the arrival in the new key returns in the tonic. The emphatic articulation of this arrival is vital to the sonata style; but it is in the nature of articulation to cut off, to segregate. The problem, then, is to balance a striking gesture of articulation with a sense of continuity of motion that spans the entire exposition and leads convincingly into its closing cadence.

In the classical style, the solution to this problem was usually found in the relative pacing of the first and second groups. As Rosen has pointed out, the pace of some element of the second theme—the surface rhythm, harmonic rhythm, or phrase structure—is generally quicker than that of the opening of the movement.[16] This seems to be true even of openly lyric second themes and is, in fact, a source of their characteristic expressivity. The first movement of Beethoven's C-major Piano Sonata, Op. 53, the "Waldstein," presents an instructive example of this principle.

The second theme of the first movement, with its slow-paced, hymn-like character, is clearly less agitated than the pulsing intensity of the opening theme. But the harmonic rhythm of the second theme moves roughly twice as quickly as that of the first theme. The relaxation of the surface rhythm is counteracted by the increased pace of harmonic activity, which in turn greatly increases the range of expressive dissonance available in the setting of this "lyric" second theme and intensifies the forward thrust of the exposition.

Beyond its expressive potential, an increased animation at the beginning of the second group acts as a surface manifestation of the tonal polarity established between the tonic and the secondary key in the exposition. The increase in surface animation, which normally entails an increase in the quantity of surface dissonance, reflects in detail the large-scale dissonance inherent in that polarity. It is this coordination of surface and underlying structure—dramatizing the course of the harmonic design—that makes the necessity for explicit resolution a central element in the sonata style.

Even when the composers of the classical period indulge in openly lyric second themes, they seem to take special care to undermine the closed, self-contained structure of these themes, insuring that the forward-driving continuity of the exposition is not lost.

Haydn, after about 1780, is particularly circumspect about thematic articulations of the secondary key, often marking the arrival with what appears to be a full-blown tune only to wander off into new matters after no more than two or three measures of the theme have been heard. The first movements of the Quartets in A major and F minor, Op. 55, Nos. 1 and 2, are instructive examples of this procedure.

The treatment of the second group in the first movement of Beethoven's F-minor Piano Sonata, Op. 57, the "Appassionata," represents a particularly dramatic application of this technique. The A♭-major second theme—a variant of the opening gesture of the movement—begins in m. 36 as a broadly paced eight-bar period, but the continuation after the half cadence in the fourth measure of the theme never reaches a full close back to the tonic. The periodicity of phrase structure is interrupted after only one measure of the second limb of the phrase, and the continuation quickly dissolves into a chain of anticipatory gestures that only settle into a surging A♭-*minor* theme in m. 51. The regularity of structure implied by the beginning of the A♭-major theme—a regularity that is essential to the articulative function of a thematic statement—is realized only later, and only in the tempestuous minor-mode theme. This, in turn, displaces the articulative weight of the latter part of the exposition from the implied lyric stability of the A♭-major theme to the pressing agitation of the A♭-minor; the explicit disintegration of the calm hinted at in the opening of the lyric theme into the impetuosity of the minor-mode theme is, of course, a central element in the relentless dramatic intensity of the movement, and of the work as a whole.

A similar technique involves a change of mode either at the arrival in the secondary key or immediately following this arrival. This seems to have been a favorite practice of Mozart's, providing a means of maintaining the forward momentum in an exposition shaped by elaborate melodic articulations.

In the first movement of the "Prague" Symphony, K. 504, the half cadence at the close of the first part of the second theme (m. 104) leads immediately into a shift to the minor mode of the dominant key for a new, though related, thematic continuation. This in turn leads to yet another new theme (which retains the original "second theme" as an accompaniment figure) that reestablishes the major mode. Each cadence within the opening of the second group is the occasion for a change of mode, necessitating further elaboration that overrides the relaxed regularity of the themes themselves.

The first movement of the Clarinet Quintet, K. 581, offers a striking example of the expressive potential of this technique. At the arrival in the dominant (m. 42), the strings begin a ravishingly unruffled eight-measure theme. The theme is absolutely complete within itself—it is carefully set off from the preceding transition by a delicate introductory vamp in the cello— and it is difficult to see what the clarinet, which has been silent throughout these eight measures, can bring to this remarkable outpouring of melody. Mozart's solution to this problem exploits the expressive quality inherent in the contrast between the clarinet and strings. The clarinet, rather than simply ornamenting the already florid theme, is given an impassioned minor-mode version of the theme: the entrance of the soloist—and the clarinet is naturally the solo voice on which our attention focuses in this work—instantly widens the emotional range of the theme and disrupts its placidly self-contained wholeness. This treatment of the relation between the clarinet and strings is itself part of a larger design, gradually integrating the contrasting instrumental voices, that runs through the entire exposition: in the first theme, the clarinet only plays between the phrases of the theme, which are given to the strings; in the second theme, as we have seen, the clarinet answers, and intensifies, the statement by the strings; in the closing theme, the strings and clarinet alternate at the half phrase, shaping between them a single melodic gesture (mm. 65ff.).

Harmonic expansion of the second group was not, of course, a uniquely Mozartean technique. The treatment of the second theme in the first movement of Beethoven's F-major Symphony, Op. 93, is one of the composer's most sophisticated exploitations of this kind of effect, and reveals the traditional roots of at least one of the formal elements characteristic of his "third period." The second theme is often described as beginning in the wrong key, and indeed, the tune does begin in D major, only swinging around to the dominant key, C major, in its second phase. But the theme does not sound as though it is in the wrong key: D major has been prepared with absolute clarity in the preceding transitional material. An understanding of this passage cannot be gained simply by appealing to expectations purportedly aroused by a textbook notion of form; rather, we must examine the specific role it plays within the larger design of the exposition.

What Beethoven has done is to telescope the transition and the second theme into a single gesture: the modulatory progression that underlies the passage as a whole turns out to be perfectly regular. A shift from the tonic to the submediant is a common first step in initiating the move from the tonic to the dominant: VI is taken as V of V of the dominant, and a straightforward sequential progression normally leads quickly to the new key. What seems to be the bridge passage in this work (roughly mm. 20–37) only reaches V of VI, however—the motion to the dominant is completed by a circle of fifths progression within the antecedent phrase of the second theme itself: the theme serves to articulate both the modulation and the arrival. It is characteristic that in the recapitulation Beethoven does not simply transpose this material so that it will come out automatically in the tonic. Instead, the first phrase of the theme returns in the subdominant, providing a touch of harmonic stabilization that is common in the classical style, but which is rarely accomplished with such economy. A new cadential pattern at the end of this phrase leads to the tonic for the continuation of the second group (mm. 234–42).

Even when a composer of the classical period uses a complete, fully rounded second theme, there is generally some element of the texture that is manipulated in a way that contributes to the larger continuity of the exposition. One of the most common of these manipulations is simply the avoidance of a solid cadence to a root position tonic chord in the new key. In the first movement of Mozart's "Jupiter" Symphony, K. 551, for example, the opening of the G-major second theme (m. 56) is perched on a first inversion chord that never settles onto a root position local tonic. A stable arrival on a G-major triad does not occur until the opening measures of the cadential theme, forty-five measures later.

Similarly, in his A-minor Piano Sonata, K. 310, the first stable root position chord in the secondary key, C major, appears only in m. 49, the last measure of the exposition, although C major was clearly established in m. 23, at the start of the second theme. In fact, the return to the lowest register of the bass at the cadence to C major in m. 49 completes, in register, a cadence implied—but not carried through—in mm. 22–23. In m. 23, the lower register established in the half cadence to V of C major is dropped abruptly, and the second theme begins in the middle register with a conspicuously lighter texture—note especially the leap in the left hand to a first inversion C-major triad in the middle of the keyboard. The entire course of the second group carries out a gradual filling-in of this abrupt registral disjunction—a process summarized and rounded off in the elaborate cadential flourishes at the end of the exposition (Example 1).

A large-scale upper-voice registral connection plays a crucial role in the organization of the exposition of the first movement of Mozart's A-major String Quartet, K. 464. The drop from b'' at the end of the transition (m. 36) to b' at the start of the second theme (m. 37) leaves the upper register established in the transitional passage unconnected to what follows. The rest of the second group is concerned with returning to that upper register to carry out a cadential linear descent from b'' to e'', a motion only completed in m. 83, four measures from the end of the exposition. An important provisional step in this process is the arrival at e'' in m. 69, but the apparent stability of this event is undercut by a sudden shift to C♯ minor—a truly deceptive cadence. (The disruptive quality of this cadential feint is emphasized by the disappearance of the bass register at the moment of the harmonic shift.) The return to E

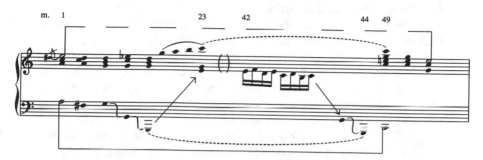

Example 1.   Mozart, Sonata in A minor, K. 310, I, mm. 1–49.

major in m. 83 is marked by a cadence that restabilizes e'' within its expected
harmonic context, apparently closing off the registral explorations of the second group. The link created by the large-scale motion from b'' in m. 36 to the
e'' of m. 83 arches over the entire second half of the exposition, engendering
a process that counteracts the closed structure of the second theme itself—an
eight-bar period that is immediately repeated with ornamental variations—
and presses continually toward the final measures of the exposition. But after
finally achieving the stabilization of e'' that closes this upper-voice motion,
Mozart proceeds to establish another registral gap, shifting the first violin
from e'' to e' to begin the final cadential phrase of the exposition (m. 83).
Given the structural significance of registral disjunction over the course of
the exposition, this obviously raises a new issue that will have to be dealt
with in closing off the generating impetus these disjunctions embody.

   In the recapitulation, the registral gap at the beginning of the second theme
is even more pronounced than it was in the exposition: the bridge passage
closes to e''', and the second theme begins on e' (mm. 197–98). This initial
leap encompasses, then, the entire three-octave registral issue of the second
half of the exposition in a single gesture. The main body of the recapitulation
of the second group carries out a linear descent from e''' to a''—or rather to
the initial a'' that is supported by the deceptive cadence in m. 230 (corresponding to m. 69). At this point, there is an interpolation that repeatedly
initiates—but immediately subverts—a direct motion from a'' to a'. In fact,
the upper voice eventually regains d''', setting off another motion to a'' in
preparation for a final cadential summing up. In the course of this, the first
violin's abrupt move from a'' to an inner-voice a' in m. 262 corresponds to
the e''–e' leap at the end of the exposition, but this time the cadence four
measures later is to vi instead of the tonic, explicitly identifying this registral
disjunction as a digression. To close the cadential circle Mozart adds a final

four-measure passage that carries out a linear descent from a'' to a'—with a quick detour to d''' that links back to the e''' of m. 197—gathering the entire registral field of the movement in a gesture of almost effortless grace.

This brief summary obviously can only begin to indicate the range of articulative devices that were available to composers working in the classical sonata style. As we shall see, the coordination of surface thematic events and underlying harmonic structure these devices supported was threatened in the romantic sonata style, where the pointedly song-like melody typically found at the beginning of the second group introduces a distinct lowering of tension—a slackening of pace to the gentle amble of a square-cut lyric tune.

This emphasis on the lyric nature of the second theme reflects the central role of themes and of specifically thematic processes for every genre of music in the nineteenth century. Our understanding of the romantic sonata requires not only an understanding of this centrality, but also of the formal problems it entails.

As Ratner, Rosen, and Tovey have all made it clear, thematic contrast could offer a vital means of articulation in the classical style. The introduction of a striking new theme is obviously an impressive way to mark the establishment of the secondary key area. But it must be emphasized that this contrast is primarily articulative, and does not in itself represent a generating principle of the form.

With the increasing interest in melodic invention and originality in the early nineteenth century, the precise nature of the relation between themes in a movement did itself become a structural issue, however. Typically, the second theme was expanded into a large, slow-paced structure, with a distinctly lyric character that stood in pointed contrast to the opening of the movement, and it was this dialectic contrast—often sharpened through explicit motivic linkages between the themes—that provided the structural motivation of the form. Carl Dahlhaus pointed out that this process reaches its extreme limit in the transformation of the second theme into a miniature slow movement within the exposition in works like Tchaikovsky's Fourth Symphony or the Second Symphony of Borodin.[17]

Mendelssohn's earliest works, which will be the subject of the second part of this chapter, provide particularly clear evidence of the difficulties an emphasis on thematic relations within sonata form entailed, while the procedures he developed in later works to accommodate the conflicting demands of sonata-form procedures and thematic processes reveal the individuality of his synthesis of romantic and classical tendencies.

But the problem of pacing and continuity within the exposition of a romantic sonata-form movement is only part of a larger problem engendered by a fundamental misunderstanding of the functional relation between the exposition and recapitulation.

By the end of the eighteenth century, the beginning of the recapitulation was almost invariably marked by the return of the tonic key and the main theme of the movement, a conjunction of elements that has come to be called a "double return." As Tovey has pointed out, this is in part simply the most efficient way to identify a crucial harmonic event, marking the return to the tonic key with material the listener cannot help but associate with the original establishment of that key.[18] In order to set this event in sharp relief, the end of the development section normally provides an emphatic and broadly laid-out harmonic preparation for the structural reacquisition of the tonic, making the tonal significance of this moment particularly striking.

In addition to its function of clearly marking the tonic arrival, the return of material from the opening measures of the movement serves as an unmistakable reference to the beginning of the distinctly memorable sequence of events that made up the exposition. In general, such a return normally arouses the expectation that what follows will be somehow related to that original sequence: as Smith has observed, when we hear what we recognize to be a return to the beginning of an integral structural unit within a work, we tend to expect that the rest will follow.[19] The opening of the recapitulation— the point at which the central tonal crisis of a sonata-form movement is resolved and the large-scale reaffirmation of the tonic is begun—functions, then, as the revelation of the promise of closure, and the concentration of expressive energy at the beginning of the closural process is a principal element in the dramatic character of the sonata style. Rosen has stressed the crucial importance of the clarity with which this moment is articulated, and the fundamental difference from the baroque style it reflects:

> An emphatic and marked return to the tonic at a point *no more than three-quar-ters of the way through a movement* is basic to the late eighteenth-century style. Its placing is almost always an event and it is never glossed over as the earlier eighteenth century tended to do.[20]

The relation between the exposition and recapitulation this implies can be relatively straightforward, as in many works of Mozart and Beethoven, where the thematic designs of the exposition and recapitulation are often almost identical, or the pattern of the exposition may serve as a springboard for the establishment of a new pattern, as is often the case with Haydn. But even the most remarkable effects in Haydn's recapitulations normally play off the expectations of organization aroused by a clearly articulated double return; without these expectations to guide us, we would not, after all, be in a position to be surprised by Haydn's rearrangements.

The nature of the relation between the exposition and recapitulation on which the present study concentrates is really very simple: the return of the thematic pattern of the exposition so strongly implied by the double return establishes a framework of events within which the process of closure—of tonal resolution—can take place. In the exposition, this thematic pattern had articulated an unresolved harmonic structure, moving from the tonic to a secondary key that functions as a structural dissonance and therefore requires resolution. The implied repetition of this thematic pattern after a return to the tonic so impressively played out as to form, in most works, the climax of the movement, indicates that the function of the repetition will involve a reworking of the harmonic structure that will accomplish this large-scale resolution: the force of the tonic return is simply too great to allow any further independent harmonic action. At the same time, the more or less exact repetition of the thematic pattern creates a predictable sequence of events within which this process of resolution will be carried out, thereby establishing the "principle of organization or design that implies the existence of a definite termination point" that Smith has identified as an essential characteristic of closure.[21] (It should be obvious that this implied pattern is, by its nature, flexible enough to accommodate a wide range of modifications that would reflect special closural issues developed over the course of the movement.) As I have suggested, this principle is not particularly obscure; I have examined it in some detail for two reasons. First, the thrust of analytical method over the last half-century has sharply downplayed the role of the thematic pattern in sonata form, and second, a misunderstanding of the role of the recapitulation led to some of the most severe problems the composers of the early romantic generation faced in trying to adapt what had become codified as "sonata form" to their individual musical styles.

It should be clear that the role of the thematic structure outlined above is not dependent on the notion of sonata form developed over the course of the nineteenth and early twentieth centuries, according to which the structure of a movement is generated by the dialectic antagonism of two contrasting themes. It is not the themes themselves, but rather the harmonic structure the thematic pattern articulates that is of primary significance for the process of closure. It is the misunderstanding of this principle that created such a difficult problem for the romantic composers. If the relation between the themes of a movement is taken to be the principal organizing agent of the form, the thematic parallelism between the exposition and recapitulation that is essential to the closural process of sonata form will naturally seem to be an unwarranted repetitiousness that undermines the fundamental generating principle of the work.

A striking example of the consequences of this attitude for analytical practice can be found in an article by Viktor Urbantschitsch in which he singles out Brahms's solution to the "recapitulation" [*Reprisenproblem*] as one of the composer's most impressive achievements.22 According to Urbantschitsch, Brahms, like Beethoven before him, found the "traditional" three-part sonata form handed down from Haydn and Mozart—a form reflecting the varied manipulations of thematic material in the exposition, development, and recapitulation—hopelessly stiff. Faced with the prospect of plodding through a recapitulation that was nothing more than "the inflexible repetition of that which has already been said"23 forced upon them by "an obligatory symmetrical analogy to the first part [the exposition],"24 these later composers were compelled to experiment with an ever-expanding variety of ploys in an effort to render this unfortunate but unavoidable formalism as palatable as possible.25

The problem is clear: a conception of sonata form in which the organic development of the thematic design plays so central a role easily leads to the conclusion that the relation between the exposition and recapitulation is essentially without function—an assumption that might seem to place the "obligatory" nature of the thematic repetition in some doubt. If a sonata-form movement is to be understood as a coherent whole, the role of one-third of the movement in establishing that coherence cannot be reduced to the essentially meaningless status of obligatory but meaningless repetition. (It is instructive that Schenker used the same designation, "repetition" [*Wiederholung*], apparently without dissatisfaction, to identify the recapitulation in the most elaborate of his late analyses, that of the first movement of the "Eroica."26 It is not surprising that he found traditional formal categories uninformative.)

As a corrective to this attitude, it is necessary to examine more closely the role played by the recapitulation within the dramatic structure of a sonata-form movement. On the one hand, if closure can be secured through a "regular" recapitulation—one in which the thematic pattern follows that of the exposition closely—that regularity must be understood as a functional element in the structure of the movement. On the other hand, the various ways in which that regularity can be disrupted must be understood not as isolated attempts to escape a distasteful symmetry, but as manifestations of significant formal processes running through the entire course of a movement—processes that require special treatment if they are to be contained within a sonata-form structure.

Mozart, in particular, made frequent use of an essentially regular recapitulation in the organization of his forms. The resulting large-scale symmetry provides an expansive field that mirrors, in formal terms, the broadly laid-out harmonic and thematic processes characteristic of his style. Beethoven, too, employed largely regular formal designs in a substantial number of works. Some of these are early works in which the influence of Mozart is strong; Tovey expressed particular admiration for the Bb-major Piano Sonata, Op. 22, likening the careful balance of formal elements that animates the perfectly regular recapitulation in the first movement to the skill displayed by a sculler "who has got his boat to a difficult landing-place without changing his stroke."[27] Later in Beethoven's career, essentially regular recapitulations are often found in the most explicitly dramatic of the "middle-period" works. The conflict between the interweaving of intensely dramatic content and implacably regular form in the first movement of the Fifth Symphony or the "Appassionata" Sonata, for example, is an important source of the uniquely Beethovenian power of these works. It is characteristic of Beethoven's sense of form that the regularity of the recapitulation itself becomes a source of tension in these works, accumulating energy that must eventually spill over into an extended coda and even into the movements that follow.

More often, however, the course of the recapitulation in a classical sonata-form work will be marked by divergences, both small and large, from the pattern established in the exposition. Some of the modifications that alter the parallelism between the exposition and recapitulation have an explicitly cadential character, and serve to reinforce the sense of tonic stability in the closing section of the movement.

In the first movement of Mozart's Eb-major Symphony, K. 543, the reworking of material in the recapitulation is particularly subtle, revealing the significance of surface detail in the mechanism of closure. In the exposition, the transition to the dominant is accomplished in the course of an agitated modulatory passage that begins in the tonic and moves rapidly through vi of Eb-major to V of Bb-major (beginning in m. 29 of the Allegro). In the recapitulation, the first part of this material is altered so that the transition will begin in the subdominant, Ab major (mm. 187–203). The later stages of the passage could, therefore, simply follow the course laid out by the transition as it appeared in the exposition—at the end of the passage, the tonic would be reestablished automatically. Indeed, the harmonic progression that underlies this later passage is an exact transposition of the earlier one, but the voice leading and the disposition of parts have been altered in the recapitulation to provide a slightly stronger emphasis on the tonic. In the exposition, the bass line circles around the tonic at the beginning of the transition and then moves abruptly to a pedal on the dominant of the new key; this method of organization, which emphasizes the lingering hold of the tonic, strengthens the sense that the dominant key is juxtaposed to the tonic as a structural dissonance. In the recapitulation, this bass line is replaced by an almost completely stepwise descent that moves from A♭ through E♭ and on to a pedal on the dominant of the tonic key. This change both sharpens the focus of the modulatory progression by establishing the beginning and end points as the boundaries of a clearly defined linear motion and gently reinforces the tonic key by providing an intermediary arrival on a root position E♭-major triad within the transition itself. The organization of the upper-voice line also helps sharpen this focus on the tonic. In the exposition the upper-voice line centres on f''' in the second part of the transition, and the approach to the second theme picks out a tonic triad in the new key: f'''-d'''-b♭'', with b♭'' serving as the first note of the new theme (mm. 58–73). In the recapitulation, the focus in the upper voice is shifted to E♭ rather than to the B♭ that would correspond to the earlier passage (mm. 211–29). As a result, the opening of the second theme (on e♭'', m. 230) sounds as a reverberation of this quietly sensitized pitch, reflecting the role of the second group as a reconfirmation of the already established tonic. Given the large-scale symmetry of exposition and recapitulation in this movement, these changes within the transitional material are not likely to attract much attention, but they delicately shift the balance of the passage in response to the closural processes that govern the recapitulation.

In some cases, special characteristics of material in the first group engender alterations at the opening of the recapitulation. Normally the join between the end of the development and beginning of the recapitulation marks the climax of a sonata-form movement. The heightened intensity at the end of the development section—intensity which can be generated through the manipulation of harmonic, motivic, and rhythmic elements—and the strongly articulated resolution into the tonic stability provided at the double return serve as an immediately comprehensible representation of the larger process of tension and resolution that underlies the movement as a whole. The opening of the recapitulation both announces the beginning of the process of closure and foreshadows the functional organization of that process. Examples of the normal form of this effect range from the broadly paced motion from dominant to tonic that typifies Mozart's practice—for example, in the first movement of the D-major Symphony, K. 504 (mm. 195–208)—to the abruptness of the first movement of Haydn's C-major quartet, Op. 76, No. 3 (mm. 65–79), or the explosive intensity of the first movement of Beethoven's Fifth Symphony (mm. 195–252) or his E♭-major Piano Sonata, Op. 81a, (mm. 94–110). Since alterations that affect the elements of the double return might seem to threaten the coherence of one of the most crucial moments in the closural process, I would like to consider some representative examples of this procedure, paying particular attention to the larger structural principles involved. As we shall see in later chapters, similar techniques animate Mendelssohn's finest works of the 1820s and represent a characteristic element of his style. Even the critic Henry F. Chorley, whose obtuseness often attained an astonishing depth and purity, noticed this aspect of his friend's works, observing that the composer "had a shy way of his own of returning to his first subject as if his humor was to perplex, not to satisfy, the ear."[28]

The first movement of Haydn's Quartet in B minor, Op. 33, No. 1, offers a famous example of a work "starting in the wrong key." The opening measures seem to establish a fairly clear, if somewhat unsteady, D major; the real tonic, B minor, is not firmly stabilized until m. 11. Rosen has pointed out that this opening gambit allows Haydn to move to his secondary key, which is, of course, D major, without having to bother about a formal modulation.[29] The continuation of the first theme reaches a half cadence to V of B minor in m. 17, pauses for a moment, and then is swept away by an exact restatement of the tune from the opening of the movement, now played *forte*, over a rock-solid pedal on D in the depths of the cello. The resulting harmonic jolt is a surprise, but one prepared by the musical material itself.

This opening creates a delicate problem at the beginning of the recapitulation, however: which key is to be prepared, the tonic or the key in which the movement began? At the end of the development, there is a feint toward D major (mm. 53–55), but the passage immediately moves on to an augmented sixth chord with G in the bass (m. 58). This presses strongly toward V of B minor, and the development closes, *forte*, on an anticipatory i_4^6-V cadence in the tonic. What follows, however, is an exact return of the opening measures of the movement, with their oddly perched D major. The preparation for this return—the half cadence on the dominant of B minor, and in particular the disjunction between the low register established in the bass at that cadence and the relatively high and closely spaced D^6 chord that supports the opening theme—suggests that this double return is not absolutely stable. An indeed, the move toward the tonic in the ensuing passage, although corresponding in a general way to the parallel spot in the exposition, is greatly expanded, becoming, as Rosen has noted, the climax of the movement before leading to a solid cadence to B minor in m. 72 (corresponding to m. 11 of the exposition).[30] A crucial event in this passage is the reacquisition of the lower register by the cello in m. 67, where an octave doubling brings back the low G abandoned in m. 58. This drops immediately to the F♯ root of V of B minor in m. 71 through which the cadence to the tonic key is finally accomplished. This registral coupling in the lower voice establishes a parenthesis around the statement of the D-major tune at the "double return," linking the end of the development to the tonic arrival in m. 72, and allows Haydn to preserve the thematic shape of the opening of the exposition while adjusting the relations between its elements, reinterpreting the harmonic ambiguity of the opening

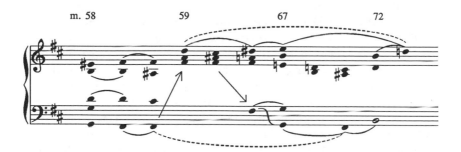

Example 2. Haydn, String Quartet in B minor, Op. 33, No. 1, I, mm. 57–73

measures in response to the closural processes of the recapitulation (Example 2).

Since the point of this ambiguity, which allows the almost literal restatement of the opening measures of the movement to articulate the establishment of the secondary key area in the exposition, depends on the absolute pitch identity of the two thematic statements in the exposition, a transposition of the "second theme" to the tonic in the recapitulation would be meaningless. Instead, since the D-major implications of the opening theme have been neutralized by isolating the beginning of the recapitulation as an acutely unstable digression on the way to the structural tonic arrival, the "second theme" version of this material is simply eliminated from the recapitulation: the resolution of the harmonic tension established in the opening measures of the exposition has already been provided by an almost literal restatement of the material that initially generated that tension.

In the first movement of Beethoven's Fourth Symphony, Op. 60, the sense of harmonic arrival at the opening of the recapitulation is clouded in a subtle, almost intangible way. The end of the development forms an extended playing-out of the F–G♭ neighbor-note relation first heard in the opening measures of the movement's introductory Adagio. This passage settles, finally, on an F in the bass (m. 307) supporting a cadential B♭$^6_4$ that pointedly refuses to resolve to V; instead, the bass simply disappears, while the timpani rumbles on an extremely indistinct tonic root that persists throughout the ensuing thirty-measure retransition. (This idiosyncratic handling of the tonic $^6_4$ at so crucial a structural join is itself an echo of the striking avoidance of an upper-voice resolution, in register, of a I$^6_4$–V–I cadence in mm. 49–51 and 59–65 of the exposition. These upper-voice cadential motions figure prominently in the coda, where cadences based on mm. 49–51 are pounded out in mm. 475–83, just before the final tonic fanfare that closes the movement.)

The immediate effect of the events at the end of the development is a sense that there is no definite moment of arrival in the tonic in connection with the reappearance of the opening theme (m. 337): the tonic was achieved, without the intervention of a normal cadence, some thirty measures before the thematic return. In fact, a strong cadence to the tonic is avoided until the return of the second theme, now transposed to B♭ major (m. 381). This might seem to suggest that the arrival of the second theme will finally provide and unambiguously articulated tonic arrival, serving as the real climax of the movement. But the second theme is not a particularly stable representative of the tonic, since the most prominent feature of the theme is an internal modulation to the local submediant. In the end, the avoidance of tonic stability must be recognized as one of the fundamental generating principles of the later stages of the movement. It is not until the cadences in mm. 475–83 mentioned above that stability is finally and unambiguously achieved. The handling of the double return, then, is just one manifestation of the operation of this principle, transforming the expected moment of structural resolution into a moment of quiet uncertainty.

In the opening of the recapitulation of the *Coriolan* Overture, Op. 62, Beethoven completely disengages the elements of the double return: the main theme returns in the subdominant, F minor, rather than the tonic. This obviously makes the reacquisition of the tonic matter of tremendous urgency *within* the recapitulation; as we shall see, it also places a powerful dramatic focus on the question of the mode of the tonic. Urbantschitsch identified this as the work in which Beethoven first presented a comprehensive solution to the "recapitulation problem" (it is worth noting that he describes this solution only in terms of thematic pattern):

> He solved it in the Overture to "Coriolan," in which he transferred the "confrontation" and with it the highpoint of the work from the development to the coda; the development remains an Intermezzo, and the recapitulation functions almost as a repetition.[31]

His characterization of the development section as an "Intermezzo" might seem strange given the intensely dramatic character of the work as a whole, but it points to a crucial element in Beethoven's design. Unfortunately, the rigidity of Urbantschitsch's underlying analytical presupposition—that sonata form was exclusively a matter of thematic organization and that for any composer after Haydn and Mozart recapitulation was simply a meaningless restatement of "that which has already been said"—prevented him from exploring fully the implications of his insight. Indeed, that insight and Urbantschitsch's analytical tools seem to yield sharply contradictory results: the solution to the "recapitulation problem" is achieved in a work in which the recapitulation functions simply as a repetition, a situation that has been identified as the principal characteristic of the problem itself.[32]

The power of Beethoven's design lies precisely in the ambiguity that arises from the interrelation of the seemingly straightforward thematic design of the recapitulation and the remarkable harmonic process with which it is intertwined: the main theme returns in the minor subdominant (m. 152), while the second group begins in what might seem to be a perfectly normal place—the tonic major (m. 178ff.). But the structure allows Beethoven to treat this latter event in a way that destroys the normal quality of the tonic major as a resolution for the instabilities of the minor mode. Closure is only accomplished with the reestablishment of C minor, which clears up an inflectional problem that has plagued the second group both in the exposition and in this ostensibly normal recapitulation, and which plays a crucial role in the movement's central "Intermezzo."

The inflectional problem centers on the relative stability—and corresponds inflectional tendencies—of Eb, the minor third degree of the tonic, C minor. The preparation for the second group in the exposition hinges on a diminished seventh chord, Eb–F♯–A–C, that wavers momentarily between V of G minor—the key toward which the passage clearly seems to be leading—and V of V of Eb major (mm. 40–41). (In the expected cadence to G minor, Eb would be the characteristic b6th degree, which normally acts as an upper leading tone to the dominant, implying a resolution from Eb to D.) The continuation leans toward Eb major, but Beethoven carefully retains the Eb–D half step in a grating Eb–D neighbor-note figure in the lower voice. This is, of course, the leading tone-tonic pair in Eb major, and the lyric calm of the opening of the second theme would seem to stabilize the relation around Eb. But Beethoven avoids a full cadence at the beginning of the theme (m. 52), and the lower-voice Eb of the accompaniment is shifted abruptly to an inner part, obscuring slightly the sense of stability at this crucial juncture: this blurring of the harmonic arrival prefigures the unusual treatment the continuation of the theme will receive, and, as Robert P. Morgan points out, the gentle ambiguity surrounding the articulative function of the opening of the second theme will prove to be quite useful at the corresponding cadence in the recapitulation.[33]

The theme quickly proves to be distinctly unstable: instead of confirming the newly won Eb major, it immediately sets off on a stepwise sequential ascent—in which each step is propelled by the stepwise ascent in the opening gesture of the theme itself—leading to statements of the theme in F minor (mm. 64ff.) and G minor (mm. 72ff.) (see Example 3).

Example 3. Beethoven, *Coriolan* Overture, Op. 62, mm. 52–72.

The second group closes in G minor, then—the key toward which the transition had originally seemed to be leading—and the final pages of the exposition play continually on E♭ as the upper neighbor to D, reversing the relation of these two pitches once again and explicitly sweeping away the resolution suggested by the E♭-major arrival at the opening of the second theme. The move to E♭ major proves to be a diversion on the way to G minor; a diversion that intensifies the minor-mode bias of the exposition by emphasizing the inflectional sensitivity of E♭—the pivotal pitch that is the third of the tonic, C minor, the ♭6th degree of the dominant key, G minor, and the root of the strangely ephemeral mediant, E♭ major.

Given this modulatory structure—in conjunction with Beethoven's unusual gambit of opening the recapitulation in the subdominant—it would have been possible to fashion a recapitulation in which the second theme could return without referring to the tonic major at all. After the return of the main theme in F minor, the second theme could return in A♭ major and move naturally through B♭ minor to C minor in an exact parallel to the design of the exposition. This is, in fact, the kind of symmetrical arrangement Beethoven normally used in movements in a major key to recapitulate a "three-key" exposition—an exposition in which an extensively elaborated subsidiary key area stands between the tonic and the eventual harmonic goal of the exposition; examples include the first movements of the Fourth and Fifth Piano Concertos and the D-major Piano Sonata, Op. 10, No. 3. In the *Coriolan* Overture, this arrangement would mesh perfectly with the opening of the recapitulation in the subdominant, creating, with Schubertian tidiness, an absolute parallelism between the C-minor–E♭-major–G-minor sequence of the exposition and an F-minor–A♭-major–C-minor pattern in the recapitulation.

But Beethoven apparently wanted to make a special point about the role of the tonic major in the dramatic structure of the movement: each of the major formal junctures in the recapitulation hinges in one way or another on the appearance of an acutely unstable C-major triad in which the inflectional stability of the major third, E♮, is repeatedly undermined. The groundwork for this is laid in the movement's central "Intermezzo."

The development section moves almost immediately to F minor, which naturally involves the support of C major as its dominant and in particular E♮ as the leading tone. The C major we glimpse in this context is obviously a subordinate element within F minor, and it cannot, therefore, register as a resolution for the inflectional problems that have accrued to the E♭ that is the minor third of the tonic key. Indeed, the extension of F minor over the boundaries of the development section into the first part of the recapitulation intensifies those problems by focusing them at what normally would be the work's decisive tonic resolution. The minor-mode orientation of the movement is, in fact, intensified by a gesture that requires the functional support of the tonic *major*. The identity of the third of the tonic triad has itself become the central formal issue of the movement—is it the E♮ of C major or the inflectionally troubled E♭ that was threaded through the exposition? (It is the elaboration of the subdominant, F minor, over the entire course of the development section—an elaboration that is most clearly revealed by an examination of the middle- and background structures—that gives the section its strangely gentle "Intermezzo" character.)

As Morgan has pointed out, the articulation of the return of the main theme in m. 152 is curiously weak—in fact, it does not represent a real harmonic arrival at all. There have already been full cadences to F minor in mm. 144 and 148, and neither the dynamic level nor the instrumentation of the passage changes when the main theme shows up.[34] Rather than marking the climax of the formal design, initiating and foreshadowing the larger process of closure that will be carried out over the course of the recapitulation, the return of the main theme is strangely disorienting—abrupt and unexpected, unprepared, and perched on a key that intensifies rather than resolves the urgent problem of establishing a stable mode for the tonic key itself. Beethoven has deployed the articulative landmarks of the formal design in such a way that the opening of the recapitulation necessitates rather than embodies closure, and the problems only intensify as the recapitulation continues.

The restatement of the first group and transition are drastically curtailed and rewritten to focus continually on F minor, but a shift of harmony at the end of the transition leads abruptly to C major for the opening of the second group (mm. 163–78). In the context of the enormous elaboration of the subdominant over the middle of the movement—extending back to m. 123—this

C major still seems to reverberate within that F-minor realm, where E♮ is only a temporary chromatic substitution for E♭. The literal restatement of the second theme actually intensifies the problem surrounding E♮, establishing it as the root of a patently unstable E minor in the third statement of the theme (m. 198). But at this critical point, the mirage simply vanishes: the change of a single note—from E♮ to F, naturally—transforms the E-minor triad into the dominant seventh of C minor (mm. 200–201). That C minor can be reestablished instantaneously in m. 201 reveals how near the surface it has lurked throughout the middle stages of the movement. As Morgan points out, the enormous subdominant spread over the middle of the movement proves to be an expansively laid out lower neighbor to the dominant established at the end of the exposition—with the return to the dominant in m. 201, that neighbor motion is completed: F minor and its attendant C major (with its E♮) are reabsorbed into an overarching cadential progression toward C minor, and the minor third, E♭, is restored to a stability it has not known since the opening measures of the exposition.35

With the reestablishment of E♭, the stepwise bass motion that underlies the recapitulation of the second theme is carried up through F and F♯ to the dominant, G (mm. 201–6), initiating a restatement of the closing paragraphs of the second group (Example 4).

But the E♮–E♭ tension that has haunted the development section and recapitulation reverberates once more in the coda, where a last statement of the second theme in C major is broken off to be answered—and resolved—by a counterstatement in C minor, with E♭ explicitly replacing the pathetically hopeful major third (mm. 244–54).

"Pathetically hopeful" suggests a programmatic significance for all this. The openly literary associations Beethoven himself conjured for the work by identifying it as the "Ouvertüre zum Trauerspiel Coriolan von Collin" suggests at the very least that the sharp contrast of character between the two

Example 4.   Beethoven, *Coriolan* Overture, Op. 62, mm. 152–276.

principal themes of the work in some sense reflects the central dramatic issue of the play—the tragic conflict between pride and love of country that eventually destroys Coriolanus. Paul Mies, for example, identifies the sequential presentation of the second theme with the successive scenes in which the Senator Minutius, the old Sulpitius, and the hero's wife and mother plead with Coriolanus to renounce his decision to betray Rome.[36] Whether the expressive character of the overture is tied this literally to specific events in Collin's play or not, the unending inflectional uncertainties surrounding the mode of the tonic—uncertainties that revolve around the inflectional stability of E♮ and E♭ both within the tonic and across the entire tonal plain of the work—seem to reflect a particularly subtle means for conveying this confrontation of uncertainty, hope, and inevitable tragedy.

Whatever the programmatic implications of Beethoven's procedures, it should be clear that the recapitulation is not simply a "repetition." Nor does the role of F minor in this work bear more than a superficial resemblance to the ambling efficiency of Schubert's subdominant-to-tonic recapitulations. The form of the movement reflects the unusually dramatic role Beethoven establishes for the tonic major within the structure of the movement and reveals the suppleness with which formal processes could be treated in the classical sonata style. As we shall see, in the finest of his early works Mendelssohn was able to recapture some of the freedom in coordinating tonal structure and thematic pattern—the interrelation of detail and structure—that underlies Beethoven's strategies.

In both the Fourth Symphony and the *Coriolan* Overture, closure is withheld until the coda, where an important cadential gesture closes off a structural problem that has been threaded through the course of the movement. The role of the coda is obviously an important issue in the classical sonata, and it is of absolutely crucial significance for the romantic sonata style. Some sort of coda is a normal feature of most movements in the classical style, ranging in scope from a few measures of cadential emphasis to the complex events and enormous waves of cadential affirmation at the end of the first movement of the "Eroica." In the romantic sonata style, the coda often tends to become the focus of the movement, serving, as James Webster has pointed out, to provide the main climax of the structure.[37]

But if sonata form represents a closed, self-generated structure in which the process of closure is set in sharp relief by the various relations established between the recapitulation and the exposition (and development), a coda— and additional complex of closing gestures at the end of the movement— would seem either to be somewhat irrelevant adjunct to the "real" structure of the movement or to offer evidence that the closural processes generated by the form are not sufficiently persuasive to bring the movement to a conclusion. The usual explanations of the role of the coda, typified by the following (presumably authoritative) comments tend toward the former view, although the analytical problems inherent in the resulting conception of sonata form—a "real" structure with additional material more or less gratuitously tacked on—are generally ignored with an innocence that should arouse immediate suspicion.

> Coda [It., tail]. In instrumental music following regular musical forms, a concluding section extraneous to the form as usually defined; any concluding passage that can be understood as occurring after the structural conclusion of a work and that serves as a formal closing gesture.[38]

> Since many movements have no codas, it is evident that the coda must be considered as an extrinsic addition. . . . In fact, it would be difficult to give any other reason for the addition of a coda than that the composer wants to say something more.[39]

If the recapitulation has at times been taken to be a necessary evil, the coda would appear to be a mysterious option.[40]

Of course, a tendency to broaden the pace in approaching the final cadence of a movement is common to most musical styles. The additional emphasis this gives to the cadence helps break the flow of the surface rhythm, reflecting the stability represented by the final close into the tonic and reinforcing the sense that, as Smith puts it, "we are prepared not for continuation but for cessation."[41] As we have seen, this broadening, in the form of a pedal or of a breakdown—or a sudden intensification—of imitative part-writing, is one of the most common terminal modifications in fugal style. But a similar tendency can be found even in works with more clearly discernible processes of formal closure. In the closing ritornellos of the first movements of the second and third *Brandenburg* Concertos, for example, short interpolations serve to delay the final cadence slightly, intensifying the effect of concluding stability by momentarily disrupting the anticipated drive to the final tonic chord.

This effect is reproduced in several of the early string quartets of Mozart, where one or two measures of cadential harmony are inserted immediately before the closing chords of the recapitulation. The emphasis these tiny interpolations provide reflects the terminal function of those final chords within the structure of the movement, differentiating them from the corresponding material at the end of the exposition. The first movement of the Quartet in A major, K. 169, or the more elaborate expansion at the cadence in the first movement of the Quartet in F minor, K. 158, offer delightful examples of this procedure.

In the mature classical style, small-scale interpolations like these are not particularly common; however, movements that close in the tonic minor represent a special case in which the brevity of the cadential elaboration plays a special expressive role. A remarkable example occurs in the first movement of Mozart's G-minor Symphony, K. 550: a four-measure aside just before the end of the movement makes a pathetic move toward the tonic major (as V of iv) that is immediately crushed back to the tonic minor in the final cadence—the hint of resolution cannot be sustained against the weight of the minor mode that has throbbed throughout the movement.

In general, codas, if they do appear at all, become increasingly elaborate through the end of the eighteenth century and the first decades of the nineteenth. If sonata form is taken to be a static framework—a jellymold to be filled with whatever materials the composer has at hand—an explanation of the role of the coda like that suggested by the perfunctory analytical observations cited above would be sufficient to understand this development: a structurally meaningless accretion of formal elements is simply extended by the addition of one more element. On the other hand, if the process of closure is taken to be significant for the form, the presence of an extensive coda is a signal that the closural processes of the movement have been blocked or left uncompleted, and that the causes of this are being dealt with in the coda.

In one relatively straightforward type of structure, for example, the end of the exposition does not come to a full close, but leads directly to a repetition of the exposition, and the transition back to the tonic forms an integral part of the cadential group. The end of the recapitulation, restating this process, naturally requires at least some additional material to effect a full close. In the simplest cases, this can be accomplished with a short cadential extension that usually does little more than place a strong emphasis on a stabilizing subdominant, as in the first movement of Mozart's A-major Symphony, K. 201. In more complex designs, this type of coda may be intimately linked to important structural elements of the movement.

In the first movement of Mozart's D-minor String Quartet, K. 421, for example, the short coda pushes to a climax on the Neapolitan, E♭ major (m. 114), that echoes and subsumes into the closing cadence the striking effect of E♭ major both at the opening of the development section (m. 42) and in the movingly subtle reworking of the second theme in the recapitulation (mm. 94ff.).

Another functional role played by the coda may involve the adjustment of registral relations within a movement. In its least subtle form, the notion of recapitulating material originally played at the dominant simply suggests transposing that material down a fifth from the position of its first statement. But one of the elements of texture that can be most effectively exploited to stabilize the secondary key at the end of the exposition is register, and the treatment of registral relations creates special requirements for the achievement of closure at the end of the recapitulation. The cadential brilliance so often found in the closing material of the exposition naturally calls for an expansion of register, placing particular emphasis on the upper ranges of the solo instrument or ensemble. To simply replay this material a fifth lower would clearly weaken its effect, dulling the brilliance and undermining the closural energy of the end of the movement, which would, as a result, sound considerably less impressive than the end of the exposition; this is not acceptable, apparently, within the terms of the classical sonata style.

In the first movement of Beethoven's D-major Symphony, Op. 36, the registral balance between the exposition and the end of the movement is restored in the coda, and the return to the closing register unleashes a brilliant climax. In the closing cadential material of the exposition, the upper-voice line reaches a''' (Flute I, mm. 126–30), the highest point of the movement. The recapitulation tends to bring back second-group material a fourth above its original register, but at the beginning of this closing material, the upper voice suddenly drops to a lower level, answering the a''' from the end of the exposition with d''' (Flute I, m. 298). The change is slight, perhaps, but it does render the closing cadences considerably duller in tone than they were at the end of the exposition, especially in the context of a recapitulation that has consistently stressed the upper reaches of the orchestral range. That this change does not simply reflect orchestrational pragmatism—the avoidance of potentially shrill extremes of the upper register—is revealed by the events of the coda. This final section begins as a parallel to the opening of the development, since this is one of those movements in which the transition leading to the repetition of the exposition is built into the structure of the cadential material. The coda soon embarks upon a strongly emphasized upper-voice ascent, beginning on c♮''' (m. 324) and leading directly to a''' (m. 334), reestablishing a registral link to the high point achieved at the end of the exposition. This touches off a brilliantly orchestrated climax—the most impressive moment in the entire movement and one of Beethoven's most exhilarating orchestral gestures—that in turn unleashes a powerful linear cadential descent from a''' to d''' (mm. 335–40), and the closing cadences of the movement hammer away triumphantly at this long-withheld upper-voice arrival.

In the first movement of Mozart's D-major String Quartet, K. 499, the coda accomplishes a similar registral linkage, this time reaching back to an important event at the beginning of the development.

The opening of the development moves rapidly from A major through A minor and F major to D minor, where the second violin brings back the main theme (m. 111). The theme is immediately taken up by the first violin in a conspicuously high register. In fact, the initial f''' of this statement, which links back to a brief encounter between g''' and f''' in the first measures of the development, represents the highest point in the movement, giving the D-minor statement of the theme a gentle, but striking, emphasis. This registral peak is alluded to again in the closing measures of the development section, but g''', which is now taken as the seventh of the home dominant, is left unresolved in register when the opening theme returns in D major, beginning on f♯'' (m. 142).

The three-line register is touched upon a number of times in the course of the recapitulation, but in ways that underline the need for an unambiguous gesture liking this register to the opening theme and to the tonic key. In mm. 209-11, g''' and f♮''' turn up prominently in connection with a statement of the opening theme, but the theme is in B♭ major—a "purple patch" which acts as a large-scale appoggiatura to the dominant. In the coda, the main theme reappears in the "D-minor" version—that is, the theme begins on f♮'''—but the harmonic support for this statement is V^7 of V, so the f♮''' is no longer even a relatively stable element of the tonic (minor) triad, but an appoggiatura to e''' (mm. 250ff.). At the arrival in D major that completes the ensuing V^7 of V–I_4^6–V–I cadence (m. 253), a new cadential version of the head of the main theme establishes a''' as a new highpoint, and the closing measures of the coda fill the entire registral space set out over the course of the movement before returning to the three-line register for a closing flutter around f♯''' that finally—at the last possible moment—replaces in register the conspicuous, and increasingly sensitive, f♮''' that has so strongly colored the development and recapitulation.

For Beethoven, the coda often serves to pull together musical processes that run throughout an entire movement but, for various reasons, do not lend themselves to resolution within the terms of sonata form, requiring instead special closural procedures that necessarily expand the scope of the form. Since the interrelation of a movement's formal articulations and the events that unfold such large-scale musical processes is not always immediately evident, it might seem that the coda actually is "extrinsic" to the fundamental structure of the piece. I hope to show that the influence of these processes on the formal articulations of the movement is normally so strong that the coda represents an essential element in the formal process of closure.

Since an investigation of these interrelations is necessarily complex, the following discussion will focus on only some of the many threads that are pulled together in the coda of one of Beethoven's most elaborate designs— the first movement of the "Eroica." In particular, I will concentrate on the reworking of aspects of the opening of the recapitulation in the course of the coda.[42]

The events surrounding the opening of the recapitulation are marked by a series of crises that undermine the foundations of the closural process. At the end of the development section, the strain of anticipation becomes so strong that the horn cannot wait for the cadence to the tonic, and jumps in with the main theme in the tonic while the strings are still hovering quietly on the dominant (mm. 394–95). This premature entry is immediately broken off and absorbed by the massive tonic cadence that follows, initiating a proper restatement of the main theme; but the exact point at which the double return occurs has been obscured, since the thematic and harmonic returns are calamitously out of synchronization with one another. As a result, a residue of instability colors this otherwise overwhelming reacquisition of the tonic, engendering a breathtaking expansion of the range of harmonic action just at the moment when the passage finally seems to have settled into a "regular" recapitulation.

As Tovey pointed out, this expansion centers on a reinterpretation of the delicately colored C♯ embedded in the opening measures of the main theme.[43] At the beginning of the movement, the motion through C♯ is simply a chromatic detail, momentarily "clouding" the harmony, but leading immediately back through D to the tonic. In the course of the first group, however, C♯ (respelled as D♭), gradually becomes the pivot on which the modulation away from the tonic hinges (mm. 18–20 and 37–45).

At the opening of the recapitulation, C♯ is reinterpreted as an appoggiatura to C♮: the harmony swings around to a magical F major, and the horn plays the main theme once again (mm. 408ff.). Both Tovey and Rosen have written of the paradox that this F major cannot be heard as the V of V it might seem to represent. What appears to be a dominant function has been transformed by its context into its opposite, "a chromatic coloring of the subdominant," that leads not to V but to ♭VII.[44]

The initial events of the coda are concerned with establishing a more functionally normal role for this extraordinary supertonic scale degree. The three block-like statements of the head of the main theme in E♭ major, D♭ major, and C major that open the coda pick out the crucial pitches of the progression leading to F major in the opening measures of the recapitulation, transforming them into harmonic slabs starkly juxtaposed to one another. When C major eventually proves to be a dominant (m. 574), however, it leads to the more normal supertonic, F minor, which is marked by a return of the "new" theme from the middle of the development. As the minor supertonic, F minor retains a relatively uncomplicated cadential function within the tonic key and leads immediately to E♭ minor (m. 589), where the new theme is repeated. In this opening section of the coda, then, the supertonic step, which had blossomed so exotically as F major at the opening of the recapitulation, is explicitly directed back toward the tonic in the aftershocks of a stupendous restatement of the E♭–D♭–C hinge. (It is an instructive example of Beethoven's economy of means that two of the most significant structural elements in the movement—the strong emphasis on the supertonic and the "new theme" first introduced in the development section—are linked in this gesture, which entwines them within the movement's massive process of closure.)

The return from the tonic minor to the final reacquisition of the tonic major recalls another element from the opening of the recapitulation—the strange harmonic problems that plague the attempts of the horn to play a theme that is clearly a horn-call. In m. 615, the second and third horns play a version of the head of the main theme (e♭'–g♭'–e♭'–e♭) that seems clearly enough to be in E♭ minor. But the harmony surrounding this statement centers on a diminished seventh chord (G♭–A–C–E♭) that implies a cadential V^6_5 of V of the tonic: the minor third of the theme, G♭, which is doubled, *espressivo*, by the clarinet and bassoon, is really an appoggiatura to the unstated harmonic root, F, and the root-tone of the thematic statement, E♭, is actually the seventh to that unstated harmonic root. As at the end of the development, the statement of the theme in the horns cuts against the grain of the harmonic context, but now the friction generated by this harmonic impasse will be harnessed into the triumphant affirmation of the tonic that blazes through the final pages of the movement.

The minor third, G♭, eventually moves by the way of F (m. 618, first violin) to G♮ (m. 623), but this initial melodic arrival is swallowed up in a deceptive cadence to C minor. The major third is only stabilized within the tonic at m. 631, where the horns finally are allowed to present a harmonically coherent statement of the main theme in the tonic. This moment, which sets off the final cadential waves that ground the tremendous energies that have animated the movement, resolves both the ambiguity surrounding the E♭-minor statement of the theme in the coda and, at longer range, the disastrous attempt of the horn to take up the theme in the measures preceding the opening of the recapitulation.

With respect to these structural elements of the movement, then, the coda serves both to subsume the harmonic disruptions that buffeted the opening of the recapitulation into a massively stable cadential apparatus—rounding off a process set in motion in the opening measures of the movement—and, as Joseph Kerman has pointed out, to establish, in a triumphant final gesture, the proper instrumental garb for the main theme—a theme which is obviously a horn call, but which the horns somehow cannot manage to play without either coming in at a catastrophically inappropriate moment or turning up in a functionally mysterious key.[45]

In general, then, it seems clear that the coda of a sonata-form movement in the mature classical style serves to complete an important element of the structural design; it is not simply some more music that could not be stuffed in somewhere else—a remark "sur l'escalier," as Kerman has characterized Mozart's codas.[46] That the design remains incomplete through the course of the formal processes of the recapitulation intensified the problem of closure, and consequently the events of the coda powerfully reinforce the "clinch" of the final cadence. Since these events often refer to the striking or unusual articulation of important formal junctures of the movement—the upper-register relations that frame the development (and prepare, but do not fully connect with the openings of the recapitulation) in Mozart's D-major Quartet, or the massive disruptions at the opening of the recapitulation of the "Eroica"—the coda also serves to pull together the formal structure, resolving important issues generated in the act of articulating that structure.

For the composers of the romantic generation, withholding a decisive sense of closural stability until the last possible moment seems to have been a fundamental element of style, and the impressive codas Haydn, Mozart, and Beethoven were able to fashion while preserving the dramatic coherence of sonata form undoubtedly represented an attractive and influential model. But as we have seen, the rearrangement of formal balance that gives these codas their meaning depends on the coordination of processes that run through the entire course of a movement, and it is precisely this large-scale control that seems to have been particularly difficult to achieve in the romantic sonata style. The intricate harmonic vocabulary and the elaborate thematic designs that style supports normally generate textures that are too rich in detail to accommodate the finely calculated inflectional play Beethoven stretches across a design like that of the first movement of the "Eroica." At the same time, the concern for strongly individualized themes that characterizes every facet of the romantic style makes it difficult to sustain the delicate balance between the localized stability that allows the themes to establish themselves most effectively and the processive subordination that subsumes the thematic pattern as an articulative agent within the formal design. Similarly, an ever-growing fascination with instrumental technique and variety of tone-color tended to make details of orchestration and register matters of purely local effect that could not be exploited as elements of a larger formal structure. Since the climax does not, then, necessarily represent the closural juncture of a network of structural processes and surface articulations, the coda of a romantic sonata-form movement often does seem extrinsic to the "real" structure of the movement, inevitable only because it is wearisomely predictable.

In general the problems of the romantic sonata style are problems of coordinating surface elements that have become increasingly self-sufficient—interesting and original—with the structural processes of sonata form. The symptoms of this condition are, on the one hand, the stiffly regularized classicist forms typical of the mid-nineteenth century, in which the form is simply a jellymold into which a mixture of attractive themes is poured, and, on the other, the wild eccentricity of a work like Schumann's Fourth Symphony, in which the form is treated as a problem that must be solved, even if the solution seems to reduce formal coherence to the level of the unity displayed by a string of colored beads.

The majority of Mendelssohn's early works—or perhaps they should be identified as "pre-early," since the last of them was written when the composer was fifteen—offer an unusually detailed view of the process of hardening of the textures that characterizes the classicist style.

The first group of works in this pre-early canon is the series of string symphonies Mendelssohn wrote between 1821 and 1823. (The C-minor Symphony, Op. 11, written in 1824 and scored for full orchestra, was originally identified as *Sinfonia XIII*, forming, apparently, the culmination of the series.) As R. Larry Todd has observed, the string symphonies are best understood as a continuation of Mendelssohn's studies in counterpoint under Zelter, forming a transition from the stricter discipline of fugue and ornamented chorale that formed the basis of Zelter's fervently conservative program to the freer deployment of textures characteristic of the contemporary sonata style.[47] In fact, the pedagogical intent that lies behind these works seems to involve a traversal of the range of transformations the North-German style had undergone in the half-century of Zelter's own compositional activity. The self-conscious sense of style that permeates these works is clearly expressed in a letter in which the twelve-year-old composer's mother comments on his productivity during the preceding six-month period (!): in addition to two operas, as well as most of a third, and a number of large-scale choral works, she reports that he had written "six Symphonies in the old manner, without wind instruments."[48]

The old manner referred to is that of the mid-eighteenth-century Berlin school—the style in which both Zelter and Mendelssohn's mother herself had been trained. In fact, Karl Nef's description of the symphonic style of the leading figure in the development of that style, J. G. Graun, could be used as an enumeration of some of the principal characteristics of the earliest Mendelssohn's string symphonies:

He wrote a large number of "chamber symphonies" in which he contributed a richer, full instrumentation—in which more real voices were deployed—to the development of sonata form; in particular, he created an effective multi-choral style, and introduced fugal and canonic techniques into this previously lighter form. . . . In contrast to the Mannheim school, the Berlin composers favored the old three-movement form; among the symphonies of J. G. Graun there is only one four-movement work with a minuet. There are also many works which are written for strings alone, in a simple deployment—works which today we would identify as quartets.[49]

Both the slightly archaic setting of these works and the continual emphasis on contrapuntal part-writing link Mendelssohn's earliest large-scale works to the symphonic style of the 1750s. His tendency to treat the double-bass as an independent part represents only a trivial divergence from this model; the first symphonies even do away with a Minuet.

Another piece of evidence concerning the historical-pedagogical orientation of these works is given in the memoirs of Heinrich Dorn. Dorn, a native of Königsberg, became Zelter's student in 1824 or 1825. A composer, conductor, writer, and teacher—Schumann studied thoroughbass and counterpoint with him in 1831–32—Dorn's most prominent role in the history of nineteenth-century music is that of tormentor of Wagner. The story begins innocently enough, with Dorn conducting the first public performance of an orchestral work by Wagner, an Overture, on Christmas Eve, 1830. But in the late 1830s, both men were in Riga, Dorn as Kapellmeister and Wagner as Musikdirektor of the opera. Wagner's situation—both personal and professional—was unusually precarious—even for Wagner—at this time, and in 1839 Dorn took over his position in the theater. Wagner's narrative of the events is almost hopelessly muddled, but he never wavered from his conviction that Dorn had betrayed him, conspiring with his enemies to secure his dismissal.[50] For his part, Dorn later had the "meanness" to clarify his side of the affair in his memoirs by publishing a number of letters written to him by Wagner—letters Cosima described with characteristically ambivalent frankness in her diary as "downright childlike."[51]

In these same memoirs, Dorn writes of the Sunday concerts held in the Mendelssohn house in the early 1820s, where he heard "the latest works of the prodigy, mostly symphonic movements for string quintet with piano accompaniment."[52] Admittedly, relatively old-fashioned ideas about the use of continuo had managed to take root in Berlin; Johann Julius Hummel produced special editions of chamber music for the Berlin market with added figured bass (even including Haydn's Op. 17!) well into the 1770s.[53] But by the early 1820s writing for strings with continuo can only have represented an anachronism motivated, presumably, by pedagogical concerns. Of course, the experience gained in this way would soon prove invaluable to the young composer as he began his exploration of Bach's larger choral works, again under Zelter's (at times grudging) guidance. And again, in 1829, during his first trip to London, which apparently was even more old fashioned than Berlin, Mendelssohn led the first performance of his C-minor Symphony from the keyboard.[54]

But it is not only in matters of scoring and general stylistic characteristics that these works exhibit emphatically old-fashioned tendencies. The concentration on formal problems and the curious stylistic incongruities inherent in this pedagogical project reveal much about Mendelssohn's initial conception of sonata form.

The exposition in the first movement of each of the first five symphonies avoids a clear articulation of the arrival in the second key area. The textures in these movements are uniformly contrapuntal and essentially seamless. As a result, although the second key is in each case marked by a statement of the opening theme—or of figures derived from that theme—this statement is woven into an imitative motivic fabric in which it does not stand out with any great clarity, and the initial establishment of the secondary key is only weakly articulated. A strong articulative break is reserved for the end of the exposition, where the texture coalesces into a unison statement of a cadential version of the opening theme—or, again, of its principal figures.

The general shape of these expositions, with their imitative textures and sense of a gradual drift to the new key confirmed only at the final cadence of the first section, is reminiscent of baroque binary forms. Unlike binary forms, however, the second half of each of these movements falls into two clearly differentiated sections: a development and a recapitulation introduced by a relatively emphatic double return. The expositions have not, however, established a strongly contoured thematic-harmonic shape on which the recapitulation can be based, and as a result the recapitulations are quite free, almost kaleidoscopic, in their treatment of materials, and the surface flow is, again, broken only at the end of the movement by a cadential—unison—statement of the opening theme.

If the sense of a closural process in sonata style depends, at least in part, on expectations concerning the shape of the recapitulation engendered by the organization of the exposition—a shape that provides the general framework in which that process unfolds—it is clear that these earliest string symphonies can have only a vague relation to sonata-form processes. The recapitulation cannot depend on references to the pattern of an exposition the shape of which, aside from its opening and concluding gestures, is inherently unmemorable. To compensate for this, there is usually a slight elaboration of the final cadence of the movement, in the manner of the baroque techniques discussed earlier.

A significant change in structural premise becomes apparent in the first movement of the Sixth Symphony. The first theme is still the basis for a continuous imitative texture, but there are sharp breaks in that texture to articulate the move away from the tonic (m. 13) and the arrival in the dominant, which is marked by a new tune (m. 21). It is, perhaps, not entirely accurate to call this a tune, however; it is more in the nature of a cantus firmus in whole and half notes with faster-moving figures in the accompaniment. The effects most closely resembles the chorale style Mendelssohn had studied under Zelter a few years earlier.[55]

Although the break in texture at the beginning of this material is sharply articulated, the chorale texture, with its very slow rate of harmonic motion, allows Mendelssohn to avoid a clear sense of a stable arrival in the dominant, since the "tune" in no way suggests a periodic phrase structure. As in the earlier symphonies, the secondary key is not clearly established until the end of the exposition, which, once again, is marked by a unison statement of the opening theme.

It is revealing that the central issue of the nineteenth-century sonata style—the problem of relative pacing—appears in the first of these works to make use of a striking textural articulation at the arrival in the new key. In addition to the absence of a clear phrase pattern, the vagueness of the new theme results from a sudden slowing of the surface rhythm; it becomes very difficult to follow the melodic line after the bustle of the first part of the exposition, and the promising vitality of the movement seems to be swallowed up in an articulative murk. Coming on the heels of this breakdown, the eventual return to continually rushing eighth notes in the concluding section of the exposition seems unmotivated, introduced only to prevent a complete cessation of motion.

In the recapitulation, this kind of structure will tend to weaken the importance of any tonic arrivals before the final cadence, so that again, a baroque sense of overall shape, although modified by a new tendency toward textural articulation of the harmonic design, rubs against the underlying sonata-form shape of the movement. The resulting tension between form and gesture is not necessarily a weakness, however; when Mendelssohn has its elements under control—as he does in the fourth movement of the Octet, for example—it is one of the principal sources of his unusual success in handling sonata forms in the works of the late 1820s.

In the Seventh Symphony, in D minor, Mendelssohn manages to exploit the slightly amorphous outline of his second theme to create a striking effect in the recapitulation that plays off a delicate intermingling of major and minor modes in the closing cadence of the exposition.

The continuation of the second theme in the exposition is notable primarily for its remarkable vagueness of contour; it is a slowly wandering cantus firmus theme like the second theme of the Sixth Symphony. Eventually, continual references to the ♭6th degree in the more animated closing material of the exposition create a strong pull toward the minor mode that gently disrupts the stability of the new key.

In the recapitulation, the beginning of the second theme marks a solid arrival in the tonic, D major (mm. 153–56). Given the shapelessness of the theme itself, the fact that the continuation moves off in entirely new directions is not immediately striking. But this new excursion places a strong emphasis on the tonic minor, even introducing a new theme in D minor (m. 198—the theme is developed from elements of the preceding material). After this elaborate D-minor episode, the return of the cadential material, with its ♭6th degree, no longer functions simply as a chromatic coloring within a clearly established major mode, as it had in the exposition. Now the minor mode recalls the impressive minor-mode expansion just heard, and in this precarious context, the D major with which the movement ends is rendered extremely unstable—it threatens to fall back to D minor at any moment. It is left for the second movement, an Andante in D major, to absorb this instability into its lyric diatonic clarity. The vagueness of contour of the second theme, which allows Mendelssohn to drift effortlessly into new harmonic regions in the latter stages of the recapitulation, enables him to create a delicate functional link between the first and second movements, giving the lyricism of the second movement, which resolves the lingering harmonic uncertainties of the first, a special serenity.

The first movements of the Eighth and Ninth Symphonies are monothematic, and are remarkable for their thematic economy, recalling the ritornello structure of the pre-classical symphonic style. In each of these movements, the first and second themes are not merely related: they are, except for key, identical. In addition, it is a quirk of Mendelssohn's style that the retransition leading into the recapitulation in each work is a transposition of material that had led to the second theme in the exposition. Since this material is destined to turn up yet again, leading into the recapitulation of the second theme, the effect of all this economy is, unfortunately, less that of a masterful deployment of a minimum of material than of a rather tiresome paucity of means. And, since the second theme is an exact replica of the first, there is none of the reworking of pacing that allows Haydn to differentiate the functional identity of thematic statements in his "monothematic" expositions. In neither of these symphony movements, however, is the effect as distressing as it is in the first movement of his G-minor Piano Sonata (given, like all of Mendelssohn's previously unpublished juvenilia, a deceptively high opus number, 105, in the complete edition of his works assembled between 1874 and 1877). In the Sonata, monothematicism is pursued so rigorously that the second half of the exposition is little more than an almost literal restatement of the first half transposed to the mediant. The recapitulation then dutifully plods through all this material—unaltered aside from essentially decorative changes—twice in the tonic.

In fact, Mendelssohn does manage a striking transformation in the reca- pitulation of the second theme in the Ninth Symphony that reflects the imagi- nation with which he was beginning to approach even the most un- promisingly stilted formal designs. The theme—there is only one—divides into a sequential pattern of four measures on the tonic answered by four measures on the second degree. At the recapitulation of the "second theme," the first four measures are shifted from the tonic to V^7 of ii, which pushes strongly toward the harmony of the second limb of the theme. The thematic arrival, then, does not coincide with a clear harmonic arrival in the tonic; in- stead, it marks the beginning of a cadential motion toward the tonic that is only completed at the end of the consequent phrase. This evasion of a crucial structural articulation, undercutting the principal tonic arrival within the re- capitulation, is effected with a minimum of fuss, but it represents a signifi- cant attempt to bridge the gap between formalism and the dynamic essence of form. It is characteristic of Mendelssohn's later style that the transformation is rooted in the nature of the theme itself.

The sectionalization that characterizes the Eighth and Ninth Symphonies becomes even more distinct in the Tenth Symphony, in which the second group begins with a pointedly lyric contrasting theme introduced by a long, and rather static, patch of dominant preparation. The expansiveness of this arrival in the new key not only fails to introduce an increased rate of motion, but quite distinctly slows the pace, so that any energy generated by the tonal polarity of the exposition is swallowed up in the gentle lyricism of the tune. Once again, the more animated closing theme that follows seems to have been tacked on, almost as an afterthought.

With the thematic pattern of this work, Mendelssohn has arrived at the fundamental structural design of the romantic sonata. Not only does this rep- resent a fundamental contradiction of the harmonic basis of the form, but the admirable energy of the end-directed shapes achieved in the earliest sympho- nies, with their essentially baroque sense of articulation, can only be main- tained through an artificial play of surface animation that strengthens the impression that the movement consists of accumulations of thematic mate- rial arbitrarily lumped together.

Of the remaining symphonies, the Twelfth and the fragment referred to as the Thirteenth—as distinct from the C-minor Symphony, Op. 11—are strictly fugal. The use of fugue presents obvious problems for the articulation of structure, since the structural principles of fugue make no provision for the articulative deployment of texture. Mendelssohn's solution to this problem in the Twelfth Symphony, a complete break at the arrival in the secondary key followed by a new fugal exposition, is, in essence, simply an extension of the thematic principles that characterize the preceding symphonies. The fully worked out fugal exposition is just another, particularly elaborate, self-contained melodic structure, one with an emphatically closed, melodically defined structure that is fundamentally unassimilable to the articulative requirements of the sonata style.[56]

This is not to deny, of course, the impressive assurance of the writing; the technical polish in this movement is astonishing, but it has little to do with sonata-form procedures. In fact, after the entrance of the "second theme" in the exposition, the movement continues to its conclusion in a purely fugal texture, with no hint of a recapitulation.

The classicist tendencies revealed in these later symphonies are realized with rigid explicitness in the series of chamber works for piano and strings Mendelssohn wrote during this same period. In the first movement of each of the Piano Quartets, Opp. 1, 2, and 3, and in the Sextet, Op. 110—and progressively more markedly in each of these works—the formal design is broken up into separate melodic structures that are fundamentally unrelated to the underlying tonal dynamic.

In each of these movements, the opening theme is followed by a lengthy transition that closes into a leisurely cadenza for the piano on V of the secondary key. This cadential pause eventually leads to a contrasting lyrically organized tune that is presented twice over, first by the piano and then by the strings. The close into the local tonic at the end of the second statement serves as a hook on which an extended passage of virtuoso cadential figuration for the piano is hung to close the exposition. The increasing breadth of these various formal elements is revealing and startling: in the C-minor Quartet, Op. 1 (completed in October, 1822), the elaboration of V of III is ten measures long, the second theme, thirty-one, and the closing passage of cadential fireworks twenty-five; in the F-minor Quartet, Op. 2 (December, 1823), the halt on V of III covers eleven measures, the second theme, twenty-four, and the closing section forty-one; in the D-major Sextet, Op. 110 (May, 1824), V of V is marked by both a new theme and a cadential vamp, the combined length of which is nineteen measures, the second theme, thirty-one measures, and the close, fifty. In the B-minor quartet, Op. 3 (January, 1825), the proportions become gargantuan. The transition itself is extremely brief: the move to D major is accomplished in only three measures. The new key is then marked by two distinct themes. The first, which does not reappear later in the movement, is eleven measures long and serves to establish a half cadence on V of D major; this anticipatory dominant is then prolonged through the next twenty-five measures. The second theme itself is fifty-four measures long, and its relaxed lyric flow is emphasized by the insertion of an eight-measure echo of the main theme between its antecedent and consequent phrases. The cadential passagework at the end of the exposition covers sixty-three measures.

The point of this survey is not the measurement of musical shapes as though they were spatially defined objects, of course; these figures do, however, offer a rough indication of the relation of the various elements of those shapes to one another and of the strain these relations are put under as the proportions of the form are expanded.

The first movement of Op. 1 can serve as an example of the procedures through which this expansion is accomplished—procedures found, more or less unchanged, in all four of these works.

The opening theme is an antecedent-consequent structure, with the first phrase moving to a half cadence in m. 4, answered by a four-measure phrase that returns from V to I (Example 5). The continuation from this opening, set off by the overlapped entrance of the piano in m. 8, expands itself seamlessly by avoiding a stable cadence until m. 32, exhibiting a subtlety of phrase structure not normally associated with Mendelssohn's style.

After this admirable beginning, the pace slackens with jarring abruptness, coming to a dead halt on V of iii in a leisurely cadenza-like passage for the piano that extends from mm. 46 to 56. This sudden dilation inflates a perfectly ordinary touch of dominant preparation out of all proportion with what has gone before, draining energy from the push to the secondary key rather than intensifying it; but this expansiveness proves to be a necessary part of the thematic structure of the movement.

The second theme begins as though it were a transcription of the cabaletta of Rossini's "Una voce poco fa," and offers a clearly defined contrast to the nervous fragmentation of the main theme. In fact, the problem with the structure of the movement is that the lyricism of this material is a little too pronounced: the harmonic rhythm of the second theme moves at exactly half the rate of the first theme, coming to a half cadence after eight measures and covering another eight measures in the return to this tonic (Example 6). Given the underlying expansiveness of this structure, the increased pace of surface activity provided by the eighth-note filigree in the melodic line cannot alter the impression that this leisurely theme marks the secondary key area as a region of repose rather than of large-scale dissonance.

In this design, then, the cessation of motion on V of iii in mm. 46–56 serves to brake the modulatory momentum generated in the opening of the

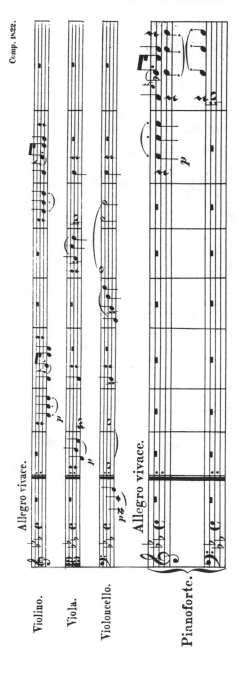

Example 5. Mendelssohn, Piano Quartet in C minor, Op. 1, I, mm. 1–9.

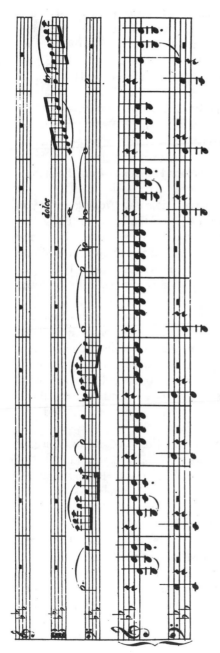

Example 6. Mendelssohn, Piano Quartet in C minor, Op. 1, I, mm. 45–66.

movement in preparation for the lyric calm of the second theme. The ten-measure cadenza frames the thematic compartments of the exposition, throwing the contrast of character between them into particularly sharp relief; this is crucial to the design because it is this contrast that is the central generating principle of the exposition. The profile of the second theme is almost identical to that of the first theme; indeed, the second theme is a calmer, more stable version of the first theme, pulling the sharply segregated motives thrown out in the opening of the movement into a single, flowing line (compare Examples 5 and 6). The thematic process is at least in part directly responsible for the unusual length of the transitional passage, as well: the filigree pattern of the second theme is developed gradually from the piano's meandering arabesques in mm. 46–56.

After this expansive confirmation of the secondary key, rounded off by an eighteen-measure codetta, Mendelssohn introduces the seemingly obligatory passage of virtuoso figuration that serves to close the exposition in each of these works. The sudden increase in surface rhythmic animation is almost completely unprepared in the preceding material, and harmonically this passage only confirms a key that has already been confirmed with too much breadth and solidity.

Although this sort of cadential virtuosity seems somewhat out of place in these works, it does play an important role in one type of sonata form. In the classical concerto, a closing expanse of passagework is part of a system of gestures that allows the solo instrument to counterbalance the weight of the orchestral forces, not only contributing to the harmonic stability of the end of the solo exposition, but providing the solo with the one kind of texture that is uniquely soloistic, and which cannot fail to give the solo the upper hand in its "contest" with the orchestra.

The closing section of the solo exposition in Mozart's C-major Concerto, K. 415, for example, is laid out along lines essentially identical to those of Mendelssohn's Op. 1, and the two large-scale concertos for two pianos Mendelssohn wrote at about the same time as Op. 1, in E major and A♭ major, follow this plan exactly, but with even more leisurely exuberance.

This cross-genre borrowing of formal gestures is inherently problematic, however: chamber works are not concertos. There is no large tutti ritornello at the beginning of the movement against which the "solo" piano must assert itself to balance the formal structure. As a result, the prominence given to the piano, especially in the later stages of the exposition (and recapitulation), tends to throw the movement wildly off balance. The skewed proportions that naturally result are primarily responsible for an unfortunate impression of empty display in these charming works. It seems ill-tempered to criticize a fourteen-year-old virtuoso's exuberance in writing for his instrument—it seems slightly mean-spirited to fault these works at all—but it is necessary for an understanding of Mendelssohn's later accomplishments that we have a clear idea of the problems to which his later works represent solutions.

Of course, it is not impossible to adopt virtuoso elements from the concerto style to other genres, but the function of these elements must be carefully integrated into the processive design of the particular movement. It is instructive to compare Mendelssohn's efforts along these lines with a series of concerted chamber works by another young composer-virtuoso, Beethoven. The first movement of each of Beethoven's Op. 1 trios exhibits a tendency to break into cadential fireworks near the end of the exposition. In each of these works, however, Beethoven either plants the beginning of an increased rhythmic animation within the second theme, so that it seems to spill over into the cadential material, or else arranges that the final affirmation of the secondary key will follow a digression away from that key, justifying the outburst of virtuosity as a gesture of structural articulation and stabilization. In fact, Beethoven's normal procedure combines these two techniques, so that in the first movement of Op. 1, No. 1, for example, the digression from the new key is marked by continually increasing animation that culminates in the passagework that celebrates the return. This is very different from the leisurely expansiveness of Mendelssohn's tunes, in which both the rhythmic busywork of the surface and the richness of harmonic vocabulary are fully subsumed within the elastic regularity of the lyric design. Furthermore, since the harmonic rhythm of Beethoven's second themes normally moves more quickly than his first themes, the increased animation at the end of the exposition does not represent an artificial injection of energy, as it does in Mendelssohn's works. Rather, it is part of a larger design manifesting the energy generated by the tonal polarity that underlies the exposition; the thematic pattern reflects the harmonic structure of the movement. Mendelssohn, working with a form organized around melodic relations, simply could not generate anything like this integration of structure and gesture.

The Symphony in C minor, Op. 11, is in every respect the most accomplished of Mendelssohn's earliest works; it was with Op. 11 that the composer chose to introduce himself to the London musical scene, leading a performance—from the piano—with the Philharmonic Society during his first trip to England in 1829. (For this occasion, Mendelssohn replaced the original Minuet with an orchestral arrangement of the Scherzo from the Octet.) Tovey dismissed the symphony as "clever,"[57] but in every movement there are strokes of genius that mark the path to the great works to follow. Even in the Minuet, the lush stillness and finely shaded textures of the Trio stake out new ground, and the romantically evocative transition back to the main body of the movement looks forward to elements of the scherzo style that Brahms employed throughout his career, from the early piano sonatas to the C-minor Piano Trio, Op. 101, and, in a subtly elusive form, in the Clarinet Quintet, Op. 115.

The thematic design of the Symphony reveals an attempt to generate all of the material of the work through manipulations of a fundamental motivic cell. The cell is a half-step relation first presented as the g''–ab'' figure (and its inverted transposition, db'''–c''') embedded in the opening measures of the first movement (Example 7). (The figure seems to have been a favorite of Mendelssohn's at this time; versions of it stalk relentlessly through the B-minor Piano Quartet, Op. 3, from 1825, and the A-minor String Quartet, Op. 13, from 1827, as well.) Throughout most of the work, the derivation of various themes from this figure is perfectly straightforward, but at times the process of interconnection is only crudely accomplished. In the finale, for example, a half-step neighbor motion centering on the fifth and flatted sixth degrees is inserted rather arbitrarily at cadences and between phrases of otherwise unrelated thematic figures. In the first movement, on the other hand, the motive is central to both the thematic process and the large-scale harmonic structure.

The move away from the tonic in the exposition is accomplished quickly, leaving C minor and reaching V of III in only six measures in the course of a counterstatement of the main theme. In a procedure that has become familiar in these early works, the ensuing sixteen-measure passage of animated dominant preparation leads to a broad anticipatory cadence that abruptly brakes the headlong pace of the opening pages of the movement.

This cadential passage is made up of an arching phrase thirteen measures long that overlaps with a lightly rescored repetition of itself. Each of these limbs divides into two almost equal subsections, the first *fortissimo*, with a triadic "rocket" figure in repeated eighth notes in the strings, the second *piano*, with primarily conjunct half-note motion in the winds. These juxtaposed contrasts are then balanced within the second theme, where strings and winds answer one another to weave a flowing cantabile in quarter notes that glides over a rustling eighth-note accompaniment figure (Example 8).

This generalized process of mediation, although impressive for its sensitive balance of detail, represents only one functional aspect of the passage. The cadence at the end of each of the two large sections places a gentle emphasis on a neighbor-note figure, Bb–Cb–Bb (mm. 53–54, clarinet, mm. 65–66, cello), which recalls the principal motive of the main theme and introduces a touch of minor-mode coloring to the preparation for the secondary key. The opening of the second theme (m. 67) immediately takes up this figure on the third and fourth steps of Eb major, g''–ab''–g'', reestablishing the major mode while retaining the half-step figure—and even restoring the motive to the pitches of its first appearance in mm. 1–2. Since the continuation of the second theme immediately touches on c''' (m. 69), the general outline of the second theme proves to be identical to that of the first (see Example 8). As was the case in the C-minor Piano Quartet discussed above, the structure of the exposition centers on what Carl Dahlhaus called "the history of a musical theme"[58]—the fragmented, agitated version of the primary motivic material presented in the main theme is transformed, its elements consolidated, in the smooth lyricism of the second theme. The explicit thematic contrast established in the exposition, and the eminently romantic concern for unity within variety that governs the thematic process are the underlying organizational principles of the movement. The expanses of preparatory material serve less to support the harmonic action of the exposition than to frame these form-determining thematic events, establishing their functional significance as emphatically as possible.

The cadential passage in mm. 43–67 is central to this process. What is curious, and revealing, about this material is that although it obviously serves as a transition between the agitation of the first group and the Italianate lyricism of the second theme, it is firmly rooted in the secondary key from the outset: the arrival in E♭ major is established with complete stability in m. 43, at the opening downbeat of the passage. This disjunction between harmonic and thematic functions reflects in the clearest possible manner the transfer of the principal organizational impulse from the emphasis on harmonic structure that characterized the classical sonata style to the thematic process that governs the romantic sonata. "Transition" has become a primarily thematic function that can—it seems—be carried out at any point in the harmonic design: it is the logic of the thematic process rather than the dynamic of the tonal polarity that generates the processive coherence of the exposition and of the work as a whole. The works created according to these principles often attain what Rosen has called a "noble, expansive, relaxed, and academic beauty unattainable . . . in the late eighteenth century."[59] What is lost, of course, is the tight coordination of thematic and harmonic processes that animates the classical sonata style; the bustling agitation of much of the movement seems more nervous than powerful.

Mendelssohn, however, unlike most classicist composers, handles the recapitulation of his design with considerable subtlety, convincingly reworking elements of the harmonic structure within a strictly maintained thematic framework.

The passage of dominant preparation (mm. 263–83) and the beginning of the cadential passage (mm. 283–88) remain firmly in the tonic, C minor. This is, of course, a common procedure in preparing for the recapitulation of a major-mode second theme, and simply follows the course laid out in the exposition. The end of the shortened cadential passage does not lead to C major,

Example 7. Mendelssohn, Symphony in C minor, Op. 11, I, mm. 1-9.

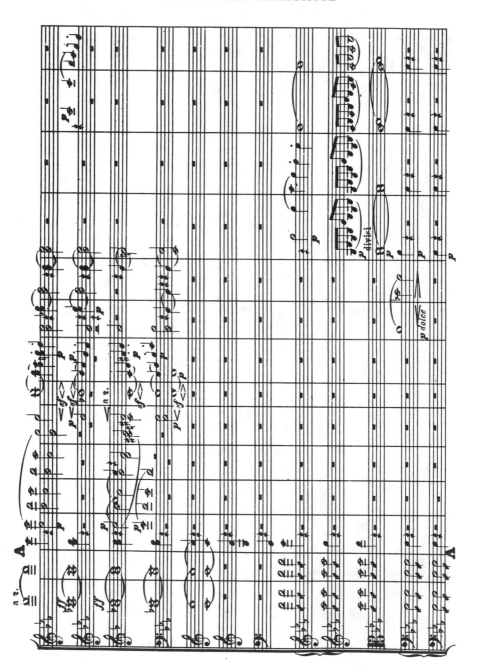

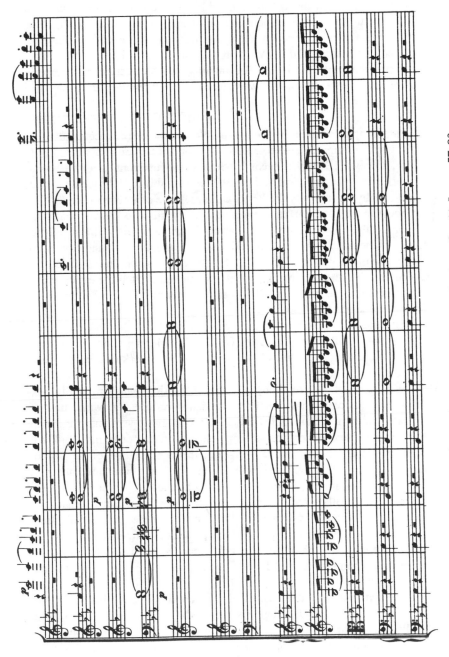

Example 8. Mendelssohn, Symphony in C minor, Op. 11, I, mm. 57–80.

however. The A♭ of the G–A♭–G neighbor motion is taken as a pivot: a modulation to A♭ major is suspended from it, and the neighbor-note figure is shifted to C–D♭–C in the cadence to this new, and unexpected, key. The second theme is recapitulated in ♭VI, then, organized around A♭ (as the temporary tonic root) and C–D♭–C (as the opening melodic gesture) restoring the motive to the pitches of its *secondary* center (see m. 4) while setting them in a new harmonic context (Example 9).

This diversion naturally postpones the establishment of the tonic major until the recapitulation of the triumphant closing theme (a brusque intrusion of the G–A♭–G figure in the coda forces the end of the movement back to C minor, however). The lyric second theme, then, functions as a transitional element in the recapitulation, and the expansive stability of the theme serves, paradoxically, to intensify the larger cadential role of its A♭ major (♭VI to the home tonic, C minor) as a massive appoggiatura to the dominant. By combining this powerful secondary harmonic development with a strictly reproduced thematic framework, Mendelssohn recaptures, in an idiosyncratic way, some of the dynamic quality of the classical sonata. The effect is in itself impressive and convincing, but it is achieved only at the expense of a harmonic structure in the exposition that seems at least inefficient, if not slightly incoherent, by comparison.

It is in the slow movement of the Symphony—and in the slow movement of the earlier F-minor Piano Quartet, Op. 2—that Mendelssohn begins to develop a more supple control of the thematic framework of a sonata-form movement.

The Andante of the Symphony is a monothematic sonata form with an exceptionally elaborate transitional section that introduces its own distinctive thematic material. Initially, the first- and second-group versions of the main theme are identical except for scoring—strings in the tonic, mm. 1–8, and winds at the dominant, mm. 33–40—but the continuation of the second theme version differs significantly from the opening of the movement.

For all its Italianate lyricism, the opening theme is oddly compact. Until the close into a full cadence in the seventh and eighth measures, what turns out to be the entire theme sounds like it will be the antecedent of a full-blown sixteen-measure tune. But in place of a consequent phrase to complete this design, the continuation of the first group consists of a series of cadential figures that soon lead to ♭VI for the expansive bridge passage mentioned above (Example 10).

At the sixth and seventh measures of the second-theme version of the tune, on the other hand, the full cadence is replaced by a half cadence to V of the local tonic, leading into a consequent phrase that realizes the regularized phrase structure implied at the opening of the movement. The lyric char-

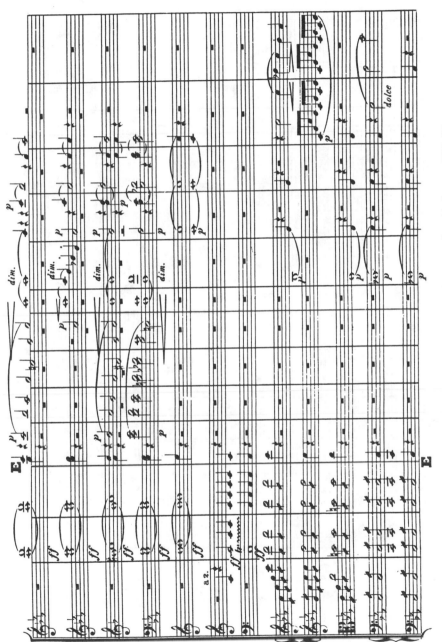

Example 9. Mendelssohn, Symphony in C minor, Op. 11, I, mm. 280–92.

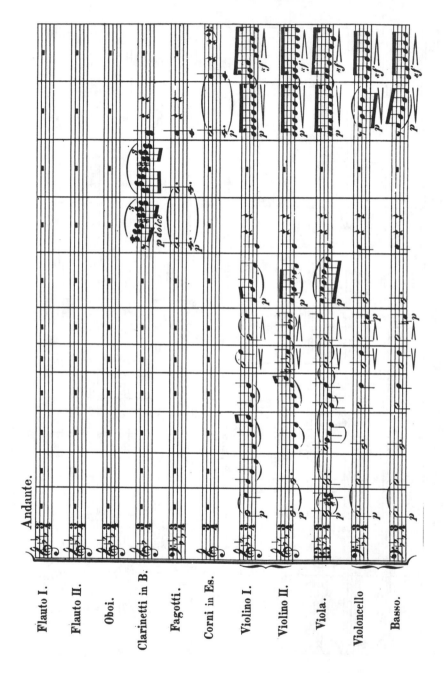

Example 10.   Mendelssohn, Symphony in C minor, Op. 11, II, mm. 1–11.

acter of the second theme, then, does not function as a contrast to the main theme, but as the realization of the lyric structure latent in the theme itself (Example 11).

The main body of the development section of the movement is given over to a restatement of the transitional material—the passage on ♭VI in the exposition—at its original pitch level. A slight change at the end of the passage transforms this C♭ major (notated as B major) into an appoggiatura to the home dominant, B♭ major, leading into the opening of the recapitulation. This unusual procedure seems to have the effect of resolving this material; it does not reappear later in the recapitulation.

The recapitulation opens with the first-theme version of the main theme— identified by its scoring for strings alone—but at the sixth measure it follows the harmonic plan of the second theme, closing to a half cadence. This opening phrase is then answered by the consequent phrase of the second-theme version, rescored for winds alone (in the exposition, it had combined winds and strings). The opening of the recapitulation, then, combines the first and second themes into a single gesture, and the thematic element of the double return takes on a new significance, persuasively coordinating the thematic and tonal designs of the movement by integrating the moment of tonal resolution with the complete realization of the expansive—but at first only latent—lyricism of the first theme.

In the wake of this, the thematic framework of the recapitulation is radically altered: there is no necessity for—nor sense in—a return of the second theme, and the sixteen—measure version of the tune at the opening of the recapitulation leads directly into the closing theme, while the cadential material from the end of the first group (mm. 8–16) is used as a short coda.

The Adagio of the F-minor Piano Quartet is even more radical in its treatment of thematic material. The movement is not, strictly speaking, monothematic, but the second theme is very closely related to the main theme, which in turn is derived from the main theme of the first movement (Example 12).

At the return to the tonic at the beginning of the recapitulation, the piano retains an accompaniment figure from the development section (the development has dealt almost exclusively with the descending-third figure of the second theme). The main theme returns over this accompaniment, but it is presented in the scoring and register of the second theme (Example 13).

Given the sharp differentiation between the first and second themes—the first is introduced by the piano, alone, in the middle register, the second by the violin in an upper register, accompanied by the piano and lower strings— this simple transformation is particularly striking, representing an interpenetration of characteristics of the two themes at the climax of the

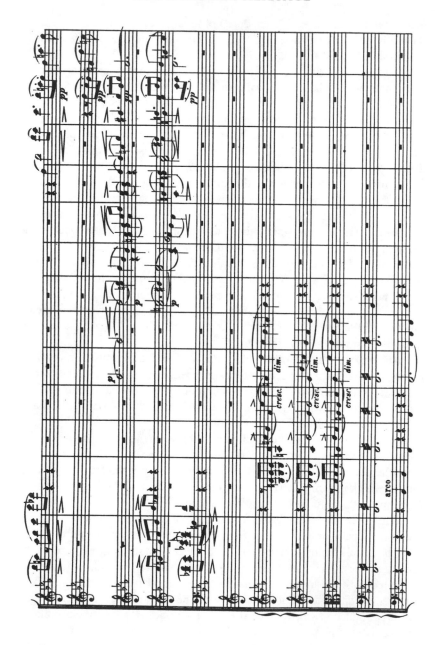

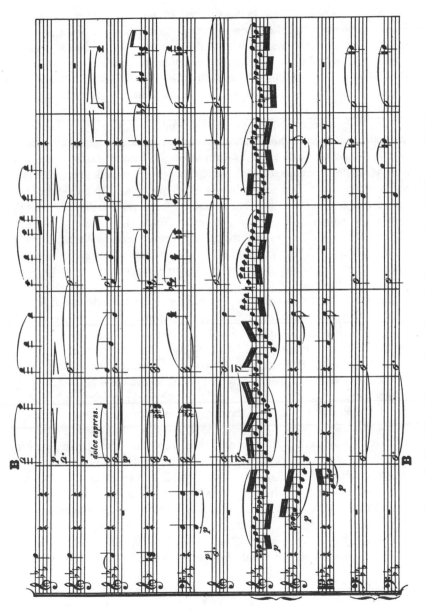

Example 11. Mendelssohn, Symphony in C minor, Op. 11, II, mm. 27-45.

movement. As was the case in the Andante from Op. 11, the opening of the recapitulation resolves the second theme by combining elements of it with the first theme. But in the Quartet there is a distinct second theme, and that theme never actually reappears in the recapitulation; the resolution is accomplished simply by making the implicit relation between the themes—the similarity of their underlying contours—explicit at this central moment of the form.

For all the unruffled lyric grace these movements display, the formal strategies that underlie them represent a radical break with the classicist style of Mendelssohn's earlier sonata-form works; to rework Tovey's formulation, Mendelssohn manages, with astonishing delicacy, both to practice form and to demolish it. But, as we have seen, Tovey found in Mendelssohn's forms only a pursuit of "easy short cuts to effect" that he dismissed as the regrettable evidence of apparently incurable artistic immaturity. If we simply take Mendelssohn—even at the age of fifteen—seriously as a composer, these manipulations emerge as evidence of an attempt to reshape the symmetries inherent in a thematically organized form to match the dynamic processes of the classical sonata style.

It is worth noting, of course, that these procedures are deployed in lyric slow movements, where problems of pacing and large-scale structure are in large part subordinated to the unfolding of the melodic design. Thematic process always remains central to Mendelssohn's conception of form—the opening of the recapitulation in these two movements is certainly more striking as a thematic event than as a tonal resolution—but the melodic pattern in which these processes are played out need not necessarily contradict the structural dynamic of the form. In each of these movements, the climax of the tonal process, the reacquisition of the tonic, is coordinated with the climactic moment of the thematic process, and the melodic shape of the recapitulation is extensively reworked to reflect this. The formal manipulations through which this integration is accomplished are certainly clever, and even drastic—although, characteristically, they are carried out with an air of complete normality—but they clearly are not simply the symptoms of boyish impertinence.

It was in his next major work, the Octet, Op. 20, that Mendelssohn extended his mastery of the sonata style to every element of his writing.

Example 12a. I, mm. 1-9.

Example 12b. II, mm. 1-6.

Example 12. Mendelssohn, Piano Quartet in F minor, Op. 2. (Continued.)

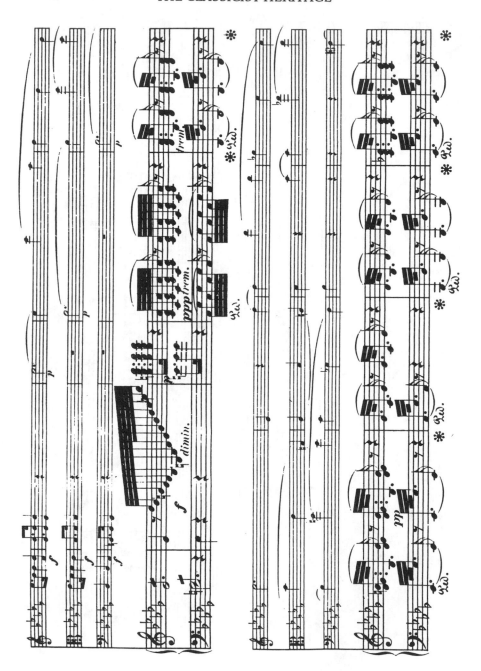

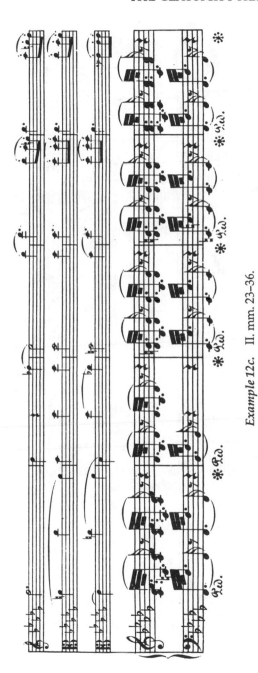

Example 12c. II. mm. 23-36.

Example 12. (Continued.) Mendelssohn, Piano Quartet in F minor, Op. 2.

Example 13.   Mendelssohn, Piano Quartet in F minor, Op. 2, II, mm. 68–73.

CHAPTER 3

THE OCTET, OP. 20

The Octet, Op. 20, written in 1825, is Mendelssohn's first unquestionable masterpiece. The brilliance of this work lies not only in the richness and energy of its thematic material and the virtuosity of its instrumental writing, but in the conception of sonata style that animates all four of its movements. The sense of form manifested in each of these movements has its roots in the composer's earlier works, of course, but those works only occasionally sustain the level of integration of form and gesture found throughout the Octet. It is the consistency with which this coordination is maintained that marks the beginning of the brief period during which Mendelssohn's creative achievement clearly stands outside the classicist approach to form that characterizes the romantic sonata style.

The last page of the manuscript of the Octet is dated "Berlin d. 15 Oct./1825," but the work did not appear in print until January, 1833 (parts only, with a four-hand piano version in March or April of the same year; the score was not published until 1848).[1] At some time between 1825 and 1833, Mendelssohn subjected the work to a thorough revision that addressed both details of the part-writing and fundamental issues of formal structure.

Few of Mendelssohn's sketches have survived, but in a number of cases early versions of works are preserved in completed manuscripts. A comparison of these manuscript versions with the printed score invariably reveals that the final shape of a work—even a work like the Octet or the *Hebrides* Overture that seems to be the embodiment of youthful spontaneity—was the result of sweeping revisions of the composer's original conception.[2] In the case of the Octet, a comparison of the manuscript version of the work and the printed score is particularly informative. In every movement except the Scherzo, a significant reorganization of formal proportions was accomplished in the published version, primarily through the elimination of large blocks of material from the manuscript version. A close examination of the passages involved discloses a pattern of recomposition in which Mendelssohn systematically abandoned the schematic formal regularity characteristic of the works preceding the Octet in favor of a more flexible formal design; and in each instance, the revision serves to clarify the role of the fundamental structural premises that control the large-scale organization of the movement.

FIRST MOVEMENT: ALLEGRO MODERATO, MA CON FUOCO

The formal proportions of the first movement of the Octet are unusual: the exposition is 131 measures long, the development 89, the recapitulation only 60, and the coda 43. In the manuscript version, the large formal subdivisions are somewhat more evenly balanced. (The note values adopted for the printed score are half those of the manuscript, so the comparison of the two versions is a little complicated: in the manuscript the exposition is 295 measures long, the development 173, the recapitulation 179, and the coda 84.) The principal change, then, is in the recapitulation, which, already relatively short in the original version, is whittled down to less than half the length of the exposition in the published score. This would seem to contradict the notion of symmetrical balance that underlies the sonata style—especially the classicist style that has emerged in the chamber works considered in chapter 2. It will turn out that the relation of formal elements within the movement reflects the influence of organizational principles that control almost every aspect of the musical design.

The first part of the exposition, up to the arrival in the dominant in m. 68, falls into two large sections—mm. 1–37 and mm. 37–68—each beginning with a statement of the opening theme in the tonic. The first section itself is divided into two main subsections—mm. 1–21, ending with a full cadence to the tonic that is followed by a short pause, and mm. 21–37, introducing new material (derived from the main theme) that seems at first to initiate a modulation but eventually leads back to a cadence to the tonic. The second section, mm. 37–68, repeats almost all of the melodic pattern of mm. 1–37, but the harmonic structure is completely different, and a number of small elisions weaken the articulation of the subsections within this material slightly. Figure 1 shows, in summary form, the melodic-harmonic action of the entire sixty-eight measure passage.

This structure bears an obvious resemblance to the common practice of initiating the modulation to the dominant within a counterstatement of the main theme, but a closer analysis will reveal the influence of a different formal principle.

The first theme, although unusual in its exuberance, is based on one of the most common opening gambits of the classical style: a phrase in the tonic is repeated sequentially on the supertonic, closing into a ii–V–I cadence. The seemingly innumerable realizations of this progression in the classical style range from the brisk formality of the opening of the Allegro in the first movement of Beethoven's First Symphony to the calm expansiveness of the opening of his C-major Quintet, Op. 29. This same pattern acquires an air of mystery and foreboding in the opening of the "Appassionata" or the E-minor Quartet, Op. 59, No. 2, where the tonic is minor and the second step is the Neapolitan. In the Octet, this harmonic structure, providing a strongly-directed foundation for the exuberant sweep of the first violin, gives the opening of the movement a forward-pressing urgency not always associated with Mendelssohn's melodic style (Figure 2).

The second subsection begins in m. 21. The articulative gestures at this point—a full close to the tonic followed by a short pause to round off the preceding section, the introduction of a new texture and of material animated by a faster-paced harmonic rhythm, and an immediate sequential motion through the submediant—are all signals that normally mark the initiation of the modulation away from the tonic toward the secondary key area of the exposition. Harmonically, the passage does not move decisively away from the tonic, however. Normally, this modulation would lead immediately to the minor submediant, which would be taken as a pivot, becoming the supertonic in a ii–V–I cadence in the dominant key. Convenient examples of this procedure can be found in the first movement of Haydn's Symphony No. 85, mm. 23–31, or Beethoven's G-major Quartet, Op. 18, No. 2, mm. 25–35. In the Octet, however, the initial move is to the major submediant, C major. This seems to undercut the modulatory impulse of the section, which at first certainly sounds like a transition, since in this context C major tends to push toward F minor, which is more strongly oriented toward the tonic than toward the dominant key. Nonetheless, it would not be impossible for this passage to lead eventually to a cadence in Bb major, although it would take a certain amount of additional material to establish and confirm this new key; Haydn uses this more elaborate modulatory scheme in the first movement of the Symphony No. 101 (mm. 49–65). By sitting on the minor supertonic throughout mm. 24–27, Mendelssohn contrives to suspend its functional identity with relation to both Eb major and Bb major, suggesting for a moment the unlikely possibility that the supertonic might actually be the goal of this transitional effort.

Thematic material:	A	B		A'		B'	C
Eb major:	I	I–vi–ii–V	–	I – modulating to		–	V
Measure:	1	21		37		52	68

Figure 1. Mendelssohn, Octet, Op. 20, I, mm. 1–68.

Phrase:	a1	a1	a2	a2
Eb :	I – – vi – ii–V– I		cadential to I	extended through sequence, leading to a full close on I
Measure:	1 – 5	5 – 9	9 – 13	13 – 21

Figure 2. Mendelssohn, Octet, Op. 20, I, mm. 1–21.

The cadence in mm. 27–29 leads abruptly back to Eb major, however, and the return to the tonic is confirmed in an extended cadence in mm. 29–37, which repeats the F-minor material from mm. 25–26, now firmly drawn back into the tonic orbit. In retrospect, as Figure 3 shows, the underlying harmonic structure of the entire "modulatory" passage in mm. 21–37 proves to be an expansion of the progression played out in the opening theme, but with a curiously strong emphasis on the supertonic.

With the restatement of the opening theme beginning in m. 37, this unusual emphasis on the supertonic suddenly takes on structural significance. The harmony in the fourth measure of the first phrase of the theme is altered slightly, and in turn the opening of the second phrase is shifted from ii to V7 of ii; as a result, the cadence at the end of the phrase (m. 45) is planted firmly in F minor, finally achieving the initial modulatory foothold that had proven so strangely elusive in mm. 21–37. The degree of structural dissonance inherent in the tonic-supertonic relation embedded in the opening measures of the main theme and elaborated in the ambiguous modulatory passage in mm. 21–37 is gradually intensified to provide the impetus for the modulation away from the tonic (Figure 4).

The sequential pattern from mm. 16–21 returns after the first statement of the cadential material (mm. 45–47, labeled a2x in Figure 4); but instead of leading back to the local tonic (now F minor) as it did originally, the sequence leads abruptly to V of G minor in m. 52: G minor is, of course, the supertonic of the just-established F minor. Since this arrival is marked by a restatement of material from m. 25, which has originally been associated

Eb major:	I – vi –	ii–V– I	(I – I)	:	I –	VI –	ii –	V –	I
Theme:	a1	a1	(a2 a2)	:	b1		b2		a1x
Measure:	1 – 5	5 – 9	9 – 21	:	21	23	25	28	37

Figure 3. Mendelssohn, Octet, Op. 20, I, mm. 1–37.

Eb major:	I – vi –	ii– V– I	I – –		I –	V/ii –	ii
	a1	a1	a2	has become	a1x	a1x	a2x
Measure:	1–5	5–9	9–21		37	41	45

Figure 4. Mendelssohn, Octet, Op. 20, I, mm. 1–21 and 37–45.

with the uneasy emphasis on ii of Eb major discussed above, an overall parallelism between mm. 1–37 and the section starting at the return of the opening theme in m. 37 begins to emerge: the emphasis on the supertonic in the opening section is taken up first in the establishment of F minor as a key in its own right early in the restatement, and this in turn leads to the supertonic of this supertonic key in a passage that pointedly recalls the modulatory feint toward ii in the first section. The harmonic structure of the exposition seems to be unfolding increasingly expansive, interlocking realizations of the step motion from I to ii first enunciated in the opening measures of the movement.

This pattern—suggesting a process of growth and transformation—is more than vaguely reminiscent of the vision of organic growth Goethe had propounded in this *Die Metamorphose der Pflanzen*, in which the development of a plant is held to reveal the progressive transformation of a single, fundamental cell.[3] Goethe and Mendelssohn had become close friends at their first meeting—through Zelter—in 1821. It is not, I think, unreasonable to find evidence of Goethe's influence in the structural organization of the composer's first fully mature work.[4]

The abrupt arrival in G minor in m. 52 retains much of the functional ambiguity that colored the F minor of mm. 21ff.; in fact, this G minor seems less arrived at then simply insisted upon. It is this curious insubstantiality that gives the eventual emergence of Bb major (in m. 59), seeming to rise out of this G-minor mist, a particularly romantic character. The cadences in mm. 55–58 place a gentle emphasis on the first violin's bb as the third of this strange G minor at just the point where the original F-minor version of the passage had swung back from the supertonic to Eb major (compare mm. 54–55 and 27–28). The written-out ritardando in mm. 57–58 intensifies this sensitive moment by prolonging the b♭ of m. 58 as a suspension over what sounds like the leading tone, the F♯ (respelled, however, as G♭) in the second cello, implying the initiation of a strongly directed cadential gesture that should close to G minor in m. 59.

But when the second viola climbs to e♮' on the last half-beat of m. 58, G minor simply vanishes. E♮ forms an augmented sixth with the F♯/G♭ in the bass, and the resulting French sixth expands to a B♭$^6_4$ in m. 59, leading into a long cadential preparation for the arrival in B♭ major in m. 68. The B♭ of the first violin in m. 59, suddenly transformed into the tonic root of the new key, is swallowed up in the textural expansion of this cadential preparation and only reemerges, spread over three octaves, at the beginning of the second theme in m. 68.

The G-minor passage serves, then, as a particularly subtle preparation for the move to the dominant. The cadence in mm. 555–58, which seems to be intent on establishing G minor, places a special emphasis on B♭; B♭ is a perfectly stable element within G minor, of course, but the harmonic realm defined by that cadence is itself distinctly precarious. As a result, the enharmonic shift in m. 58 can pivot around this already sensitized B♭— which is paradoxically both consonant and unstable—creating a new tonal orientation that instantly clarifies and stabilizes its functional identity.

This method of preparing a modulation by emphasizing the eventual harmonic goal within a tonally ambiguous context is an important element in the gentle smoothness of Mendelssohn's style. The modulation is not engendered by the intrusion of an actual dissonance, but by the instability of a larger harmonic context that is in itself structurally dissonant; the modulation in turn functions as a resolution, supplying a restabilized tonal orientation for this complex of ambiguous relations.

At the same time, as Figure 5 indicates, the entire passage from mm. 45–59 plays out a long-range neighbor-note embellishment of the bass note, F. Like the motion through G minor, this process builds on implications suggested in the parallel passage of the first part of the exposition, where F was tentatively established as a possible tonic before falling back to E♭ major.

The overall shape of this lower-voice motion, F–G–F, retains the contour of the E♭–F–E♭ motion of mm. 1–37, but it transforms the function of its elements: in the earlier passage, the move back to E♭ marks the return to the tonic; the later passage begins in F minor, but after the excursion through G returns to a dominant seventh on F (m. 45) that initiates the cadence to the secondary key.

On an even larger scale, Figure 6 shows that the entire modulatory process of the exposition is based on the same interlocking harmonic pattern that has threaded through every level of the first part of the movement, hinging on the

Eb	–	F	–	Eb	becomes	F	–	(F♯)	–	G	–	(F♯/Gb)	–	F
1–21		24		37		45		54		55		58		59

Figure 5. Mendelssohn, Octet, Op. 20, I, mm. 1–37 and 45–59.

| Main Theme: | I–vi– ii–V–I | | | | | | |
| Measure: | 1 | 5 | 9 | | | | |

| Mm. 1–37 | I | – – – – – | VI–ii–V–I | | | | |
| Measure: | 1 | | 23 25 37 | | | | |

| Restatement | (| |) I – | VI – ii – | VI/ii – | ii/ii – | V |
| Measure: | 1 | | 37 | 41 45 | 52 | 55 | 68 |

| First Group | I | – | | VI– ii | – | | V |
| Measure: | 1 | | | 41 45 | | | 68 |

Figure 6. Mendelssohn, Octet, Op. 20, I, mm. 1–68.

tonic-supertonic step motion embedded in the main theme. Again, Goethe's vision of the progressive metamorphosis of a fundamental cell would seem to provide an illuminating analytical metaphor for the intertwined harmonic and thematic processes as they unfold in the first part of the movement.

As was mentioned earlier, the broad outlines of this design suggest an unusually elaborate realization of a normal classical practice—initiating the structural modulation in the course of a counterstatement of the main theme. This is a technique particularly common in Haydn's works, in connection with which H. C. Robbins Landon has called it "double presentation."[5] An interpretation along these lines would plot out the large subdivisions of the material accurately enough, but it would fail to illuminate fully the functional processes unfolded in this remarkable passage.

The significance of this opening does not lie in the fact that the theme reappears, but in the way that every element of the two versions of the material plays a role in shaping the processive design of the movement. Measures 21–36 are not simply filled with elaborately deployed but essentially extraneous material standing between the two statements of the tune: it is the carefully balanced ambiguity of this material that generates the modulatory energy for the decisive motion away from the tonic. And what occurs in mm. 37–68 is not simply a restatement of the head of the main theme that leads on to new transitional material. Rather, this later passage reworks and reinterprets the entire thematic-harmonic structure of mm. 1–37. The modulation tentatively implied and ultimately thwarted in the first part of the exposition is realized and expanded upon in the second, while the impetus of this continuous process of harmonic transformation is controlled by the framework established through the repetition of the thematic patterns laid out in the first section. Seen in this way, Mendelssohn's procedure seems less closely related to sonata-form techniques of double presentation and modulation than to the double exposition characteristics of the classical concerto.

Much of the power of the double-exposition form arises from the relation between the opening ritornello, which generates a tremendous potential energy by presenting the principle thematic material of the movement while simultaneously implying and withholding any fully organized modulation away from the tonic, and the solo exposition, in which this modulatory potential is realized as the material of the ritornello is organized into a sonata-form exposition. In the Octet, this structural principle is adopted to allow the work's modulatory impulse to develop gradually out of the relatively neutral harmonic pattern that underlies the main theme: mm. 1–37, implying but ultimately withholding a strong modulatory impulse, serve as the ritornello, and mm. 37–68, where that impulse is reinterpreted and realized, as the first part of the "solo" exposition.

At the same time, the double-exposition structure provides a formal basis for the expansive—almost symphonic—scope of the movement, and even for the unusual brilliance of the instrumental writing. In this, Mendelssohn is following a long-standing tradition: gestures borrowed from the concerto can be found in instrumental genres throughout the eighteenth and early nineteenth centuries. Bach's *Italian Concerto* is, of course, essentially a concerto transcribed for a solo keyboard instrument, while Beethoven's C-major Sonata, Op. 2, No. 3, combines sonata-form procedures with some of the more flamboyant elements of the Viennese concerto: the extraordinary virtuosity of the keyboard writing in the first movement finds its natural culmination in a full-blown cadenza for the "soloist." Haydn's E♭-major Sonata, H. 52, from 1798—his most elaborate and most broadly designed keyboard work—represents a somewhat more subtle realization of the same principle. The first eight measures of the first movement present a neutral "ritornello" version of the main theme which momentarily feigns a modulation in the sequential passage in mm. 6–7. An elaborately virtuoso "solo" presentation of this same material begins in m. 9, and in the course of this new version, the sequential passage is transformed into a modulatory transition that leads to a restatement of the main theme firmly entrenched in the dominant—itself an articulative gesture typical of the ritornello concerto.

Both the brilliance of the instrumental style and the expanded proportions of the movement, which result from the systematic repetition of large blocks of material in "ritornello" and "solo" guises, are directly motivated by the underlying concerto-form structure introduced in the opening measures.

The sophistication of Mendelssohn's adoption of the structural principles of concerto form in the opening pages of the Octet is particularly impressive in light of what seems to have been his lifelong difficulties with the genre. In the Concerto for Two Pianos in A♭ major, written in 1824, for example, the opening ritornello contains an elaborate transition to the dominant, and the new key is duly marked by a statement of the second theme. This scheme, which is also followed in the Concerto for Violin and Piano in D minor (1823) and the Concerto for Two Pianos in E♭ major (1823), simply obliterates the dynamic relation between the potential implied by the opening ritornello and the structural process realized in the solo exposition: the solo exposition can do little more than repeat the pattern established in the ritornello—there is no room for the process of reinterpretation that differentiates the solo and tutti in the classical concerto. As Tovey and Rosen have pointed out, the procedure Mendelssohn follows engenders a premature realization of the flow of tension and resolution that underlies the movement, playing out the tonic-dominant polarization and resolution within the ritornello—before the solo has played a single note.[6] In his later concertos Mendelssohn simply eliminated the opening ritornello, replacing it with a short introductory flourish in the orchestra. It is striking, then, that the double-exposition principle underlies two of Mendelssohn's most satisfying formal designs—the first movement of the Octet, and the first movement of the "Italian" Symphony; in this latter work, there is even a cadenza near the end of the recapitulation introduced by a general pause on a tonic $^6_4$.

In the Octet, the "solo" exposition gradually moves toward the dominant, and the arrival is marked by a new theme related, as Krummacher and Todd have pointed out, to material from mm. 21–36.[7] As we have seen, the handling of the second theme caused Mendelssohn a certain amount of trouble in his earliest works, where the arrival in the secondary key invariably broadened into an expansive lyric tune. The internal self-sufficiency of these tunes tends to bring the movement to the brink of a complete cessation of motion and dissipates the energy generated by the large-scale dissonant relation between the tonic and the secondary key. In the Octet, Mendelssohn contrives for the first time to integrate a lyric second theme into an exposition that moves with steadily increasing animation toward its closing cadence.

In relation to the expansive scale of the first part of the movement, the second theme is surprisingly compact, consisting of two almost identical four-measure phrases that hinge on cadences to the tonic at every second measure.

Supported by these continual returns to the tonic, the phrase structure gives the theme a strangely motionless quality (Example 14).

Like the first theme, this Bb-major tune begins with a strong downbeat accent in the accompaniment that serves as a springboard for the motion of the melodic line. Unlike the first theme, however, the end of the first phrase of the second theme does not overlap onto the initial downbeat of the second phrase to supply a new opening accent. Instead, the first phrase comes to a dead halt on the downbeat of its fourth measure (m. 71), and the gap between this closing accent and the beginning of the next phrase is filled in with the head of the opening theme.

As a result of its constricted, almost static character—the second half of each phrase is almost an exact retrograde of the first half—this undeniably lyric theme does not really provide the broad stability needed to establish itself as the goal of the expansively laid-out design of the first part of the exposition. In contrast to the lyric coagulations that were spread over the secondary key in the earlier works, this theme—really a thematic cell circling back repeatedly on itself—seems to act like a coiled spring, its compactness necessitating continuation and its quietly gathering energy providing the impetus for the propulsive brilliance of the final stages of the exposition.

The continuation of the second group takes the form of an animated developmental passage based on fragmentation and recombination of elements of the second theme and rapid harmonic shifts. This too marks an advance over the earlier works, where the animation of the latter stages of the exposition seemed to have been tacked on. Mendelssohn's developmental expansion is, in fact, reminiscent of Beethoven's procedure in the first movement of the "Waldstein"—another work in which the second theme is remarkable for its concision.

Mendelssohn arranges the continuity between the end of the lyric theme and the continuation of the second group with great care. In place of a full close, the cadence at the end of the second phrase of the new theme is undercut by a sudden shift from Bb major to the submediant, G minor; the animation of the developmental passage is the persuasive surface manifestation of this disruption of the newly established key center and of the need to return to it. And in contrast to the clear closing-accent-then-upbeat articulation at the end of the first phrase, the closing accent of the consequent phrase is elided with the opening accent of the continuation. This dovetailing further alleviates the sense of static juxtaposition of closed blocks of material that had characterized the second group in the works considered in chapter 2.

The nervous abruptness of the harmonic and textural shifts in the ensuing passage might at first seem bewilderingly unstructured, like the developmental digressions in Dvorak's symphonic expositions, but they prove to be care-

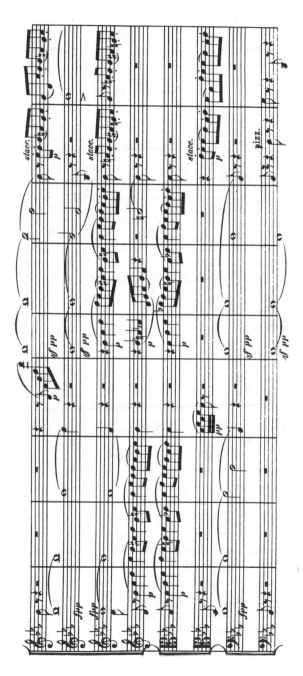

Example 14. Mendelssohn, Octet, Op. 20, I, mm. 68–76.

Bb major:	I	–	–	vi	–	VI	–	–	ii–V	–	(V/vi)	–	I^6_4
	2nd theme		dev.		2nd theme			dev.	1st theme		2nd theme		
Measure:	68		75		77			84	90	92		96	

Figure 7.   Mendelssohn, Octet, Op, 20, I, mm. 68–96.

fully integrated into the structural processes of the movement: as Figure 7 shows, the harmonic design of this section, articulated by the changes of texture, turns out to be yet another realization of the progression that has controlled every important aspect of the movement so far.

The first part of this section moves from Bb major to G minor (and then on to a G major that is strongly biased toward its own minor submediant, C minor) reestablishing, in a new guise, the relation between G (major/minor) and Bb major played out in the modulation in mm. 52–59. At the end of the passage, an enharmonic play on Gb and F♯ in the bass of mm. 90–92—setting off a momentary shift from V of Bb to V of G minor—pointedly recalls the lower-voice pivot that forced the move from G minor to Bb major in that earlier passage.

The drive toward Bb major is supported by an underlying regularity of two- and four-bar phrases, and seems, at first, to be quite straightforward. But continually shifting patterns on the rhythmic surface cloud this underlying regularity and eventually undermine the clarity of the cadential motion. Because rhythmic complexity and formal irregularity are not attributes normally associated with Mendelssohn's style, it will be useful to examine this passage in some detail.

The first stage of the developmental passage (mm. 84–87) establishes a metric pattern in which the downbeat accent in each measure serves as the springboard for a motive (labeled x in Example 15) beginning on the second beat; this is the pattern that has governed most of the exposition.

As Example 16 shows, this design is continued in mm. 88–89, with a change from eighth notes to sixteenths (x′) and the introduction of a dialogue between the first and second violins alternating statements of x′ at the distance of one measure. In m. 90, the rhythmic figure is shifted onto the downbeat (x″). This "anticipation" coincides with the reestablishment of V of Bb, and lends the final stage of the cadential drive a special urgency. This is in turn intensified by a compression of the dialogue between the two violins, with the alternations of x″ entering at every half measure. This stretto makes the two-beat fragment of x″ (y in Example 16) the most prominent melodic figure.

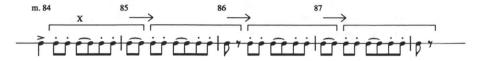

Example 15. Mendelssohn, Octet, Op. 20, I, mm. 84–88.

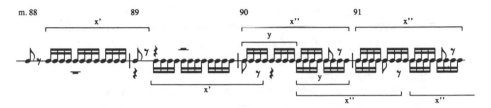

Example 16. Mendelssohn, Octet, Op. 20, I, mm. 88–91.

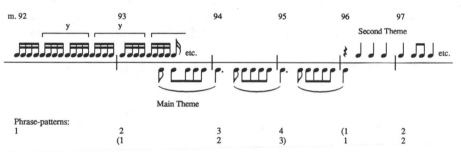

Example 17. Mendelssohn, Octet, Op. 20, I, mm. 92–97.

Example 17 suggests that the pattern established in mm. 90–91 seems to be carried over into m. 92, but the first violin overlaps itself, beginning a new statement of y on the second beat of the measure; this new disruption coincides with the shift to G minor—touched off by the enharmonic switch from Gb to F♯ in the bass—mentioned above. Coming on a weak beat and in connection with an unexpected harmonic deflection, this latest rhythmic shift seems particularly disorienting, although it is simply a continuation of the process of compression that animates the entire passage.

To add to the confusion, the head of the main theme slips in on the second beat of m. 93 and is repeated in mm. 94 and 95. Previously, each statement of this striking figure has been touched off by a strong downbeat opening accent, but, as we have seen, Mendelssohn has been carefully eliminating downbeat accents from the metric tangle of this passage. Lacking its initial springboard, the entrance sounds distinctly precarious, almost like a mistake; the need to establish a clearly articulated, unambiguously stabilized arrival in Bb major is becoming a matter of compelling urgency in these later stages of the exposition. This continual infusion of new energy at the most troublesome spot in the formal design is a remarkable achievement, and it provides a particularly clear measure of the distance that separates the Octet from the amiable classicist rambles of the composer's earlier works. The control with which Mendelssohn harnesses this energy is equally impressive.

The head of the main theme becomes its own springboard, setting off reverberations of itself in mm. 94 and 95. Together, these three statements of the theme form an extended upbeat to m. 96, where the next stage of the cadential process begins.

The lower-voice line settles onto a strong downbeat F in m. 96, which serves as springboard for a new statement of the second theme, finally suggesting a re-coordination of phrase accent, metric accent, and harmonic focus: the narrow compass of the second theme, now perched over a dominant pedal, will be exploited, apparently, to channel the cadential impulse of the second group into a strongly articulated confirmation of the secondary key that can close off this remarkable exposition.

But a new problem quickly appears: the three-bar pattern introduced by the triple upbeat in mm. 93–95 superimposes itself on the theme, transforming its balanced 4 + 4 grouping into an overlapped 3 + 3 and recomplicating the hoped-for clarity of the approaching cadential affirmation.

As we have seen, the second theme already contains the seeds of a three-bar structure: the antecedent phrase normally closes on the downbeat of the fourth measure, and the rest of that measure is filled in with the same fragment of the main theme that has just turned up in mm. 92–95. The explicit three-bar pattern now introduced simply eliminates the "empty" measure that had stood between the two phrases of the theme, dovetailing the closing accent of the first phrase into the opening accent of the second (m. 99). In itself, this might seem to reflect the headlong urgency of the cadential drive that has built up throughout the second group, but it engenders a problem concerning the stability of the end of the second phrase—the point at which the return to Bb major was presumably to be completed.

In each of the previous statements of the second theme, the end of the consequent phrase has been dovetailed into the opening accent of the next section (mm. 75 and 84). This treatment of the phrase-accent pattern is obviously useful in generating the destabilizing momentum of the developmental texture of the entire passage, but the ambiguity of stress that has accrued to the closing accent of the phrase could threaten the stability of the structural arrival at the end of this cadential statement of the theme. The

Bb major:	I_4^6		I_5^6	IV	V	I
Phrase pattern:	1–2–3–(4)		1–2–3 –	1–2–3–4 –	1–2–3–4 –	1
		1–2–3–(4)				
Measure:	96	99	102	105	109	113

Figure 8. Mendelssohn, Octet, Op. 20, I, mm. 96–113.

dovetailing in m. 99, bringing this ambiguity of phrase accent into the antecedent phrase as well, intensifies the threat by emphasizing the potential for instability inherent in the structure of the theme. As a result, the cadence to Bb major in m. 102 so elaborately prepared through the latter stages of the second group has suddenly come to seem a distinctly precarious point of arrival.

Mendelssohn seizes on the implied double function of the downbeat in m. 102—as both closing and opening accent—to transform this long-awaited confirmation of Bb major into the beginning of yet another cadential expansion. In place of a straightforward Bb-major triad, the downbeat of m. 102 lands on a *fortissimo* V_5^6 of IV, initiating a cadential progression that rushes with brilliant energy toward its by now strongly anticipated goal. As Figure 8 indicates, one crucial element in the clarity of this new extension is the realignment of phrase structure, coordinating the next arrival on Bb with an unambiguous opening accent to set off the final cadential gesture of the exposition.

The arrival on a stable Bb-major chord on the downbeat of m. 113 is not simply the correct thing at the proper point in the formal design—the right sort of ingredient to pour into the sonata-form jellymold; it is the goal of an enormous process of harmonic and thematic expansion initiated in the concentrated energy of the second theme, establishing the secondary key area as a persuasive counterpart to the tonic so broadly laid out in the first part of the exposition. Appropriately, details in the structure of the closing theme introduced in m. 113 pull together important threads that have run through the texture of the second group, helping to close off this sprawling design.

First, the strong downbeat in m. 113 sets off a new version of the head of the main theme in the lower voices, restabilizing that figure within a four-bar phrase pattern that corrects the off-kilter entrances in mm. 93–99.

Second, the soaring ascent of the upper-voice line links into a registral process that provides a conclusive "clinch" for this last part of the exposition and that will play a vital role in the final stages of the movement. The final cadential impetus initiated in m. 102 was set off by the first violin's leap to ab''', which transformed the expected Bb-major triad into a dominant seventh. This pivotal moment marks the registral highpoint of the movement to this point (aside from a brief ab''' in m. 8). The tumultuous upper-voice descent in mm. 102–5 leaves ab''' hanging, unresolved—as it was in m. 8, as well. The cadential theme introduced in m. 113 climbs immediately to the three-line register (note the octave leap in the first violin, m. 113), and its highest note, g''', is hammered out four times in the next seven measures during the repeated upper-voice cadential motions to bb''. The details of the inner-voice parts are altered under each of the g'''s, and with the last of them, in m. 122, which returns to the *fortissimo* dynamic level of m. 102, the connection to that earlier plateau is clinched, and the ab''' of m. 102 is finally resolved in the closing cadence of the exposition (Example 18).

Aside from minor changes in the part-writing, the printed score of the first movement differs significantly from the manuscript version at three points: the end of the exposition; the opening of the development; and the early stages of the recapitulation. The first revision, at the end of the exposition, involves the elimination of eight measures that originally stood between mm. 108 and 109. (The change in notation Mendelssohn introduced in the final version of the movement makes the comparison of the two versions cumbersome: all measure numbers in the following discussion are taken from the printed score, but the number of measures in a passage from the manuscript version will be counted in the original "double-value" measures.) The omitted measures elaborate the step from IV to V in the cadence to Bb major that immediately precedes the beginning of the closing theme, and the form of this elaboration provides a last fleeting reference to the harmonic cell that has governed the modulatory design of the exposition as a whole (Example 19).

IV in Bb major is, of course, Eb, the overall tonic of the movement, and in the first measures of the excised material, this identity is made explicit through an allusion to the head of the main theme. This fragment is led through VI of Eb (with Db substituting for the root C, as it did at mm. 41–44) and on to the I_4^6–V–I cadence of mm. 109–13. As it stood in the manuscript, then, the decisive reacquisition of Bb major contained yet another—compressed but strikingly articulated—realization of the work's fundamental I–VI–ii–V progression—in the tonic, Eb major! The problem which led the composer to strike out this material seems to lie in difficulties it would present when it reappeared within a remarkable process Mendelssohn works out at the parallel spot in the recapitulation. By eliminating this clever passage in the exposition, he avoids an unnecessary complication that could weaken the exuberant climax achieved in the coda.

The two other major revisions in this movement deal in one way or another with the reabsorption of the elaborately realized modulatory structure of the

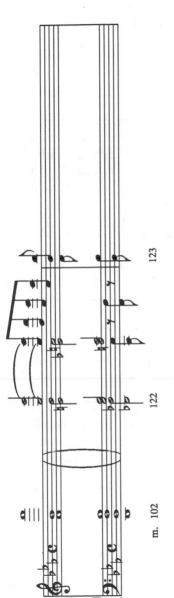

Example 18.   Mendelssohn, Octet, Op. 20, I, mm. 102–23.

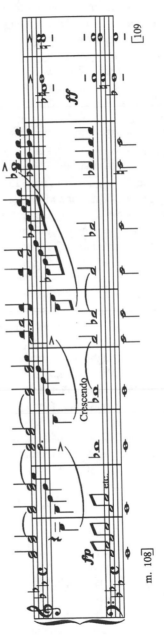

Example 19.   Mendelssohn, Octet, Op. 20, I, manuscript version, passage between mm. 108–9.

exposition into the closural processes of sonata form—a problem that seems to have caused Mendelssohn a certain amount of difficulty.

The development section in the manuscript version differs significantly from the final version only from the end of the exposition to m. 138—a matter of some ten measures (there are also some minor differences between mm. 139 and 146). The reworking of this passage does not alter the goal of the development section as a whole, but it has a profound effect on the functional significance of that goal.

The second ending of the original version was identical to the first ending of the final version—that is to say, the development section opened with another return to the tonic, Eb major. The first part of the development took up the cadential figure from mm. 123–24; the harmony shifted rapidly from Eb major to V of F minor and then sequentially to V of G minor, forming a chain of interlocking I–VI–ii progressions that picked out the decisive steps of the modulatory scheme of the exposition. The G minor at the end of this chain was transformed to major, becoming a dominant that led directly to C minor for a statement of the closing theme of the exposition (taken from mm. 113ff.). The continuation of this material was shunted once again toward G minor, and after a few measures of cadential preparation led into what would be m. 138 of the printed score.

In the final version, the opening of the development takes up a variant of the opening theme—now in the dominant—moving quickly from Bb major (m. 127) through the submediant (m. 131) and on to a strong cadence to C (minor, but taken as major, as the dominant of F minor, in m. 137). Figure 9, a sketch of the overall plan of this version of the development section, immediately reveals one important aspect of this revision.

In the final version, the development section embodies yet another realization of the I–VI–ii–V pattern that controls every level of the exposition. In fact, the coordination of thematic and harmonic patterns in this version yields a condensed restatement of the entire exposition, transferred to the dominant. Now, of course, the goal to which this progression leads is F (minor). Earlier, F minor, as ii of Eb major, was the pivotal key of the modulatory process of the exposition; now it is established as a key center in its own right, fulfilling, at last, the residual implications of the continual emphasis on the supertonic which animated that modulatory impulse.

The original version of the development section had taken up aspects of the exposition as well, but the harmonic focus of that version is not as sharply defined as it is in the later version. The relation to important moments in the exposition is clear enough in analysis, but the effect of the continual harmonic shifts is too busy, and this blurred focus is mirrored in the thematic design, which lacks the conciseness of the final version. In addition, the final

Opening theme			Transition material (from measures 21–37)	2nd theme	
Bb: I	VI	ii	prolongation of ii through a circle of fifths: note the registral link through c'' joining measures 136 and 147	v V/v v	

Mm.: 127	131	137		146	164

Figure 9. Mendelssohn, Octet, Op. 20, I, mm. 127–64.

version also eliminates the return to Eb major at the beginning of the development section, and this will prove to be very important in clarifying the tonal process played out in the final stages of the section.

The development settles into F minor in m. 164, with the arrival marked by the return of the second theme. A repetition of the theme begins in m. 170, but a delicate harmonic shift pushes the continuation of the theme into Eb major (mm. 170–71). The restatement gradually subsides into a quiet murmuring and comes to a full close in m. 177. Although the cadence establishes Eb major with absolute clarity, this is not the usual way to return to the tonic after the development section. I would suggest, rather, that this arrival in Eb major, accomplished through a juxtaposition with F minor, is a distillation of the tonic-supertonic relation that animates every level of the harmonic structure of the movement. Played out in the remarkable stillness that has settled over the passage, setting these measures in sharp relief, this confrontation gathers the supertonic back into the tonic, effecting an extraordinary resolution of this fundamental tonal opposition commensurate with its central role in the structure of the movement.

The revision of the first part of the development section contributes to the effectiveness of this moment in two ways. First, it explicitly identifies the arrival in F minor as the result of a new realization of the I–VI–ii–V pattern that was originally drawn out of the tonic-supertonic pairing that underlies the first theme: the return to Eb major through F minor closes the circle, suggesting a neutralization of the modulatory impetus that has shaped both the exposition and development.

At the same time, the revision keeps this resolution—a profound stillpoint at the very center of the movement that is unlike anything in normal sonata-form procedures—from acquiring too much stability—from simply abrogating the function of the recapitulation. In the original version of the development section, the return to E♭ major after the end of the exposition, although brief, gives the later arrival in the tonic a relatively strong sense of stability, since it is a return to what has been established, however fleetingly, as the tonal center of the entire section. The final version, retaining the dominant as the initial tonal reference of the development section, leaves the close to E♭ major in m. 177 slightly undefined. The function of E♭ major as the tonic is only gradually stabilized through a move to its own dominant in the passage that follows, and that function is confirmed only at the opening of the recapitulation, marked by the return of the main theme (m. 216).

In spite of its mysterious delicacy, however, this reabsorption of F minor into E♭ major does accomplish the principal tonal resolution of the movement: it is a restatement of the second theme—chorale-like, in augmentation—in the tonic. This resolution, which takes place well before we have any sense of a process of recapitulation being underway, both adumbrates the effect of the opening of the recapitulation as the initiation of the process of closure and undercuts the significance of the principal event of the latter stages of a recapitulation, the resolution of the harmonic polarity through the replaying of the second theme in the tonic. As a result, although the resolution has been realized only in the most veiled, decidedly unemphatic way, the final stages of the movement clearly cannot function in the manner of a normal sonata-form recapitulation; it is in the light of this that the third major revision of the movement, the elimination of sixty-two double-length measures from the recapitulation of the first group, is best understood.

This final revision has the obvious effect of shortening the final stages of the movement drastically, but once again it is not the number of measures eliminated, but the structural significance of the alteration that is important. The excised material, which followed the initial statement of the main theme, retraced the thematic outline of the vast modulatory plain that stands between the opening measures of the movement and the beginning of the second theme in m. 68; in particular, the passage explored once again the tonic-supertonic chains running through that material.

In the manuscript version of the recapitulation, the sequential pattern beginning in m. 227 corresponded more or less exactly to mm. 16–20 of the exposition and led into a long section based on mm. 21–37. In the exposition, this material had served to establish F minor as a tentative modulatory way-station, generating the momentum that eventually led to the decisive move away from the tonic. In the original version of the recapitulation, this material once again established F minor, but then moved on to G minor, and the rest of the passage wavered indecisively between these two keys before finally cadencing back to the tonic for the recapitulation of the second theme.

The point of this passage is clear—it retraced the interlocking tonic-supertonic steps from E♭ to F, then F to G, that had controlled the modulatory process of the exposition, and by turning those steps back to the tonic it assimilated that modulatory process back into the tonic. But Mendelssohn's realization of this strategy reveals two problems inherent in his procedure.

First, G minor is not made to relate directly to the tonic, remaining throughout an upper neighbor to F minor: its presence does not really bear on the underlying structure of the passage, which turns out to be nothing more than an elaboration of the E♭-F-E♭ relation of mm. 21–37. This new version does not actually reinterpret that earlier passage, then, but simply repeats it in a curiously meandering form. As a result, the entire section seems to mark time rather aimlessly before the return to the tonic for the second theme.

The second problem is that the apparent function of this passage—the explicit resolution of the tonic-supertonic opposition—has already been accomplished in the quiet passage preceding the opening of the recapitulation. As an element of the unusual tonal processes that shape this movement, the excised passage is redundant; it responds, rather, to the thematic shape of the exposition. This passage in the manuscript version, then, reflects the lingering influence of thematic pattern as the primary organizational principle in Mendelssohn's conception of sonata form. Measures 21–37 of the exposition represent a significant stage in the thematic process of the movement, mediating between the first and second themes, but the primary structural role of this material is a function of its harmonic significance, developing the modulatory impetus latent in the tonic-supertonic opposition; indeed, the intermediary role of the passage in the thematic process can be most clearly understood as a reflection of its role in that harmonic process. But the necessity for a balanced thematic design that underlies the classicist sonata requires that the thematic pattern of the exposition be followed closely in the recapitulation, retracing, in this case, a course of thematic events even though the crucial harmonic process unfolded through them has already been impressively, if mysteriously, resolved. In eliminating this passage, Mendelssohn rejects a stiffly classicist conception of sonata form in favor of a flexible formal strategy that allows him to fashion a more coherent response to the structural issues raised over the course of the movement.

To bridge the gap between mm. 230 and 233 created by the elimination of this material, Mendelssohn provided a two-measure continuation for the sequential pattern begun in m. 227; this small passage has important consequences for the sense of tonic stability over the middle stages of the recapitulation. In the manuscript, the beginning of the second theme coincided with a solid cadence to the tonic. In the final version, the thematic articulation in m. 233 is slightly out of synchronization with the harmonic

Developmental continuation:									1	2	3	etc.
New figure:						1	2	3	4	(5 – dovetailed)		
Second theme:	1	2	3	4	1	2	3	4				
E♭ major:	I_4^6			V	I			V	I			
				"poco rit"			"a tempo"					
Measure:	233			236			240					

Figure 10.   Mendelssohn, Octet, Op. 20, I, mm. 233ff.

arrival, since the cadence only reaches I_4^6 before the second theme slips in in the first viola. When the harmonic pattern finally does lead to a tonic cadence in the fourth measure of the tune, coinciding with the closing accent of the antecedent phrase, this arrival is in turn undercut, becoming the opening accent of a new melodic figure in the first violin (m. 236). An unexpected and striking gesture, this new figure imposes its own phrase structure over and against that of the consequent phrase of the tune, so that the second theme itself is made to sound like an intruding element only tangentially anchored to the harmonic and phrase-structure patterns of the passage. The whole of the second theme, then, seems to be set against the grain of its surroundings and passes by without managing to establish itself as a stable articulation of the tonic.

The point of all this, of course, is that we have already heard a restatement of the second theme in the tonic that played a central role in resolving the harmonic design of the movement—at the end of the development section. Reflecting this anomalous bit of legerdemain, the restatement of the second theme within the recapitulation is denied the structural significance it would have in a more regularly organized movement. By obscuring the articulative landmarks at this point, Mendelssohn avoids a redundant emphasis on tonic arrival, and at the same time he is able to generate a continually intensifying cadential drive over the entire span of the recapitulation—there has to be a decisive structural cadence somewhere in this final section of the movement. As Figure 10 shows, the first truly stable cadence occurs only at the beginning of the developmental continuation of the second theme, which now coincides, as a result of the realignment of the phrase structure enforced by the new figure in the first violin, with an unambiguous opening phrase accent and a return to tempo after the poco ritardando introduced by that new figure. (The new figure is already present in the manuscript version of this passage; the final version intensifies its disruptive effect on the coordination of phrase structure, harmony, and thematic articulation at this important juncture.)

The continuation of the second group, beginning in m. 240, has a slightly different sense than the corresponding passage in the exposition: its opening is marked by a stable tonic arrival supported by the phrase structure of the preceding material. But the continuation is, by its nature, unstable, so any sense of tonic arrival is instantly undercut, and after this initial change, the continuation of the passage is reworked to generate a cadential drive that completely overshoots the closing group and is only completed in the coda.

The counterstatement of the second theme in the submediant is eliminated in the recapitulation, creating a direct juxtaposition of the tonic on the downbeat of m. 240 and the supertonic of the developmental fragmentation that follows. It seems Mendelssohn is not interested in establishing the supertonic with any prominence at this stage of the movement, and so dispenses with the reinforcement that the intermediary turn to V of ii had provided in the exposition. Furthermore, in the exposition this submediant turn had carried echoes of the G-minor-Bb-major relation established in the course of the modulation from I to V. Since a corresponding relation between C minor and Eb major has not been established in the recapitulation, the connective links that had originally been woven through this I-VI-ii chain are no longer in effect.

In the exposition, the continuation of the second group seemed to push toward a decisive cadence (mm. 86ff.), but the ambiguities surrounding the resolution of that cadence in turn set off the elaborate cadential process that expanded the final stages of the exposition before the introduction of the closing theme. In the recapitulation, the continuation from the restatement of the second theme in the supertonic is immediately diverted away from the dominant, pushing instead directly toward V of vi. (In the exposition V of vi had appeared as a digression on the way to the dominant, introduced by an enharmonic shift in the bass that once again recalled the G-minor-Bb-major relation established in the course of the modulatory process.) This harmonic alteration is barely noticeable in the hectic rush of the passage, and it can hardly threaten the overall stability of the tonic at this stage of the formal action of the movement, but it does weaken slightly the cadential drive we would normally have expected here. The dominant pedal finally shows up in m. 251, but the play on V of V that had been so important at this point in the exposition—pivoting on the enharmonic shift that introduced G minor—is missing now, and the approach to the Bb pedal, instead of emphasizing a lower-voice motion directed toward Bb as a goal, involves a shift of the bass line into a middle voice that seems to leave the arrival floating with no secure foundation.

Further reflecting the curious insubstantiality of this cadential event, the arrival on I_4^6 in m. 251 is not marked by a return of the second theme, functioning as a cadential affirmation, as it was at the parallel moment in the exposition (m. 96). Instead, the sixteenth-note figure already established in the first violin simply continues, smoothing over the arrival to the extent that it probably passes unnoticed.

As a result, the uncertainties concerning the stability of the eventual resolution of the dominant pedal that had animated the cadential drive at the end of the exposition simply are not present in the recapitulation: the arrival on I_5^6 in m. 235, while paralleling the $B\flat_5^6$ of m. 102, generates none of the explosive power that marked that earlier event. In fact, the chord functions in a completely different way in this later passage. Instead of leading into an elaborate I_5^6–IV–V–I cadence, the chord in m. 235 is taken as an enharmonic alteration of V of ii that leads through II_3^4 (mm. 255–56) to V_5^6 (mm. 257ff.).

Of course, V_5^6 in E♭ major is the same collection of pitches as V_5^6 of IV in B♭ major, the explosive harmony in m. 102 that touched off the final cadential push of the exposition. The disposition of the chord in m. 257—in particular the leap of the upper voice from a♮″ to a♭‴—makes it difficult to overlook this relation; the chord in m. 257 clearly sounds like the chord in m. 102. The effect is striking, and it has important consequences for the organization of the end of the movement. (It should be noted, in addition, that in the course of the progression over mm. 251 to 257 the bass voice finally reestablishes the low register that had been abandoned in m. 249.)

Since the $B\flat_5^6$ of m. 257 now functions within the tonic realm of E♭ major, the first part of the cadential expansion from the exposition, with its strong emphasis on IV of B♭ major, can return unchanged here; a slight alteration at the end of the passage is sufficient to keep it in E♭ major for the cadence that leads into the closing theme (second half of m. 263). It is here that the rationale for the revision at the corresponding place in the exposition—the elimination of the elaborate E♭–F step from the cadence to B♭ major discussed above—becomes clear: the point is that a big chunk of cadential material from the end of the exposition, where it was embedded in the dominant, is being replayed at its original pitch as what appears to be the long-delayed cadential affirmation of the tonic. In the exposition, remarkably, the move from E♭ to F served to orient the passage toward B♭ major by simultaneously recalling the original meaning of that step relation as tonic-supertonic in E♭ major and resituating it as subdominant-dominant in B♭ major. The effect cannot be recreated in the recapitulation because the passage can be neither transposed—the double meaning of both terms would be lost—nor coherently restated verbatim. Since the point of the passage as a whole rests in its absolute similarity to the corresponding place in the exposition, it would seem that the earlier passage was sacrificed in order to strengthen the effect of this later reinterpretation.

An important aspect of that effect is the urgency surrounding the reestablishment of a stable articulation of the tonic. But the return of the closing
theme in E♭ major after a literal restatement of the harmonic and registral
preparation that had originally led to its appearance in B♭ major has an important effect on its function within the closural process. In the exposition,
the a♭''' of the chord in m. 102 had been left hanging unresolved in register,
to be picked up by g''' in the closing measures of the cadential theme. In the
recapitulation with the closing theme transposed to E♭ major, this crucial
g''' is replaced by c''' in mm. 269-75, and the hook that would secure the
long range registral link to the a♭''' of m. 257 is lost. In fact, the closing
theme, returning at a lower, markedly less brilliant registral level, and conspicuously failing to link back to the inflectionally sensitized highpoint reac-
quired in the course of the second group, clearly cannot function
persuasively as the culmination of the closural process of this movement—a
process that has been driven with such remarkable singleness of purpose toward a final tonic affirmation. As a result, the energy Mendelssohn has so
carefully harnessed and directed over the course of the movement suddenly
spills over the boundaries of the recapitulation, making a coda indispensable
for the completion of the formal design.

The coda begins by taking up the sixteenth-note figure from m. 21—which
has not yet been heard in the final version of the recapitulation—as a cadential element now apparently anchored firmly in the tonic (mm. 276ff.). In m.
280, the cello quietly swings the harmony around to F minor, however, and,
in a gesture reminiscent of the modulatory juncture in m. 51, a cadence begins that places a strong emphasis on the third of F minor (paralleling the
emphasis on B♭ in the earlier passage). This is transferred to the first violin
as a♭'' in m. 283, and F minor gradually dissolves back into the tonic under a
leisurely upper-voice ascent from a♭'' through c''' (m. 290) to e♭''' (m.
292). By sifting out the emphasis on F minor at earlier stages of the recapitulation, Mendelssohn has greatly enhanced the effect of this last shimmering
reference, while the coordination of this last return to the tonic with the reacquisition of the three-line register intertwines the various threads of the
closural process in a gesture of remarkable poetic grace.

The last page of the movement culminates in a massive cadence in mm.
311-13, in which a♭'''—linking back to m. 257 and to m. 102—is finally led
explicitly through g''' and on to f''' and e♭'''. (On the largest possible scale,
this ties the coda to the end of the exposition and to the opening measures of
the movement, where the cadence to the tonic at the end of the first statement
of the main theme establishes the significance of registral disjunctions between a♭''' and the G to which it resolves.)

The sense of culmination in these final measures of the coda is a typical enough gesture in the romantic style. What is unusual is the way in which Mendelssohn has contrived to make the entire recapitulation press toward this culmination, undercutting every tonic arrival along the way. In turn, this entire design is perhaps best understood as a response to the unusual resolution of the fundamental tonic-supertonic relation accomplished immediately before the opening of the recapitulation. The recapitulation serves less to provide the structural resolution for the movement than to sound a reverberation of that resolution—a reverberation that gradually swells into the cadential exuberance of the coda.

SECOND MOVEMENT: ANDANTE

The second movement of the Octet represents one of Mendelssohn's most unusual realizations of sonata form, although in outline it recalls a form common in the mid-eighteenth century, in which the first subject does not appear in the recapitulation; it does return in the coda, however. As was the case in the first movement, the manuscript indicates that the movement had originally been organized quite normally, with a perfectly regular recapitulation. And, as in the first movement, the fundamental generating principle of the Andante involves the working out, over the entire course of the movement, of a motivic relation embedded in the first measures of the main theme. In the original version of the movement, the thrust of this process was repeatedly blunted by the ambling symmetry of a melodically organized form; in the final version, the symmetry of the thematic pattern is discarded in order to establish a closer coordination of surface articulation and underlying structure.

The first measure of the Andante, with its quiet open fifth, C–G, in the lower register of the violas, allows E♭, echoing from the noisy cadence at the end of the first movement, to set the minor mode without actually being present in the chord. C minor seems to have come into being before the music became audible, investing it with a mysterious stability that will play an important role at the beginning of the recapitulation and at the end of the movement.

E♭ is immediately taken up as the first note of a wistful melodic figure unfolded in the cello (m. 2) and viola (m. 3). In m. 4 the melodic line is taken up by the first violin, but the harmony has shifted almost imperceptibly from the opening C minor to D♭ major. The apparent melodic continuity over this abrupt shift of key and register obscures the phrase structure for a moment, and it only gradually becomes clear that m. 4 marks the beginning of a square-cut lyric theme in D♭ major—a realization that suddenly blurs the tonal orientation of these opening measures. The continuation of the theme eventually reaches Ab major, the dominant of the new key (mm. 11-13), before sliding back through Db and into a cadence to C minor that extends from m. 16 to the downbeat of m. 27.

The curious evanescence of this opening would seem to bear out Tovey's mildly critical characterization of the movement as being "rather vague in structure and theme."[8] But vagueness of structure would seem, in turn, to imply a lack of ascertainable significance in the course of events outlined above; in the following analysis, I will suggest that, in fact, this unusual opening establishes the structural issues that shape the entire movement.

The handling of the harmonic transitions in these opening measures reveals that the Db-major passage, comprising almost the entire melodic substance of the first theme, is an enormously elaborated appoggiatura on the Neapolitan of C minor. As the theme is first taking shape, Mendelssohn seizes on the expressive melodic dissonance, ab in the viola, m. 3, and at the change of register to ab'' in m. 4, simply hangs the new key from it. The expected melodic resolution to G is withheld until m. 16, where the mysterious Db major is absorbed into a cadence back to C minor. The Db-major passage serves, then, as a wonderfully elaborate intensification of the expressive quality of the sensitive Ab-G melodic relation touched upon in m. 3, postponing its resolution by enveloping it in a precariously stabilized harmonic context.

The veiled, romantic coloring of this opening—the strange blurring of its tonal and melodic profile—is a reflection of the ambiguity that arises from expressing a melodic appoggiatura as if it implied a key, and then articulating that key—and even establishing its own dominant—within a fully developed thematic gesture, while at both the introduction and resolution of the appoggiatura emphasizing its purely ephemeral character.

The reabsorption of the ab'' appoggiatura occupies mm. 16-21 and grows increasingly animated as the passage proceeds, culminating in a sharply dissonant ascent to g'' (mm. 20-21). This links back to the ab''-g'' resolution of m. 16, and the upper-voice line is immediately led into a series of quiet cadential motions to c'' in mm. 22-26.

The Neapolitan reappears fleetingly in the last of these cadences, where the db''-c'' of m. 26 sounds a faint reverberation of the entire opening and adds a delicate emphasis to the plagal cadence and *tierce de Picardie* C-major chord that close this first part of the exposition.

The transition, beginning in m. 27, picks up the first violin's *pianissimo* triplet motive, already sensitized by the d''-c''/db''-c'' opposition played out in the preceding cadence. The subdominant tinge of that cadence spills over into the Gb–A–C–Eb diminished seventh chord that, functioning as V7 of Bb, initiates the modulation away from the tonic.

The move to the mediant is accomplished in only two measures. The arrival (in the middle of m. 29) is marked by a new thematic fragment that combines the triplets of the preceding measures with the descending fourth figure from the head of the main theme (see mm. 2, 4, etc.). This arrival, to the mediant minor, proves to be only provisional, however: the ensuing passage moves slowly through a rising sequence that swings around to Eb major in m. 41. The function of the passage beginning in m. 29, then, lies somewhere between arrival—we are already in the new key, which is marked by a "new" theme—and transition—the minor mode prevents the mediant from sounding like a fully stable key at this point. Harmonically—and, as we shall see, thematically—mm. 29ff. only foreshadow the goal toward which the exposition is moving.

As was mentioned above, the motive introduced by the first violin in m. 29 is closely related to the main theme. It is embedded in the opening of the sequential passage, but the motive itself falls away after the first two harmonic steps (Eb–F in the bass, mm. 29–31), while the sequence continues and accelerates through two more steps in mm. 33–34. As Example 20 shows, the outer-voice framework of this sequence is simply a chain of ascending tenths.

As Example 21 shows, the theme marking the arrival in Eb major in m. 41 is nothing other than this outer-voice framework of ascending tenths, transposed from minor to major and moving at twice the speed of its original presentation.

The process of thematic derivation is striking: a variant of a motive from the first theme is introduced in m. 29, but is treated as an expendable accessory to its own sequential elaboration, while it is the harmonic framework of the sequence that foreshadows the shape of the second theme. The Eb–minor passage serves as an intermediary between both the main themes and the principal key areas of the exposition. The thematic process played out in this passage involves both a relatively straightforward chain of motivic transformations and the establishment of a less obvious relation through a similarity of contour; this combination of elements plays a particularly important role in Mendelssohn's style. What is peculiar about the process, and typical of Mendelssohn's finest achievements, is the elusiveness with which it is realized. The individual steps of the transformation are clear enough, but as a result of the interpenetration of surface and middle-ground processes, no trace of a clear relation between the opening theme and the Eb–major theme remains at the end of the process.[9] The second theme is both new—calming and resolving the murmuring agitation of the preceding section—and

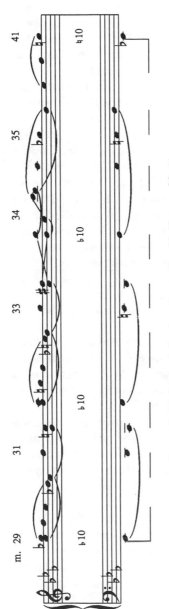

Example 20.   Mendelssohn, Octet, Op. 20, II, mm. 29–41.

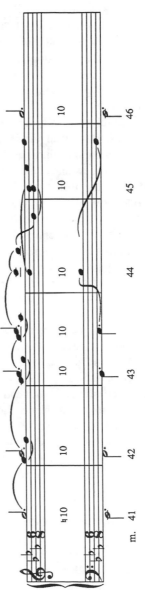

Example 21.   Mendelssohn, Octet, Op. 20, II, mm. 41–46.

vaguely familiar—its first appearance has the air of an obscure recollection. This duality invests the theme with a remarkable serenity that greatly intensifies its compact lyricism.

A detail should be noted. It is at the fourth step of the transitional sequence, with A♭ in the bass of m. 34, that the harmony shifts into a dominant preparation for E♭ major. This sequential pattern will return several times in the course of the movement; each appearance will treat the continuation from this fourth step differently, and each new continuation will have important consequences.

In addition to offering a resolution for the delicate E♭-minor agitation of the preceding material, the second theme resolves a larger-scale relation. In replacing the minor third, g♭'', of mm. 29–37 with g♮'', the second theme introduces a new and stable context for the a♭''–g'' half step on which the structure of the opening theme hinged. The luminous harmonic and motivic clarification achieved in the second theme convincingly establishes E♭ major as the goal of the exposition as a whole. It is through this overarching design that Mendelssohn is able to accommodate the essentially thematic organization of the movement to a coherent sonata-form process, linking each step of the thematic design to an extraordinarily delicate long-range harmonic and registral process: the logic of the thematic process is absolute, and that process is at every point intertwined with the unfolding process of the harmonic design.

The E♭-major theme is repeated in a counterstatement, and at the fourth step of the sequential pattern (mm. 48–49) a change of harmony leads briefly through iii and vi before the passage settles into the closing cadences of the exposition. The submediant, C minor, lingers through these cadences in the repeated evasions of a full cadence to E♭ in mm. 54–55.

Mendelssohn transplants the E♭-minor sequence from mm. 29–34 to serve as the main body of the development section, a procedure recalling the slow movement of the C-minor Symphony, Op. 11. The effect seems to be unique to Mendelssohn, and these two examples—both lyric slow movements—are the only occurrences of it in his output. Krummacher is correct, I think, in suggesting that the advantage of this design is that it allows the composer to write a slow movement in sonata form in which lyricism will not be disturbed by the normal developmental techniques of fragmentation and recombination.[10] In the Symphony, the thematic material is not particularly suited to development in the normal sense; in the Octet, a remarkable process of thematic development has already been accomplished within the exposition. The central section of the movement is given over to the culmination of the harmonic process set in motion in the opening of the main theme.

The shift to E♭ minor at the beginning of the development section replaces g♮'' with g♭'', reopening the play around this sensitive region of the scale. This shift and the sequential structure of the passage, now further emphasized by the appendage of a cadential measure (from the end of the exposition) between each step of the sequence, provide an appropriately developmental level of harmonic action, while some element of motivic fragmentation and rearrangement is, so to speak, built into the texture of this material. As was the case in Op. 11, the use of transitional material from the exposition in the development section appears to accomplish the function of resolution for that material; it does not return in the recapitulation.

The texture becomes increasingly animated as the sequence accelerates toward its fourth step, the A♭ in the bass of m. 63. This time, A♭ is introduced as the dominant of D♭ minor, the (minor) Neapolitan of the movement as a whole. This A♭ is gradually transformed into an appoggiatura to G as the upper voices ascend from the D♭-minor $^6_4$ of m. 63 through an augmented sixth chord that leads into an eleven-measure passage on the dominant of C minor that serves as the retransition to the recapitulation. (Mendelssohn manages to present yet another statement of the sequential passage within the retransition, this time moving four times faster than the original, in mm. 69–70.)

The A♭–G relation played out in mm. 63–65 bears a strong resemblance to the elaborate appoggiatura relation established in the opening of the movement. In fact, these measures represent a condensation and inversion of the central harmonic process played out in that opening: the sensitive melodic A♭ of mm. 3–16 is transferred to the bass, and the Neapolitan, which is built up from the bass instead of being suspended from the melodic line, once again swings gradually around to the tonic as A♭ presses back to G.

This new realization transforms the expressive core of that mysterious opening—the remarkable elaboration of the ephemeral A♭–G relation—into the moment of greatest formal tension in the movement, and its resolution now serves as the pivot on which the return to the tonic hinges.

Coming after this climactic transformation, a return to the opening theme, with its lyric exposition of the A♭–G relation, could at best only seem a tautology. Mendelssohn contrived a drastic abbreviation of this material for the original version of the recapitulation, with mm. 1–4 leading directly into a cadence to C minor taken from mm. 16–23, but even this seems hopelessly flaccid. To make matters worse, the continuation led into yet another leisurely exposition of the A♭–G relation: after the cadence to C minor, the figure from mm. 22–26 was repeated in A♭ major, and A♭ major proved, with distressing predictability, to be, once again, an appoggiatura to the dominant of C minor.

Furthermore, in spite of this continual play on the central structural issue of the movement, the elaborate preparation for the restatement of the second theme in the original version of the recapitulation did not establish a persuasive counterpart to the long-range harmonic, motivic, and registral processes that interconnect the principal themes in the exposition. Those processes were simply replaced by a rambling design that undercut the impressiveness of the second theme, making the latter stages of the recapitulation somewhat anticlimactic, and disengaged the carefully balanced relation between the thematic surface and the harmonic structure of the movement. As in the original version of the first movement, the emphasis fell on the pattern of the thematic succession, and the impressive continuity of the exposition was reduced to the dutiful wading-through of an arbitrarily predefined sequence of melodic events.

The final version of the movement represents a radical solution to these problems. That Mendelssohn originally wrote a "normal" recapitulation and only later reworked this formal juncture indicates the way in which his sensitivity to his materials and to form as a functional process rather than a melodic framework seems to have been gradually overcoming the classicist sense of form that had shaped his earlier works. The result is one of Mendelssohn's most convincing fusions of sonata-form principles and romantic lyricism. Indeed, the lyricism of this movement is not merely a characteristic of its thematic surface—a lyric impulse controls the underlying formal processes of the movement as well.

The exposition pointedly avoided establishing a strongly polarized contrast of elements, either thematically or tonally. The closing theme flowers, mysteriously, from the motivic seed embedded in the opening measures of the first theme, just as E♭ major emerges from the inflectional uncertainties of those opening measures, serving, already in the exposition, to resolve those uncertainties. If resolution has in some sense already been accomplished in the closing measures of the exposition, then the processes of recapitulation must take on a new meaning.

In the final version the recapitulation begins with a statement of the *second* theme in the tonic major (m. 76), and this puts a pointedly equivocal emphasis on the function of this crucial structural articulation. As the goal of the dominant preparation at the end of the development, this is obviously the climactic moment of the movement, but the serene clarity of this C major is neither a completely adequate representative of the tonic—of the complex and elusively shifting interplay of relations worked out in the opening of the movement—nor a compelling resolution of that complexity. On the one hand, the minor third, E♭, has acquired a remarkable stability in the course of a process extending, as we have seen, from before the opening notes of the movement to the closing cadence of the exposition. The strange brightness of the C major unfurled at the opening of the recapitulation sounds curiously unstable in comparison—E♮ registers as an upper neighbor teetering back toward E♭. On the other hand, the special quality of the C minor at the opening of the movement is in large part a function of the shifting relation between A♭ and G; the simple assertion of the tonic major, which focuses primarily on the shift to the major third degree (see the fourth violin, m. 76), does not really address the issues posed by the opening of the movement. The eventual establishment of E♭ major in the exposition was a natural outgrowth of those issues, embracing both E♭ and the sensitive A♭-G relation as stable scale steps; in contrast, the unexpected C major at the opening of the recapitulation simply ignores these critical interrelations.

By placing the second theme at the opening of the recapitulation, Mendelssohn makes the question of the stable mode of the tonic a pressing concern. In contrast, in the original version of the movement, the return of the second theme at the expected spot in the recapitulation was simply a matter of correspondence to the thematic pattern of the exposition. The sharper focus achieved in the final version provides a persuasive impulse for the return to C minor, which is only achieved in the coda, displacing the decisive reacquisition of the tonic to the end of the movement, while preparing the delicate ambiguity of the *tierce de Picardie* that colors the final cadence.

After only five measures in C major, the counterstatement of the second theme turns abruptly to A♭ major (m. 81). The effect is striking in itself, casting a warm shadow over the early stages of the recapitulation; on a larger scale, it sounds a reverberation of the emphasis on A♭ that has run through the entire movement. The shift was taken over from the original version of the movement, but there it had been just another in a series of digressions around A♭, its effect adumbrated by the continual retracing of the same harmonic path back to the tonic. In the final version of the movement the effect is fresh, allowing its emphasis on flatted scale degrees to intensify the C-major-C-minor problem raised in the new version of the recapitulation.

In addition, the shift to A♭ major places a new meaning on the sequential pattern that forms the continuation of the second theme. In the exposition (mm. 49-53), the continuation from the fourth step of the sequence had functioned as a short digression through iii and vi on the way to the closing cadence. In the recapitulation, iii of A♭ major is the tonic key itself—and the minor mode of the tonic; the sequential passage, reinterpreted, now functions to reestablish the tonic. In addition, the end of this passage touches briefly on the subdominant, marked by a d♭′′′/C clash in the outer voices that introduces another echo of the tonic-Neapolitan confrontation from the opening of the movement (mm. 86–87). The lingering submediant that colors the closing cadence is now, of course, A♭ major.

The opening theme reappears quietly under the last of these cadences (m. 92), and its Neapolitan-to-tonic pivot throbs through the texture in the quavering d♭′–c′ of the second viola. After a turn to D♭ major in m. 94 (paralleling m. 4), the passage immediately moves on to an elaboration of the plagal cadence from mm. 26–27. The touch of Neapolitan in that earlier cadence is intensified in the sharply expressive D♭/C clashes in mm. 97–99, reflecting a complex harmonic compression in this last part of the coda. The D♭/C clashes are both a distillation of the Neapolitan-tonic confrontation of the opening theme and the cadentially incisive ♭6–5 of a strong subdominant bias that runs through the closing measures of the coda. This subdominant bias brings with it a momentary echo of E♮—as the leading tone to F—setting the stage for the beautiful, and unsettling, effect of the *tierce de Picardie* in the final cadence of the movement. The cadential pull of the subdominant clearly marks C major as a chromatic coloring of the tonic minor that is of strictly local significance: as at the opening of the recapitulation, C major cannot register as a resolution of the inherent instability of the minor tonic, and both meanings of the D♭–C relation—as Neapolitan-tonic and as ♭6–5 of the subdominant—must be comprehended simultaneously, held precariously in balance, as the movement dissolves into the obscurity from which it emerged.

THIRD MOVEMENT:
SCHERZO, ALLEGRO LEGGIERISSIMO

The third movement of the Octet is one of Mendelssohn's most remarkable achievements. The exuberance of the thematic material and the brilliance of the instrumental writing are obvious, but the subtlety of the formal design and the refinement of technique with which that design is realized have attracted surprisingly little attention. This is particularly unfortunate since the restricted scope of the movement reflects a uniquely concentrated example of the finest characteristics of Mendelssohn's sonata style; and it is an example the success of which, though never carefully investigated, has never been seriously questioned.

To appreciate the sophistication of technique Mendelssohn brought to this movement, it will be useful to begin by tracing the elusive process of motivic transformation that is woven through the thematic design of the exposition. The most striking, and characteristic, aspect of this process is that it hinges on what appears to be a completely insignificant detail within the main theme. Since there is absolutely nothing memorable about the initial presentation of this detail, the individual steps of the transformation it undergoes flash by before it is clear where our attention should be focused, or, for that matter, that there is anything happening that requires particularly close attention at all. This intangibility is an important factor in the remarkable clarity of texture in Mendelssohn's music, allowing important structural processes to run their course without seeming to disturb the lustrous smoothness of the surface. Unfortunately—for the composer's reputation at least—this rather elegant technique seems to have fostered the impression that nothing was to be found beneath that beguiling surface.

The detail singled out in the opening of the Scherzo is the first violin's third, g''-bb'', in m. 4 (Example 22).

In the counterstatement of the theme the third is filled in, and it settles with a gentle bump on bb'' in the second half of m. 12 (Example 23). Four measures later, the rhythmic figure of this filled-in third, two sixteenth notes followed by an eighth note, is shifted one half-beat "to the right," becoming an upbeat-to-downbeat figure that is scattered across the texture for the next eight measures (Example 23, mm. 16–23).

In m. 24, this rhythmic figure is gathered back into the first violin to form an extended upbeat stepwise ascent to bb'', now firmly settled on the downbeat of m. 25 as the first note of the second theme (in Bb major). The new theme itself is nothing more than a string of filled-in ascending thirds—articulated in the rhythmic pattern of m. 12—linked to one another (Example 24).

The second theme, then, represents the end product of a motivic process that spans the first theme and transition, gradually transforming a fleeting melodic detail in the first theme into the generating motive of the second theme. Perhaps the most delightful, and typically Mendelssohnian, aspect of this process is that the themes bear absolutely no resemblance to one another; the logic of the thematic derivation is as absolute as it is evanescent. The opening downbeat accent on the bb'' in m. 25 also plays an important role in this process, restabilizing the precarious bb'' of m. 12—calming the slight ruffle on the surface that had initiated the modulation away from the tonic. In the end, the rhythm, basic intervallic content, initial pitch (and key), and even the register of the second theme are all subtly prepared through the manipulation of the g''-bb'' third embedded in the opening measures of the movement. Although this procedure obviously reflects the concern for thematic logic that is central to the romantic style, its fundamental significance does not lie in the establishment of a Rétian web of thematic unities. Rather, I would suggest that this method of foreshadowing the elements of the new theme is best understood as a gradually unfolding preparatory gesture that encompasses every element of the musical texture. The new key area—marked by this beautifully prepared new theme—emerges, organically, over the course of the first theme and transition to clarify not only a harmonic instability, but a "textural instability" as well.

The second theme begins, then, firmly settled in the mediant, B♭ major. This is the normal secondary key for a movement in G minor, of course, and it is exactly what we would expect from a composer with a reputation for conventionality in matters of harmony and form. But the young Mendelssohn had a penchant for manipulating conventional gestures to unexpected ends; the course of the latter stages of the exposition will prove to be considerably less predictable than the smoothly regular beginning of the second theme might suggest.

After six measures of purposeful bustle, the tune suddenly comes to a dead halt. The harmony shifts abruptly from B♭ major to D major, and a fragment of the first theme flashes by. Four measures later this apparition fades and is quickly absorbed back into B♭ major. But this brief digression will prove to be a central element in the design of the movement; and as is often the case in Mendelssohn's early works, much of the effectiveness of the design derives from the unobtrusiveness with which its elements are deployed.

As Example 25 shows, the first eight measures of the second theme unfold within a gradual stepwise expansion of the underlying outer-voice framework, leading from the B♭s on the downbeat of m. 25 to the widely spaced Ds on the downbeat of m. 31; when the upper voice reaches d‴, Mendelssohn simply hangs a D-major chord from it. It is the strong directional control imposed by this outer-voice frame that establishes a connection between the prevailing B♭ major of the second theme and the shimmering D major unfurled in m. 31; in fact, this outer-voice motion is so persuasive that D major almost seems to have been the goal of the passage from the start. It is characteristic of Mendelssohn that the eminently romantic effect of this abrupt harmonic juxtaposition should be so carefully woven into the voice-leading structure of the passage, and it is equally characteristic that this apparent digression will play a central role in the formal processes of the later stages of the movement.

Even the unexpected reappearance of the first theme is carefully prepared; it seems at once surprising and inevitable. The first theme began with an ascending fourth skip, d″-g″ (m. 1), and the first violin has an ascending fourth skip, a″-d‴, over the bar line of mm. 30–31. But the a″ in m. 30 still registers in B♭ major, while the d‴ of m. 31 has been enveloped in the strange new D major, so it is not easy to hear a melodic connection between these two notes. The violas, however, slip in with the accompaniment figure of the first theme under the violin's d‴, so it seems only natural that two

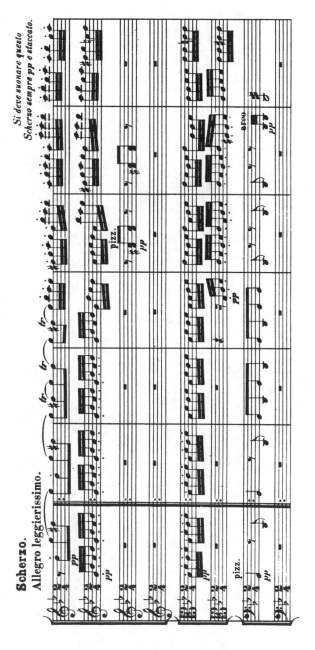

Example 22. Mendelssohn, Octet, Op. 20, III, mm. 1–7.

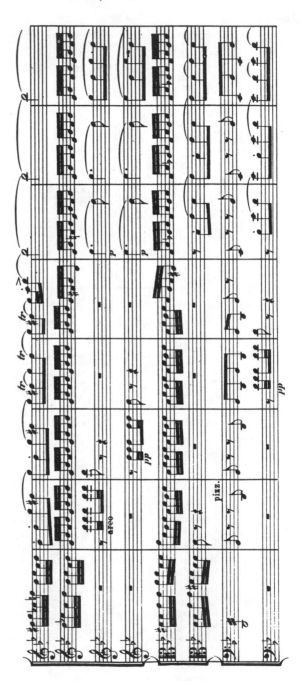

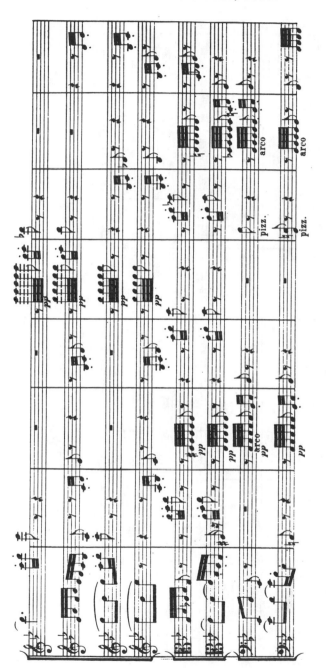

Example 23. Mendelssohn, Octet, Op. 20, III, mm. 8–23.

Example 24. Mendelssohn, Octet, Op. 20, III, mm. 24–32.

Example 25. Mendelssohn, Octet, Op. 20, III, mm. 24–32.

measures later the head of the theme pops up, beginning, of course, with the a''–d''' fourth. The thematic fragment emerges as the characteristic elements of the theme gradually coalesce in a process touched off by an almost imperceptible motivic association.

This D–major passage is quickly explained away in a circle-of-fifths sequence that leads back to B♭ major for a delicately varied counterstatement of the second theme. In due course the harmony shifts once again to D major, and, amazingly, simply stays there for the rest of the exposition, stabilized, after a fashion, by twenty-two measures of skittering cadences. (Notice the string of A–D fourths threaded through this cadential passage, now functioning as gestures of conclusion—compare this with the new d'''–a'' figure in mm. 43ff. at the return to D major. Mendelssohn's control of the functional significance of his motivic material in its various manifestations over the course of a movement repays close study.)

The overall shape of the first part of the movement, leading from G minor through B♭ major to D major, appears to be that of a "three-key exposition," in which the middle key serves as an elaborate transition, but the effect of Mendelssohn's design is fundamentally different.[11] The middle key, B♭ major, is prepared by an elaborate transition, and its establishment as a stable key is articulated by an important new theme. The third key, D major, is first introduced as a rather quirky intrusion; the only preparation for its reappearance is the fact that we have heard it before, and nothing prepares us for its retention as the key in which the expositions will close. In the end, it is primarily the unbroken regularity of four-bar phrases throughout the second theme that persuades us to accept the cadence to D major in mm. 48–49 as being in any sense analogous to the stable return to B♭ major in mm. 36–37.

This simply is not the way the tonal polarization of tonic and dominant is normally established. In spite of the cadential bustle at the end of the exposition, D major is never stabilized as an independent key area; it registers as V of i, and the entire closing section of the exposition actually functions as a transition back to the tonic. This reveals an important source of the unruffled vitality of this movement. The polarized opposition of clearly established tonal areas that animated the classical sonata style—but which was almost impossible to establish within the complexly detailed terms of the romantic harmonic language—has been replaced by a more fluid tonal structure in which the secondary key area, although apparently established with emphatic clarity, is little more than a far-flung digression that never really breaks free from the tonic. The result is a steady cadential drive that will run through the entire movement, generating a constant forward momentum more typical of baroque harmonic procedures in which, as Tovey puts it, the tonic is never made to "disappear below the horizon."[12] The quicksilver the-

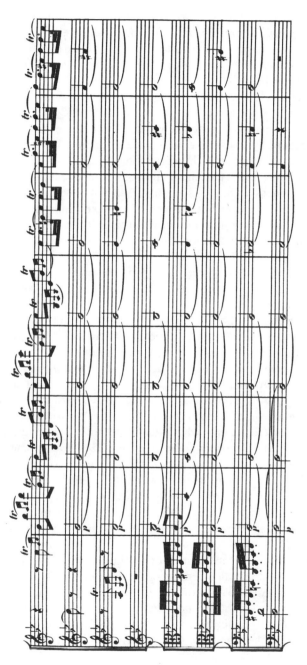

Example 26. Mendelssohn, Octet, Op. 20, III, mm. 105–19.

matic process and the technique of kaleidoscopic juxtaposition weave a texture of logic and surprise that provides an appropriately elusive network of surface articulations for this non-polarizing tonal process. The semblance of formal regularity proves to be the basis for a transformation of the elements on which the form depends.

At first glance, the development section also appears to be perfectly regular. It extends from m. 69, the end of the exposition, to m. 143, where the main theme reappears perched on the tonic, and it falls into three large subsections, each articulated by a striking change of texture: mm. 69–93; mm. 93–112; and mm. 113–43. Once again, however, things are not entirely what they seem to be. The beginning of the third section—little more than halfway through the development as a whole—is marked by an elaborately prepared cadence to the tonic, G minor. In fact, the end of the preceding section is saturated with ascending fourth skips that insistently recall the head of the main theme, and the harmonic orientation in these measures focuses with increasing urgency on the return to G minor (Example 26). These are gestures normally associated with the retransition leading into the opening of the recapitulation; Mendelssohn simply neglects to bring back the right tune when he reaches the tonic in m. 113.

In fact, the main theme only shows up thirty measures after this tonic arrival. Instead of forming the first stages of the recapitulation, mm. 113–43 are given over to a prolongation of G minor in the form of a chain of 5–6 progressions over a rising chromatic bass. This eventually comes to rest with a statement of the head of the first theme over a Neapolitan $^6_4$ (mm. 139–42). The bass note, E♭, quickly proves to be the bass of an augmented sixth chord that presses toward the dominant of G minor.

But just as the harmony settles onto what would appear to be a cadential $^6_4$, on the downbeat of m. 143, the opening theme materializes, two measures before the implied arrival at a root position tonic chord. The harmony scrambles around to G minor as quickly as possible, but the passage only regains its harmonic equilibrium after the thematic return is well under way, and the precise moment marking the beginning of the recapitulation—normally articulated by the double return of the main theme and the tonic key—has eluded us (Example 27).

Instead of providing an emphatic gesture of resolution that initiates and foreshadows the large-scale closural process of the movement, the opening of this recapitulation represents a moment of deceptively gentle instability in which the thematic articulation actually undermines the fundamental process of tonal resolution. Of course, this ambiguity is itself a reflection of a much larger-scale disjunction of harmonic and thematic arrivals—we have been in the tonic for the last thirty measures—so a strongly articulated cadence here

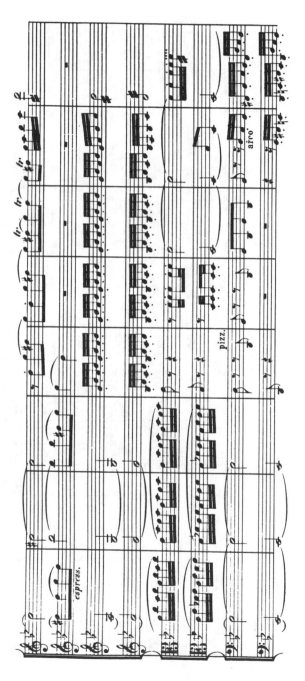

Example 27.   Mendelssohn, Octet, Op. 20, III, mm. 140–47.

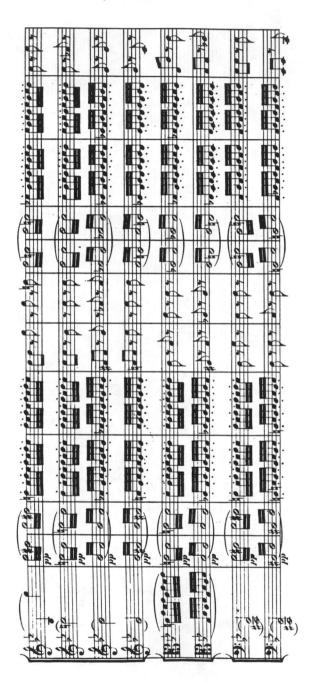

Example 28. Mendelssohn, Octet, Op. 20, III, mm. 172–94.

would be at least slightly redundant. Not surprisingly, the treatment of the opening of the recapitulation will prove to be only the first step in a uniquely conceived closural process.

The restatement of the first group is slightly longer than the corresponding passage in the exposition. The transition, on the other hand, is greatly expanded, deploying new motivic elements as it plays out an ever more elaborately delayed cadence to G minor. In the course of this expansion, the instability associated with the pivotal bb'' of mm. 12–25 is transferred through a short stepwise ascent to eb''' in m. 158, a shift prepared by the prominent d''' in mm. 147–51, and Eb, with its inflectional tendency toward D, becomes a central element in the cadential drive of this passage, pushing back toward G minor. This might seem to imply that the emphatic articulation of the tonic arrival that was so artfully forestalled at the opening of the recapitulation will instead be provided at the return of the second theme. But, of course, the structure of the second theme insures that this articulation cannot be as straightforward as its energetic preparation would suggest.

Indeed, this elaborate preparation does not lead to a tonic arrival at all. In mm. 184–85, when a cadence seems unavoidable, G minor is abruptly swept away when the second theme reappears in Eb major (Example 28). Given the prominence of Eb as an upper neighbor to D in the preceding passage, the effect of this sudden shift is that of a deceptive cadence enormously prolonged. The sense of harmonic misdirection is intensified by a surprising refusal of the first strain of the tune to make the expected move to the local mediant, which in this case would be G, the key we have been waiting for all along. Instead, a pointedly innocent cadential tag holds the tune securely in its distinctly precarious Eb major (mm. 191–92). It is left for the second strain to accomplish the expected shift, and the sense in which "expected" is an appropriate term reveals some interesting points about Mendelssohn's handling of the relation between surface detail and large-scale structure.

In the exposition, the first key of the second theme, Bb major, was prepared and stable, while the second key, D major, was an interpolation that in the end simply did not go away. In the recapitulation, where the primary issue seems to be the establishment of any kind of stable tonic articulation at all, the first key of the second theme, Eb major, is an interpolation—the prolongation of a deceptive cadence that has sidestepped the tonic—while the second key, G major, is the "right" key—the key toward which the entire recapitulation has been directed.

But G major is emphatically the wrong mode. The focus of the recapitulation—reaching back to the elaborate prolongation of G minor in the final section of the development—has stabilized the tonic minor so thoroughly that G major sounds more like a chromatic alteration than a clarification of the fun-

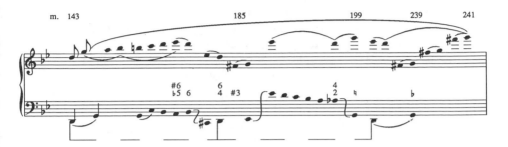

Example 29.   Mendelssohn, Octet, Op. 20, III, mm. 143–241.

damental tonal frictions inherent in the minor mode. The refusal of the first
strain to lead to G major further weakens the claim of the major mode by
eliminating the principal legitimizing agent in Mendelssohn's harmonic
merry-go-round—the repetition of the shift from one key to another within
the course of the second theme. In the end, the arrival of G major embedded
in the restatement of the theme, although it is elaborated by some twenty
measures of cadential bustle of its own, is just another evasion of the tonic in
this closing section of the movement.

In fact, G minor, although hovering in the background throughout the
cadential activity at the end of the recapitulation, is not securely achieved
until m. 239, three measures from the end of the movement—literally the last
possible moment. Two important registral details help to clinch this long-delayed close (see Example 29). First, eb‴, d‴, and g‴ have been conspicuous upper-voice landmarks at the major cadential junctures of the
recapitulation: the thwarted resolution of eb‴ to d‴ in the transition; the
eb‴ halo floating over the restatement of the second theme; the
eb‴-d‴-g‴ line leading to the cadence in mm. 197–99 (but the cadence is
to G major!); and finally the rush to g‴ in m. 223, the last G-major cadence
of the movement. Measure 224 reintroduces eb‴ and d‴, but it is only in
mm. 240–41, at the final cadence of the movement, that d‴ is led to g‴,
realizing the cadential impetus of this long-rage upper-voice connection. At
the same time, the bass line regains the lower-voice D abandoned abruptly in
m. 221, leading it to G in m. 239 to support that final cadence. These registral
connections help to close off the tonal issues of the movement with extraordinarily delicate precision.

Not only is the weight of the formal structure displaced to the final cadence, a gesture typical of the romantic conception of formal balance, but the
subtle tension between formal implications and surface processes that results
from this displacement proves to be central to the tremendous vitality of the

movement. The continual disruption of the tonic articulations in the second half of the movement and the reorganization of the relation between the keys of the second theme in the recapitulation generate a convincing analogue—in terms of a romantic sense of harmony and form—to the dynamic process of closure of the classical sonata. The delicacy of Mendelssohn's technique allows him to accomplish this transformation within what appears to be a perfectly regular formal design that somehow manages to never be quite what it seems to be.

FOURTH MOVEMENT: PRESTO

The fourth movement of the Octet is justly famous as a *tour de force* of contrapuntal part-writing, and is for this reason often compared with the finale of Mozart's "Jupiter" Symphony. Unfortunately, this comparison, with its emphasis on the deployment of fugal textures, obscures the real originality of Mendelssohn's conception, which lies not simply in the handling of these fugal textures—which represents only one element of his strategy—but in the modification of the movement's formal processes through the use of cyclic thematic organization to reflect the role of the finale within the four-movement work. As we shall see in chapter 5, the Octet is neither the first nor the last of Mendelssohn's explorations of cyclic form, but the smoothness and subtlety with which the interpenetration of cyclic and sonata-form processes is carried out mark it as one of his most brilliant achievements.

The fugal exposition of the first theme, mm. 1–25—which, with the restatement of the theme in mm. 189–213 and the opening of the development section, contains almost all of the specifically fugal writing in the movement—is only the first element in an unusually well-populated first group. In all, this thematic complex consists of four distinct but interrelated themes which are juxtaposed with a minimum of connective padding (Example 30).

The significance of this unadorned, almost perfunctory presentation of the thematic material will become clear after a brief consideration of the rest of the first part of the movement.

After theme D comes to an emphatic close in the tonic (m. 63), a short transition passage moves briskly to the dominant, reaching B♭ major in only six measures. Harmonically, this arrival is only weakly defined, however, and there is no immediately discernible break in texture that would serve to articulate the establishment of the new key. Both the transition and the arrival continue to play on elements of theme D (which are identical to elements of theme A) and on interjections of an ascending-fourth skip that sound suspiciously like the head of the main theme of the Scherzo.

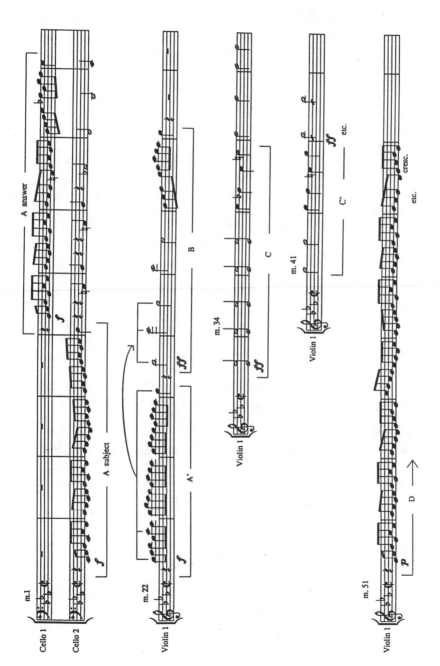

Example 30.   Mendelssohn, Octet, Op. 20, IV, mm. 1–9, mm. 22–29, mm. 34–38 and 41–43, and mm. 51–57.

The ensuing passage continues the motivic play on theme D (or A) and the ascending fourth. Theme B is soon added to the developmental jumble (m. 73), and the harmony begins to push toward V of V of the dominant key, leading into a more firmly planted cadence to Bb major in m. 89.

The thematic articulation of this arrival, although clearer than m. 68, is unusual. The arrival is marked neither by a striking new theme nor by a new version of the main theme in the manner of a "monothematic" form. Instead, the establishment of the dominant is announced by theme C, which is surrounded by a swarm of ascending-fourth figures, now in the form of filled-in scalewise gestures. This transformation of the fourth skip allows what appeared to be a shadowy motivic link to the Scherzo theme to be absorbed into the texture of the finale—explained away as an accompaniment figure—and is typical of Mendelssohn's thematic technique: the ascending fourth, its "Scherzo-theme" identity carefully obscured, can now be woven into the fabric of the movement, unobtrusively preparing the cyclic return that will shape the final stages of the work.

By using a subsidiary thematic element from the first group to articulate the structural arrival in the dominant, Mendelssohn is able to blur slightly the clarity of the formal outlines of the exposition. Theme C, although it is striking and memorable, is essentially an element of continuation—or prolongation within an established thematic and harmonic structure—rather than of initiation. As Example 30 shows, theme C originally grew out of the successive transformation of themes A and B—the outline of theme A yielding the shape of theme B, and the rhythm of theme B providing the repeated half notes of theme C. Theme C, in turn, led directly into the cadential stability of theme D, which, with its echoes of theme A, closed the circle of this progressive thematic process.

This succession of thematic elements is, in fact, subtly paralleled in the opening of the second group, since the statement of theme C beginning in m. 89 has been preceded by fragments of themes A (or D) and B. Harmonically, too, the arrival in Bb major in m. 89 recalls the function of theme C in the first group: the arrival, although more clearly marked than m. 68, is really a continuation of the Bb-major domain established—tentatively, to be sure— at that earlier point. The result of all this is a curious sense of having slipped into the new key without passing any of the distinctly memorable textural landmarks that normally articulate the various stages of a sonata exposition. The slight obscuring of the formal outline this entails will prove to have important consequences later in the movement.

The perfunctory cadential tag from the end of the original version of theme C (mm. 48–51) is replaced by a more expansively melodic but equally efficient tag in mm. 99–105 that leads into a counterstatement of the theme. The counterstatement is identical in shape to mm. 89–99, but its melodic line is dispersed among the four violins in hocket, and the stepwise ascending fourths of the accompaniment are transformed yet again, this time into skittering eighth notes. The cadential tag of the counterstatement leads on to a new, even more broadly laid out cadence to B♭ (m. 133).

At this arrival another element from the first group, theme B, returns, but in an oddly stilted version in which the melody outlines parallel fifths instead of the smooth disjunct sixths that characterized its original presentation. This tune, like theme C, receives a new cadential tag (mm. 137–45—composing out yet another ascending fourth) that leads to a counterstatement of both the theme and the tag (mm. 145–53). The tag itself is extended through another fourth before settling back into B♭ major in m. 165.

This third arrival in the dominant within the course of the second group is marked by a return of the original shape of theme B, complete with its original cadential figure (from mm. 28–29). This proves to be the closing theme of the second group, and it merges into a leisurely retransition, spun out in the first violin, that leads back to the tonic for an abbreviated restatement of the first group. The design seems to be organizing itself into a sprawling rondo, although the main theme—or thematic complex—of the movement provides none of the relaxed tunefulness or expansive symmetries we expect from a rondo theme.

What is even more unusual about this rondo is that the second group presents absolutely no new thematic material. Instead, the harmonic arrivals within the secondary key are marked by the reappearance of subsidiary themes from the first group. The themes do receive new cadential elaborations that introduce new melodic gestures, but these are clearly accessories to the themes to which they are attached. They represent little more than the replacement of briskly efficient cadential clichés from the first group with somewhat more expansively realized clichés. This treatment of the thematic design is so unusual that both Krummacher and Thomas insist that its latter stages (mm. 89–173) cannot be understood as a second group at all.[13] Although I would suggest that this reveals a fundamental misunderstanding of Mendelssohn's procedures—the formal outline is only obscured, not obliterated—it does offer striking evidence of just how unusual the articulative processes of the movement are.

In order to understand Mendelssohn's strategy, it is necessary to recognize how the treatment of the second group grows out of the organization of the first group.

At first glance, the abundance of themes in the first group is reminiscent of the type of rondo exposition Mozart often used in his concerto finales, in which the main theme is followed by a string of accessory ideas. But there are important differences between Mozart's practice and the technique Mendelssohn employs in the Octet that radically alter the significance of the thematic pattern in this later work.

For Mozart, a symmetrically organized main theme—symmetrical both in its internal repetitions and in its dual presentation, first by the soloist and then by the orchestra—establishes the character and pacing of the movement. Rosen has pointed out that for Mozart the function of a concerto finale as a resolution for the entire work "demands melodic material that will resist, rather than imply, development—in other words, a theme that gives he impression of squareness, regularity, and completeness—antiphonal treatment both brings out this character most clearly and colors it most effectively."[14] Since this material does not, by its nature, lend itself to extension, Mozart normally fills out the tonic group with a string of accessory themes (themselves often symmetrically organized) for the orchestra, providing the breadth of tonic stability implied by the opening theme and establishing a relaxed form of the solo-tutti opposition that animates the concerto style. The function of this material in providing harmonic ballast—rather than in introducing primary thematic material—was emphasized by Tovey in his observation that Mozart generally reserved a full restatement of the opening group for the end of the movement, where its tonic bulk offered a persuasively stable cadential counterweight to the looser formal design typical of these movements.[15]

In contrast, Mendelssohn's opening theme is emphatically open-ended and non-symmetrical. Instead of rounding itself off in balanced phrases in the manner of Mozart's themes, the fugal subject propels itself on into the succeeding material, which, as we have seen, is generated through a process of progressive transformation of elements of that material. These themes function not so much to flesh out a tonic expanse as to unfold a single but multi-faceted thematic gesture that spans the entire first group.

In this, and in the strangely hectic way the themes tumble out on each other's heels, Mendelssohn's procedure seems less closely related to Mozart's than to that of the opening ritornello of a baroque concerto, where the pregnant abruptness of an almost telegraphic summary of the principal thematic elements provides the basis for continual thematic elaborations over the course of the movement. In fact, Mendelssohn's technique bears a surprising resemblance to that employed in the opening of the Third *Brandenburg* Concerto. Even the gradual coalescing of independent parts into a unison passage—the progression from the contrapuntal density of theme A to the galumphing unisons of theme C—parallels the organization of Bach's ritornello; where Bach uses this unison passage to close his ritornello, however,

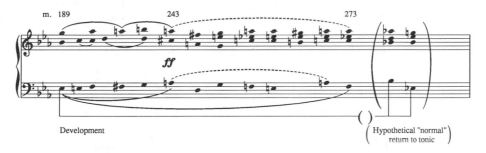

Example 31.   Mendelssohn, Octet, Op. 20, IV, mm. 189–273.

Mendelssohn strikes out on his own path, returning to a fuller texture for his cadential theme.

It is this method of presenting the thematic material of the first group that sets the stage for the slightly disorienting treatment of the second group. The baldness of the initial thematic presentation seems to make further elaboration absolutely essential, just as the brisk efficiency of a baroque ritornello lays the foundation for the elaboration of its figures that is a generating principle of the form. Mendelssohn's stroke of genius was to spread this later elaboration over the framework of a sonata-form exposition. This allows him to articulate the harmonic structure of that exposition in a functionally explicit manner while at the same time obscuring the formal outline by avoiding strongly marked thematic articulations; in place of sharply differentiated themes, Mendelssohn simply reintroduces the same material over and over. The shadowy formal contour that results from this severely restricted articulative design—which recalls some aspects of the thematic organization of the early string symphonies—is a crucial element in Mendelssohn's strategy to open the later stages of the movement into a vast cyclic design embracing the entire work.

In its largest outlines, the development section is organized around an ascending linear progression that begins in the tonic and moves toward the dominant in broadly laid-out steps. The individual steps of this progression are elaborated through fleeting harmonic excursions that are embedded in complex contrapuntal textures (Example 31). For the most part, these center on details of the chromatic relations inherent in the underlying progression—the transformation of a minor chord into a passing dominant—and culminate in the replacement of Ab, the fourth degree in Eb major, with A♮, the leading tone of the dominant key, Bb major. Through the manipulation of registral connections, surface harmonic elaborations, and abrupt changes of texture, Mendelssohn invests the entire development section with a powerful cadential drive, and the unexpected way in which he exploits this cadential energy represents one of the most remarkable formal achievements in his entire output.

Several details in the course of this long-range progression require comment, since they help prepare later events. The arrival in F minor in m. 229 sets off a short passage in stretto (on theme B) that temporarily establishes the third of F minor, A♭, as a tonic root. The part writing is arranged to place a strong emphasis on the A♭s scattered across the texture of this passage, and in particular on ab″ in the upper voice of mm. 233–36 (first violin, then third violin). But when the large-scale linear progression is resumed in m. 237, moving immediately on to G, the ab″ so prominently established is abruptly replaced by a♮″ (m. 238). This chromatic detail, carefully isolated in the upper register, brings the A♭–A♮ exchange, which is central to the cadential drive of the development section as a whole, into fleeting but sharp focus. The functionally secondary a♮″ of m. 238 serves, in a sense, as an anticipation of the *fortissimo* a♮″ in m. 242 (now doubling the triadic root), where a sharp textural break marks the beginning of the next stage of the linear progression.

In the manuscript version of the Octet, the stretto passage that follows the establishment of F minor is fifteen measures longer than it is in the printed score. The additional material fits between the second and third beats of m. 233, and the process of revision can be described as simply lifting this material out and making minor adjustments to the second viola and the cello parts to smooth over the slight gap that results.

R. Larry Todd has observed that in eliminating this material, which elaborates the stretto texture over a harmonic base that vacillates between A♭ major and F minor, Mendelssohn was exercising an admirable and all-too-rare restraint, curbing a tendency to indulge in contrapuntal display for its own sake.[16] It is true that on occasion the development sections—and even the expositions—in some of Mendelssohn's earlier works do clot into wearisome lumps of contrapuntal predictability, but the excised material in the finale of the Octet is not particularly unattractive; in fact, it provides an impressive structural ritardando for the large-scale progression that underlies the section, prolonging A♭ before the push to A♮. The revision does play an important role in the registral organization of the development section, however. In the manuscript version of this passage, the repeated ab″s of mm. 233–36 followed a welter of subsidiary modulations that generated a somewhat random upper-voice motion. In the printed score, on the other hand, the initial eb″–ab″ of the stretto (first violin, mm. 232–33) immediately sets off the reverberating ab″s of mm. 233–36, establishing this emphasis as the only significant upper-register event in the passage. The concision achieved in the revised version brings the central A♭–A♮ exchange of the development section into sharper focus.

The next step in the large-scale progression—prepared by this play on A♮—is accomplished abruptly, with a *fortissimo* eruption in A major, and marked by the sudden replacement of the contrapuntal bustle of the first part of the development with strongly rhythmicized block chords (m. 242). (The new texture recalls, in a typically unobtrusive way, the development section of the first movement.) This strongly marked articulation gives the arrival in A major an extraordinary power, reflecting the cadential tension generated by the large-scale tritone relation between the tonic, E♭ major, and A major with particular vividness, and marking the penultimate step in the large-scale motion from E♭ major to the dominant, B♭ major, as the point of greatest intensity in the movement—and, in fact, in the entire work.

The central portion of the development section is a prolongation of this impressively established A♮, organized as a circle-of-fifths progression that begins with the A major of m. 242 and eventually returns to A minor in m. 263. With the return to A (minor), the final chromatic detail of the linear progression—the replacement of C♯ with C♮ is completed, clearing the way for what will presumably be a strongly articulated move to B♭ major that will touch off a passage of dominant preparation sufficiently persuasive to pull this strange movement into the closural processes of a recapitulation. But Mendelssohn has other plans for the last part of the finale—plans that reflect its position as the last stage of the work as a whole; little of what happens from here on is what could be expected to happen.

Simply as a result of its position, the closing section of the last movement of a multi-movement work has a significance that extends beyond its immediate, self-contained formal context. Normally, in the classical sonata style, the looser textures, more square-cut phrase structure, and surface animation typical of a finale are, apparently, sufficient to accommodate this larger function of the concluding tonic area within the formal processes of the movement. To reinforce that larger function—and the sense of looser formal organization—there is a tendency for the latter stages of a finale, whether in sonata or rondo form, to broaden into a coda that provides an expanded breadth of conclusive tonic stability. In Beethoven's works, this final tonic area may be expanded far beyond the proportions suggested by the movement itself, reflecting the role of this closing section as a final cadential gesture that grounds tensions which have coursed through the entire work. The finale of the Eighth Symphony offers a remarkable example of this sort of expansion—the coda is nearly as long as the body of the movement. In the Fifth Symphony, on the other hand, the delirious affirmation of C major in the last pages of the finale is explicitly linked to events in earlier movements through the reappearance of a fragment of the Scherzo just before the opening of the recapitulation. (The cyclic design of this work will be considered in greater detail in chapter 5.) In other works—the "Waldstein," or the Eb-major Trio, Op. 70, No. 2, for example—the final tonic elaboration may take different, and often less conspicuous, forms, but its function is essentially the same.

In the Octet, Mendelssohn responds to this cumulative aspect of the multi-movement structure by transforming the entire closing section of the finale into a massive tonic cadence that in both its dimensions and its thematic organization relates it to the whole of the work. Although, as we shall see in chapter 5, the "finale problem" occupied Mendelssohn throughout the 1820s and 1830s, only once, in the "Italian" Symphony—which follows a plan similar to that of the Octet—did he manage to achieve anything approaching the brilliant animation of this first of his major works. The strategies he employs here—at once obvious and subtle—reveal the flexibility with which he was able to approach the structural issues of sonata style.

As we have seen, the development section is organized around a broadly laid out motion toward the home dominant, Bb major. With the establishment of A♮ over the central portion of the development section, and the eventual motion toward V of Bb major, this cadential drive becomes increasingly focused, and the structurally decisive return to the tonic seems to be at hand: the recapitulation, presumably, is about to begin. But just as F major (V of V) is established in m. 273, this essentially normal course of events is simply swept away, and the opening theme of the Scherzo suddenly materializes—out of thin air—bringing with it the skittering accompaniment figure from the beginning of the third movement.

It was noted earlier that the ascending-fourth skip from the head of this theme has popped up throughout the course of the finale, beginning at the transition between the first and second groups of the exposition. As a fleeting motivic allusion, this seemed to have been effortlessly assimilated into the flow of the movement, primarily in accompaniment figures woven through the second group. But now this allusion has reassembled itself into an explicit statement of a theme from one movement within the course of another—an event that is, by its nature, an intrusion in the self-generated structural processes of that movement and that cannot be absorbed so easily within its structure.

Coming at just the point where the carefully developed cadential forces of the movement seem to be converging on the final reacquisition of the tonic, the intrusion of the Scherzo theme is particularly conspicuous and, therefore, disruptive. The placement is rather subtle, and is an indication of the care with which Mendelssohn has planned the design of the movement around this moment.

The model for a work in which material from the Scherzo reappears near the end of the development section of the finale is, of course, Beethoven's Fifth Symphony. But in that work, the material from the third movement returns at the end of an absolutely gigantic passage of dominant preparation, and the sudden turn to C minor at the interruption functions, in effect, as an elaborate deceptive cadence that further intensifies the cadential drive to the tonic major for the opening of the recapitulation. Within the movement, then, this cyclic return can be understood, in one sense, as a particularly distinctive articulative texture, marking the culmination of the cadential drive to the tonic with tremendous expressive force.

Mendelssohn's Octet operates at a much lower emotional temperature than that generated in the Fifth Symphony, of course, and this is reflected in the organization and function of the cyclic design of the work. In the Octet, the articulative break created by the intrusion of the Scherzo material occurs just *before* the harmony settles into the home dominant: where Beethoven used the cyclic intrusion to intensify the drive toward the reacquisition of the triumphant C major with which the Symphony concludes, Mendelssohn has used the return of the Scherzo material to derail the harmonic process of the finale just as it seems to have settled into a clearly focused passage of dominant preparation. There is, then, a disjunction between what is certainly the most prominent articulative gesture in the movement—the appearance of the Scherzo theme—and the underlying tonal processes of the movement—the processes we would normally expect the surface articulations to be articulating. Mendelssohn seizes on the formal destabilization created by this disjunction to disengage the structural process of the finale—the carefully prepared drive toward the opening of the recapitulation—and replace it with a cadential process that explicitly embraces the whole of the four-movement work.

Four measures after its unexpected reappearance, the Scherzo theme dissolves back into the transitional rush of the finale, and the harmony finally moves on to V of Eb major. But the arrival in the tonic in m. 279 is marked by another statement of the Scherzo theme. As a result, although this tonic arrival realizes the large-scale cadential motion that has governed the entire middle section of the movement, it is stripped of its normal significance within the formal design: this new intrusion of the Scherzo theme at the return to the tonic confirms the breakdown of the thematic integrity of the finale, and consequently the tonic arrival cannot offer any sense of resolution—or even of relative stability—for the sonata-form processes of the movement. In fact, this return to the tonic functions as nothing more than a passing incident in a new design initiated at the first appearance of the Scherzo theme. The transitional rush is resumed, leading to a third, climactic, statement of the Scherzo theme, *fortissimo*, in its own home tonic, G minor (m. 291); but at this point the accompaniment figure from the third movement is replaced by theme C of the finale, which seems to have been designed specifically to work in this combination. The pair of themes marches steadily up the scale, exchanging positions half-way through an octave ascent. On reaching the upper-octave G (m. 313), the procession changes direction, and after a rushed descent in three precipitous steps, the harmony lands once again on the tonic (m. 321). In the shadow of the disorienting events of the preceding 48 measures, this abrupt arrival, marked by theme B, hardly qualifies as the clearly articulated return to the tonic that will restabilize the movement, and it is not surprising that the passage tumbles on with barely a moment's hesitation, settling onto a dominant pedal six measures later.

The manuscript version of the passage beginning at the return to the tonic in m. 321 is eighteen measures longer than the printed score. As Example 32 shows, the tonic arrival set off a circle-of-fifths progression in which fragments of theme B were juxtaposed with reappearances of the head of the Scherzo theme. I would suggest two reasons for the excision of this material. First, the original version eventually led to an exact repetition of mm. 321–22. The repetition itself is not necessarily a problem, but it points up the fact that this version placed a comparatively strong emphasis on the reestablishment of the tonic: the entire passage functioned as a prolongation of the Eb major with which it begins and ends. The problem, I think, is that this broadly laid out tonic prolongation, with its idiosyncratic, but striking, thematic content, acquired too much articulative weight, suggesting that it was, indeed, functioning in some strange way as the opening of the long-withheld recapitulation. Eliminating this material intensifies the larger cadential thrust of the passage and strengthens the sense that this final section of the movement is assuming a structural function that extends beyond the limits of the finale itself.

The second point involves the role of the Scherzo material within the overall structure of the work, a role only imperfectly defined by the generally accepted sense of cyclic procedures.

As we have seen, the texture of the finale is made to assimilate a wide range of ascending fourth figures that were generated by the fleeting but relatively overt reference to the head of the Scherzo theme first introduced in m. 64. The original version of the passage beginning in m. 321 reinforced the sense of a thematic tie between the two movements by explicitly relating that ascending fourth to the initial ascending fourth of theme B. This corresponds to the normal sense of cyclic process as a function of thematic interconnection. But the intrusion of the Scherzo material in the latter stages of the finale

Example 32.   Mendelssohn, Octet, Op. 20, IV, manuscript version, mm. 321ff.

does not simply serve to clarify an already obvious thematic relationship. On the contrary, the primary function of the cyclic return is the disruption of the course of events of the finale, and this requires that in spite of the relationship between the various thematic elements, the Scherzo material be recognized as a foreign body—as an intrusion into the structure of the finale. The repeated juxtaposition of the Scherzo theme and theme B in the original version of the passage undermined this quality by assimilating, almost too readily, that foreign body into the pattern of the finale, suggesting that after a somewhat jarring digression, everything could return to normal. The point of the movement, and of the work as a whole, however, is that there is nothing normal about these closing pages.

The extraordinary manipulation of formal elements in this final stage of the movement is not simply a naughtily clever boyish "effect." The foundation for Mendelssohn's redefinition of the role of the last part of the finale has been carefully laid down in the thematic organization of the exposition. The essential function of the recapitulation—what Edward T. Cone has called the "sonata principle"—is to resolve the tonal polarity established in the exposition by replaying in the tonic any significant material that has originally been presented in another key.[17] But as we have seen, Mendelssohn has taken great pains to avoid the introduction of any important new thematic material in the second group of the exposition; in a very real sense, there is nothing to recapitulate in this movement, since there is no material that has been associated uniquely with the dominant. Furthermore, the thematic profile of the exposition has been rendered so indistinct through the kaleidoscopic recirculation of material that the necessity for recapitulation, which is generated in large measure by the memorability of the interrelated thematic and harmonic patterns of the exposition, is too weak to shape these later stages of the movement.

In place of a normal recapitulation, the end of the movement is given over to an enormous tonic cadence covering 108 measures—slightly more than one quarter of the movement's entire length. For the thematic content of this final section, Mendelssohn employs some of the thematic material common to the first and second groups as well as figures derived from the cadential appendages that represented the only strikingly new material in the second group, so he does manage to incorporate a shadowy form of recapitulation after all. Over the course of this section, however, the thematic gestures become less and less clearly associated with the melodic material from the finale, and fragments of first movement material are gradually introduced—at first only allusively, but in the closing pages explicitly.

In outline, the cadential design is of the utmost simplicity. As Figure 11 shows, the tonic so precariously attained in m. 321 tumbles onto a dominant

E♭ major:	I^6	V^7	I^6	$I_\flat{}^6_5$	(IV)	V	I
Measure:	327	349	355	357		385	387–429

Figure 11.   Mendelssohn, Octet, Op. 20, IV, mm. 327–429.

Example 33. Mendelssohn, Octet, Op. 20, IV, mm. 335–39 and 363–68.

Example 34. Mendelssohn, Octet, Op. 20, IV, mm. 387–95.

pedal in m. 327, initiating a perfectly straightforward cadential progression, laid out over the course of more than one hundred measures.

The initial stage of this progression, beginning in mm. 339–54, brings back theme C, in a form almost identical to its initial presentation at the beginning of the movement: it is in the tonic, but over a dominant pedal. Measure 355 introduces a new figure derived from the triadic counterstatement to theme A first heard at the beginning of the development section. The slow harmonic rhythm of this passage, with a change of chord at first occurring every four measures, is reminiscent of the cadential expansion that was attached to theme C in the second group (mm. 121–32). The continuation of the melodic figure in the first violin in mm. 363–71 is new as well, but there is a curious tinge of familiarity about it that results from a particularly subtle aspect of Mendelssohn's thematic technique. The framework of this new melodic figure fills out the same registral space as the presentation of theme B (just heard in the tonic, mm. 335–39, first violin): in fact, as Example 33 shows, the new line is simply a permutation of theme B—using the same pitches, but transforming its characteristic cadential descent into a soaring ascent. The new theme is both new and already familiar. This entire passage (mm. 335–71) is repeated immediately with numerous changes of detail.

At the cadence to the tonic in m. 387, another new figure is introduced, but again, its newness is tinged with familiarity. This time it is the harmonic scheme that is familiar; in fact as Example 34 indicates, it is nothing other than the I–VI–ii–V–I progression that governed every level of the structure

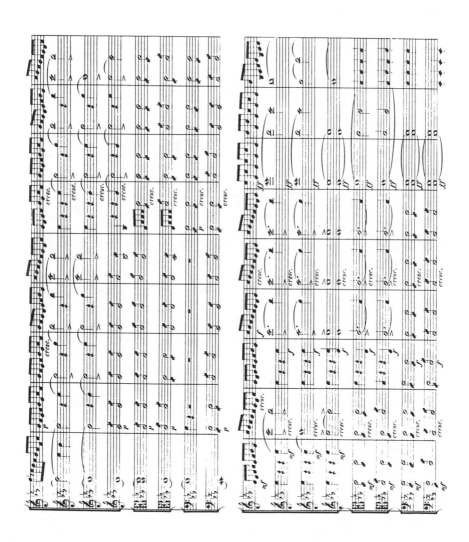

Example 35. Mendelssohn, Octet, Op. 20, IV, mm. 402–29.

of the first movement. But now the strong modulatory impulse embedded in the progression is grounded to the tonic by the unmoving E♭ pedal in the lowest voice, setting off a chain of E♭–E♮ clashes that reverse the tendency of E♮ to move to F by explicitly pulling it back to the tonic, E♭.

This veiled allusion to the harmonic design of the first movement leads to an explicit return of thematic material from the first movement. In m. 403, the closing theme of the first group of the finale, theme D, reappears for the first time since the opening of the movement. Like the subsidiary material in a Mozart concerto, this theme, with its emphatically cadential function, has been reserved to mark the final return to the tonic, clinching the elaborate cadential process of this last part of the movement. But theme D is not the only cadential element Mendelssohn brings back at this point. Just as this restatement begins, the second and third violins reintroduce the closing theme from the first movement, and it turns out, naturally, that these two themes share the same harmonic underpinning; it will probably not be surprising that this underpinning is simply a cadential form of the I–vi–ii–V–I progression (Example 35).

This final tonic cadence serves, then, a double function. On the one hand, it rounds off the sprawling design of the finale with the reappearance of a particularly emphatic cadential tune. At the same time, the closing measures of the Octet complete an elaborate cyclic design identifying the final tonic affirmation of the last movement as a cadence for the work as a whole by circling back to the cadential material of the first movement.

Of course, veiled thematic allusions—or even explicit thematic returns—are not particularly unusual in eighteenth- and nineteenth-century music: they are almost to be taken for granted in any large-scale work of the romantic period. What is unusual in the finale of the Octet—and in different ways in the other three movements as well—is the integration of these thematic manipulations with the structural processes of sonata form. In the finale, for example, the rhythm, harmony, and texture that animate the combination of the Scherzo theme with theme C generate an exhilarating climax, but the foundation that rationalizes this extraordinary effect is the expansion of the formal design generated by the cyclic intrusion. What had seemed to be a carefully controlled drive toward closure within the confines of the finale is revealed—in a thrilling instant—to be the beginning of a gigantic cadential gesture that encompasses the whole of an unusually expansive four-movement work. The effect is majestic in its scope, but it is accomplished with a lightness of touch that is breathtaking in its nonchalance.

CHAPTER 4

THE THEMATIC SHAPE

It is a revealing indication of Mendelssohn's sensitivity to the functional organization of sonata form that the revisions of the Octet examined in chapter 3 are concerned primarily with the process of recapitulation. This is most striking in the first movement and in the Andante where perfectly regular classicist recapitulations, with full repetitions of the thematic pattern established in the expositions, are drastically abbreviated, yielding less rigid formal designs that better reflect the structural processes played out over the course of each movement. This flexibility in dealing with the thematic elements of sonata form—combining freedom of gesture with the semblance of absolute normality—is one of the most characteristic, and most persistently overlooked, elements of Mendelssohn's sonata style in the works from the second half of the 1820s, distinctly setting them apart from most of the music of the early romantic generation. Unfortunately, in comparison with the struggle for formal mastery that seems to be a defining characteristic of the works of his contemporaries, the unruffled elegance of Mendelssohn's compositional method has often been mistaken for superficiality, and this in turn has engendered a critical attitude toward that method securely founded on almost total neglect.

The problems the composers of the early romantic generation faced center in large part on the difficulty of coordinating the large-scale symmetries inherent in a clearly articulated tonal dynamic of tension and resolution with the romantic ideal of a thematic process controlled by the progressive development of material over the entire course of a movement—a development that was organic and unidirectional. The establishment of thematic processes as the primary generating principle of sonata form necessarily introduces a disjunction of form and process that threatens the fundamental coherence of

137

the style: if thematic transformation is the essential vehicle of coherence, the process of recapitulation, with its return to the thematic pattern of the exposition, does indeed seem to be "the inflexible repetition of that which has already been said," signaling a pathological breakdown of stylistic principles. In the more spectacularly "romantic" solutions to this problem—in works like the Liszt B-minor Sonata or Schumann's Second and Fourth Symphonies—the formal design is radically transformed to accommodate the thematic process. But as these experiments became more individually characteristic, the relevance of the sonata-form framework—lurking somewhere in the background—to the events of the musical surface becomes increasingly obscure, and the explanatory value of an analysis based on the functional significance of that framework seems to be restricted to the cataloguing of partial congruences and—more often—fundamental but inexplicable licenses.

In a majority of the works of this period, however, the thematic symmetry of exposition and recapitulation is adhered to with discouraging consistency, invariably to the detriment of the composer's individual style.

The first movement of Schumann's F♯-minor Piano Sonata, Op. 11, offers an instructive example of the difficulties posed by the attempt to integrate a romantic musical language with the formal regularity that was apparently perceived to be appropriate for a sonata-form movement.

The structural plan of the movement hinges on the gradual emergence of the tritone A–D♯ as a decisive element in the harmonic structure of the exposition. What is particularly impressive is the care with which Schumann plants the tritone relation and develops it over the course of the exposition; what is particularly instructive is the cursory way in which he is forced to deal with this process in the recapitulation.[1]

The A–D♯ tritone is introduced in the first measures of the Allegro, forming the upper and lower limits of the initial melodic gesture of the main theme, and D♯ is carried over in an inner voice through the next six measures (Example 36). D♯—and the A–D♯ tritone—are elaborated more prominently in the second statement of the theme (beginning in m. 23 of the Allegro), and there is a D♯ on every half beat of the twelve measures that make up the third, *fortissimo*, statement of the theme and the modulatory bridge that grows out of it. The transition begins by expanding on the hint of supertonic emphasis that is built into the theme—D♯ suggesting V of ii—but eventually the harmony shifts toward V of E minor, the minor dominant of III, in which D♯ functions as the leading tone. The passage comes to a resounding climax on a B7 chord in m. 54, reuniting the three pivotal pitches of the theme: F♯, A, and D♯. But instead of leading on to a preparation that will—presumably—soon establish A major as the secondary key of the exposition, as all this

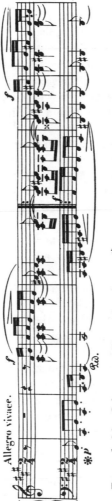

Example 36. Schumann, Piano Sonata in F# minor, Op. 11, I, Allegro vivace, mm. 1–7.

seems to be implying, the B7 is taken as an augmented sixth chord, introducing a tempestuous passage in Eb minor that brusquely reverses the inflectional thrust of the passage. D♯, the presumed leading tone, suddenly—and astonishingly—becomes the tonic keynote, while F♯ becomes the minor third. At the end of this sixteen-measure outburst the tempo slows, and a sequential passage over a stepwise descending bass accomplishes a leisurely move to A major for the lyric closing theme of the exposition. In the first steps of this sequential passage eb'' is reinterpreted as d♯'', and leads, at last, to e♮'', finally realizing the inflectional impulse that has coursed through every measure of the exposition. This entire process reverberates quietly throughout the second theme itself, in gently lingering motions through D♯ that subsume this troubling pitch within a delicate lyric gesture in the new key.

The control of harmonic and motivic resources in this structure reflects a long-range coherence that is not always attributed to Schumann's compositional method. The dissonant agent that will generate the structural modulation is embedded in the opening measures of the movement as a passing detail in the melodic line, and the strange eruption of Eb minor proves to be not simply a colorful effect, but a carefully prepared prolongation that dramatically forestalls—and intensifies—the realization of that modulatory impulse. The remarkable effect of distance and return Rosen notes in the motion from F♯ minor through Eb minor and finally to A major is the result of the subtle manipulation of inflectional relations Schumann has woven through the entire span of the exposition.[2]

The problem with this beautifully worked-out process is that a large-scale modulatory design that hinges on specific inflectional relations poses difficulties when it is translated into a recapitulation that begins and ends in the tonic. As we have seen in chapter 2, when Haydn was faced with a roughly analogous situation in the B-minor Quartet, Op. 33, No. 1, he reworked the network of harmonic interrelations established in the first group to subsume the modulatory impulse within the closural field of the tonic, and he drastically altered the thematic design, eliminating what would have been an unexceptionably regular, but processively incoherent, symmetry between the exposition and the recapitulation.

Schumann, too, alters the thematic pattern of the first group in the recapitulation, attaching the bridge passage to the end of the initial statement of the main theme: this reflects the need to avoid reestablishing the modulatory impetus generated over the course of the restatements of the theme. But the carefully worked-out network of pitch relations that controlled the harmonic structure of the exposition is not so much altered as simply derailed, swept aside rather than assimilated. The design of the main theme involves a number of fleeting subsidiary modulations; when the pattern of these modulations first swings around to V of F♯ minor, Schumann inserts a short cadential extension and launches into the bridge material, which now begins in the tonic and seems to be leading toward the unlikely eventual goal of G minor (compare mm. 298–305 with mm. 47–54). The crucial note in this passage is C♯, the leading tone to V of G minor, and continually reiterated C♯s replace the D♯s of the corresponding material in the exposition. At the enharmonic shift in m. 306 (corresponding to the move to E♭ minor in m. 55), the new tonic that crystallizes around this pivotal note turns out, of course, to be C♯ minor, the minor dominant; the large-scale interruption is given new meaning, serving now as a particularly impassioned dominant preparation for the return to the tonic at the closing theme. This reworking of the tonal perspective is impressively handled, bathing the return to the tonic for the lyric closing theme with a special tenderness. But tightly woven network of pitch relations that controlled the exposition, linking each step of the thematic-harmonic process to what had come before and to what would follow, is lost. The A–D♯ tritone is dropped rather than resolved in the opening of the recapitulation, and there is no compensating preparation for the sudden change of focus to C♯ preceding the bridge passage: since C♯ is not treated as an inflectionally sensitive pitch, the "organic" quality of the exposition as the gradual unfolding of a single process is missing in the recapitulation. Of course, the beautiful relation between the opening gestures of the first theme and the closing theme unfolded in the exposition is completely obliterated in this recapitulation.

Similar problems of reassimilation can be found in almost any of the major works of the early romantic period; the first movements of Schumann's "Rhenish" Symphony or Schubert's C-major Quintet and G-major Quartet are among the most imposing examples. The profound beauty of these works is beyond question, but it is precisely the most extraordinary moments in the expositions of these works—the gradual emergence of G major in the first movement of the Quintet, or the delicate oscillation of the second group around A♯ and A♮ in the first movement of the Quartet—that cannot be absorbed within the process of recapitulation. As a result, these carefully elaborated structural designs are sacrificed to the thematic regularity imposed by the "obligatory symmetrical analogy with the exposition," and the recapitulation does ramble along, offering little more than "the inflexible repetition of that which has already been said."

As we have seen, this conception of form governs the first movements of Mendelssohn's C-minor Symphony and the early chambers works discussed in chapter 2; but even in the Symphony, written when the composer was fifteen, Mendelssohn manages to keep the pitch structure under tighter control than Schumann can muster in the F♯-minor Sonata. Beginning with the Octet—in its revised form—Mendelssohn's treatment of thematic structure reveals a suppleness and freedom that recaptures much of the persuasive coherence of the classical sonata style.

A particularly instructive example of this new formal technique can be found in the first major orchestral work of this period—and one of Mendelssohn's most original conceptions—the Overture to *A Midsummer Night's Dream* (1825-26). G. A. Macfarren identified some of the most astonishing elements of the work when he observed that "no one piece of music contains so many points of harmony and orchestration that had never been written before as does this, and they have none of them the air of experiment, but seem all to have been written with certainty of their success."[3] But the Overture is more than simply a collection of brilliantly original orchestral effects; the formal design is, in a less astonishing way, perhaps, equally original, and seems to reflect the healthy influence a literary program provided for Mendelssohn's approach to formal organization.

The opposing poles of the world of Shakespeare's play are ruled over by the two noble couples: Oberon and Titania, with their strange intrigues and magical powers; and Theseus and his bride-booty, Hippolyta, with their solidly down-to-earth concerns. The two pairs of young lovers, along with Bottom and his troupe, move in a bewildering forest of shadow and misdirection that is the common boundary between these two royal domains. In Mendelssohn's Overture, this structure is reflected in the organization of the exposition around two interconnected sets of thematic groups.

On the largest scale, the exposition falls into the normal pattern of a thematic group in the tonic, a modulatory transition, and a second thematic group in an opposing key—in this case, the dominant. But the most immediately striking thematic (and harmonic) contrasts within this design are not established between the principal themes of the first and second groups, but between the two themes that make up the first group itself. The opening E-minor "fairy music" is one of the finest examples of Mendelssohn's almost pointillist scherzo style, a barely perceptible whir in the strings, *pianissimo* and staccato throughout. The second theme of the tonic group (beginning in m. 62), is an exuberant fanfare in E major, scored for full orchestra, *fortissimo*, that evokes the considerably less ethereal court of Theseus. A close relation is established within this strongly contrasting pair through the upper-voice cadential descent from the fifth degree, b'', around which the fairy music is centered, to the e'' at the beginning of the E-major theme: the two themes mark the boundary points for this overarching cadential gesture—a relation which the fanfare makes clear by immediately retracing the overall shape of the fairy music in one sweepingly magisterial gesture. In terms of the programmatic design, the ethereal darting of the fairy music is contrasted with (and at the same time rationalized by) the well-defined cadential stability of the Theseus music (Example 37).

The fairy music reappears at the cadence to B major, establishing the fifth degree of that key, F♯, as the initial upper-voice pitch of the second group (m. 98). The lyric second theme (mm. 130ff.), which, as Tovey suggests "may safely typify Hermia and Helena,"[4] centers on the third degree, D♯, with repeated descents toward B. But Mendelssohn has a habit of handling the exact degree of cadential stability over the course of a melodic line with particular sensitivity, and the continuation of the theme, which "grows in girlish enthusiasm," is developed out of a deflection of the upper voice from a final descent to the tonic pitch (mm. 176–94). The Bottom-as-ass music (beginning in m. 198) continues to circle through the third from B to D♯ and back, foreshadowing the conclusive motion to the tonic that is accomplished, with a great celebratory racket, at the reappearance of the Theseus music as the cadential theme of the exposition (mm. 230–50). On the largest scale, then, the entire exposition functions as a prolongation of the initial note of the fundamental line, the B established by the fairy music in the opening measures of the work (Example 38).

The opposition between the fairy music and the court music established in the first group governs the overall structure of the second part of the exposition as well: the $\hat{5}$-$\hat{1}$ upper-voice descent that links these two themes as a structural unit in the first group is elaborated over the 152 measures that span the second group, linking the initial F♯ of the restatement of the fairy music to the B of the fanfare that closes the exposition, controlling the large-scale organization of Mendelssohn's extraordinarily well-populated second group just as the intertwined actions of Theseus and Oberon suspend the various characters in a baffling world controlled by the ephemeral logic of dreams.

The task of the recapitulation will be to translate the overarching structural prolongation of the upper-voice B of the exposition into a closural motion to the tonic. Obviously, a transposition of the second group to the tonic would accomplish much of this automatically, replacing the large-scale prolongational motion from F♯ to B in the exposition with a parallel motion from B to E; in fact, much of the second group returns along the lines set out in the exposition—Tovey observed that the structure of the recapitulation was "very regular in form."[5] But a literal restatement of the first group would preempt the larger process of closure, arriving at a cadentially secure upper-voice E at the restatement of the Theseus music—before a single note of the second group has been heard. Mendelssohn avoids this problem by simply eliminating the latter stages of the fairy music and all of the Theseus music,

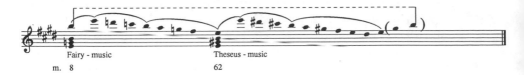

Example 37. Mendelssohn, Overture to *A Midsummer Night's Dream*, Op. 21, mm. 1–66.

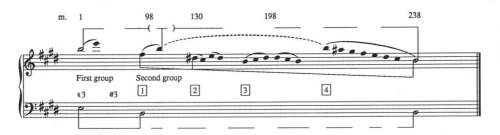

Example 38. Mendelssohn, Overture to *A Midsummer Night's Dream*, Op. 21, exposition.

in effect treating the initial statement of the fairy music as the opening of the second group and moving directly into the Hermia–Helena theme.

This scheme has several advantages over a truly "regular" structure: it strengthens the closural design of the recapitulation as a whole by clarifying the fundamental linear motion from $\hat{5}$ to $\hat{1}$ that spans the entire course of the work, and in particular, it allows Mendelssohn to exploit more fully the cadential character of the Theseus music, which is, presumably, being held in reserve to provide the summary "clinch" at the end of the recapitulation. The treatment of the thematic shape of the recapitulation reflects a coherent musical strategy, then, but it has a programmatic significance as well. After the intricately confused schemes concocted by Oberon and Puck are unraveled in the opening scene of the fourth act, Shakespeare abruptly shifts our attention away from the fairy world. As daylight returns the bewildered victims of these misguided plots—the lovers and the mechanicals—are released from their spells, leaving the forest to gather again for the wedding festivities that are the focus of the final section of the play. Theseus, the embodiment of cool reason, confirms this return to the normal order of things, dismissing the reports of their adventures as the products of the seething brains of lovers and madmen. Mendelssohn, by eliminating the restatement of the fairy music in the recapitulation and reserving the Theseus music for a jubilant, pompous, and more than a little self-satisfied conclusion, sets the balance of his Overture along these same lines: the fairy world seems to have been dismissed, and the function of resolution has been given over to the various happy endings the mortals think they have themselves arranged.

As David P. Young has observed, Shakespeare's final scenes enclose the action within a series of ever-widening circles that *appear* to restabilize the world as the audience's world.[6] After we watch the court watch the mechanicals' tedious brief scene, the mortals retire, giving themselves over to the world of sleep—the fairy world of night and magic. The fairies fill the stage, and Theseus, Hippolyta, the lovers, even Bottom and his men are brought within the embrace of Oberon's midnight blessing. Finally, in the epilogue, Puck addresses the audience directly; but as actor or fairy? Are we not also included in that blessing, encircled by a world of magic we are too dull to see?

Mendelssohn captures the magical serenity of this close, encompassing the rational order of our world in a still wider circle of delicate mystery, with breathtaking simplicity. The anticipated return of the Theseus music at the end of the second group has been delayed by an extension of the Bottom music, a new theme, and transitional material not heard earlier in the recapitulation, and is itself extended, forming a brilliant and almost overly emphatic close in E major—anchored by the timpani with its distinctly un-Mendelssohnian marking, *con tutta la forza* (mm. 586–620). After all this it seems impossible to expect anything more—cessation has unquestionably become more likely than continuation. But even as the final chord reverberates across the orchestra, the scurrying rush of the fairy music returns in the strings. An expansive cadence quickly leads back to E major and a last statement of the Theseus music, but just as in the final pages of the play the seemingly stable world of daylight and reason is enfolded once again in Oberon's embrace, the Theseus music is transformed (translated, as Peter Quince might say) by nocturnal magic, its sweeping pomp stilled to a quiet sigh of infinite gentleness. The final cadence, a last statement of the opening woodwind chords, seems to close the circle of the work, just as Puck's farewell, addressed to the audience, seems to close off the world of the play. But as Tovey pointed out, the final chord is even more delicately scored than it has been before, and the timpani rumbles on the dominant rather than the tonic, quietly unbalancing this last E–major triad.[7] The cadential circle is not fully rounded off: the end of the work vibrates with a delicate instability, and rather than actually stopping, the music seems to simply fade to inaudibility, continuing, perhaps, to sound in a realm just beyond perception.

The Overture *Calm Sea and Prosperous Voyage* [*Meeresstille und glückliche Fahrt*], Op. 27 is another work in which a programmatic subject derived from a literary source seems to have provided a healthy stimulus for Mendelssohn's treatment of sonata form.[8] The literary source is a poem—or rather a contrasting pair of poems—by Goethe, describing the oppressive stillness of a becalmed ship and the relief felt when the wind at last picks up and the voyage nears its completion.

Mendelssohn apparently conceived of the two sections of the Overture as two juxtaposed pictures of the sea, with the first section, the "Calm Sea," *not* intended to function as an introduction to the second.[9] The two sections are, however, interrelated in a number of ways. In the following pages I will sketch briefly one of the elements of this relation—the unfolding of the thematic process—and its integration into the programmatic and formal structures of the work.

All of the thematic material for both sections of the Overture is derived from the motive presented by the double basses in mm. 1–2. Over the course of the work, the constituent elements of this motivic cell will be treated as independently variable rhythmic and intervallic patterns (Example 39).

In the opening measures of this first section, the motive is presented as an initiating gesture, an open-ended descent from D to F♯ that requires continuation. This form of the motive returns in the lower voice at the end of the section, undercutting the cadence that frames this first picture (mm. 40–44), which merges directly into the transition to the second.

As Example 40 shows, the opening of the "Prosperous Voyage"—a sonata-form movement, Molto Allegro e vivace—(mm. 99ff.) adopts the rhythmic pattern of mm. 1–2 (in the quicker tempo, of course), but introduces a new intervallic pattern, suggesting, but withholding, a $\hat{3}$–$\hat{2}$–$\hat{1}$ descent in the upper voice.

A subsidiary thematic element in the first group plays on the relation between this quicker version of the theme and the opening of the Adagio, retaining the rhythm and initial pitch of the quick version, but restoring the overall profile of the Adagio version (Example 41, mm. 107ff.).

A second theme, placed over a dominant pedal in A major, picks up the diastematic shape of m. 107, but uses a new rhythmic pattern—a stretched-

Example 39. Mendelssohn, Overture, *Calm Sea and Prosperous Voyage*, Op. 27, motive, mm. 1–2.

out variant of the original—that displaces the consonant chord tones of the tune to the weak beats within each measure, again hinting at a $\hat{3}$-$\hat{2}$-$\hat{1}$ descent that is not, in the end, accomplished (see Example 42).

The opening measures of a third, more broadly lyric theme (Example 43, mm. 185ff.), now firmly settled in A major, finally integrate the original rhythmic pattern from mm. 1-2 with a straightforward $\hat{3}$-$\hat{2}$-$\hat{1}$ descent, completing, at the motivic level, the cadential impetus latent in each of the transformations of the initial motivic cell. But over the course of the melodic line, this cadential impulse is not fully realized. The half cadence at the end of the first phrase (mm. 195-96) is never answered by a full cadence in the consequent phrase; instead, the end of the exposition melts into the opening of the development section.

The course of this two-part Adagio–Sonata-allegro exposition is governed, then, by a gradual process of motivic transformations that culminates in the coordination of the rhythmic and diastematic patterns of the original motive in a stable cadential configuration. This process is organized with exceptional smoothness; it differs markedly from the schematic juxtapositions of the first movement of the C-minor Symphony, Op. 11, for example, in coordinating the intermediate stage of the thematic process (the transitional theme in mm. 149-65) with a provisional arrival in the secondary key, while the more stable cadential form of the motive is reserved for the affirmation of the new key at the end of the exposition. In the Overture, in contrast to the Symphony, the thematic process clearly articulates the harmonic structure.

The seamless flow from the end of the exposition into the development section is one of the more important consequences of Mendelssohn's revisions in this work: originally, the exposition was rounded off with an emphatically conclusive cadential tag. (This material will be considered in more detail below.) The smoother formal outline of the final version seems to be a particularly appropriate reflection of the programmatic character of the work: since the only significant events in the narrative of Goethe's second poem are the return of a favorable wind and the successful completion of the voyage, it is to Mendelssohn's advantage to downplay the internal articulations of his musical structure. And, of course, this voyage ends somewhere other than where it began, so the expectations of symmetrical balance a fully rounded exposition would imply run counter to the sense of the work's program. The coordination of this unidirectional, linear quality typical of a literary program with a symmetrically balanced form is undoubtedly the central problem of program music in the nineteenth century. Mendelssohn's solution involves a kind of "developing variation" procedure in which new thematic elements—based on the cadential process that shaped the thematic design of the exposition—will be introduced in the final stages of the work,

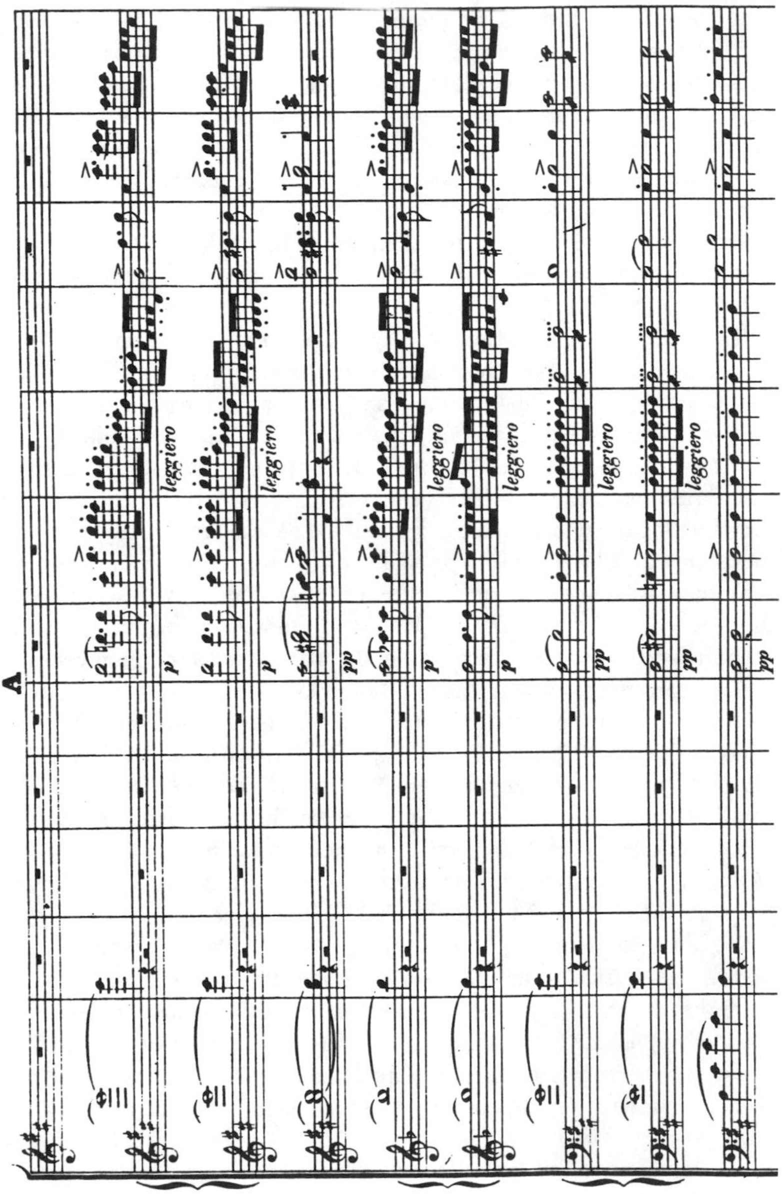
A
leggiero
leggiero
leggiero
leggiero
leggiero
leggiero

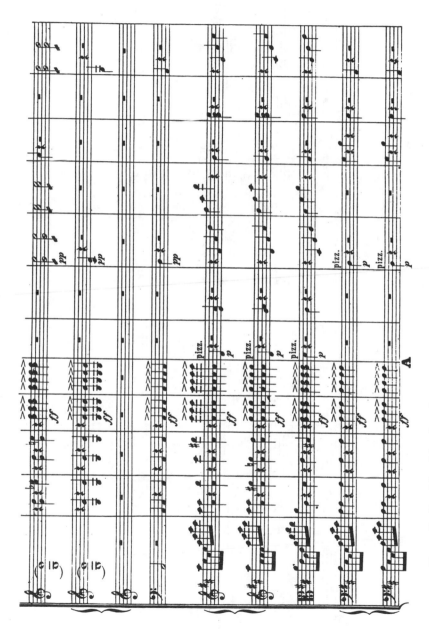

Example 40. Mendelssohn, Overture, *Calm Sea and Prosperous Voyage*, Op. 27, mm. 94-105.

Example 41. Mendelssohn, Overture, *Calm Sea and Prosperous Voyage*, Op. 27, mm. 106–15 (strings only).

Example 42. Mendelssohn, Overture, *Calm Sea and Prosperous Voyage*, Op. 27, mm. 145–53 (strings only).

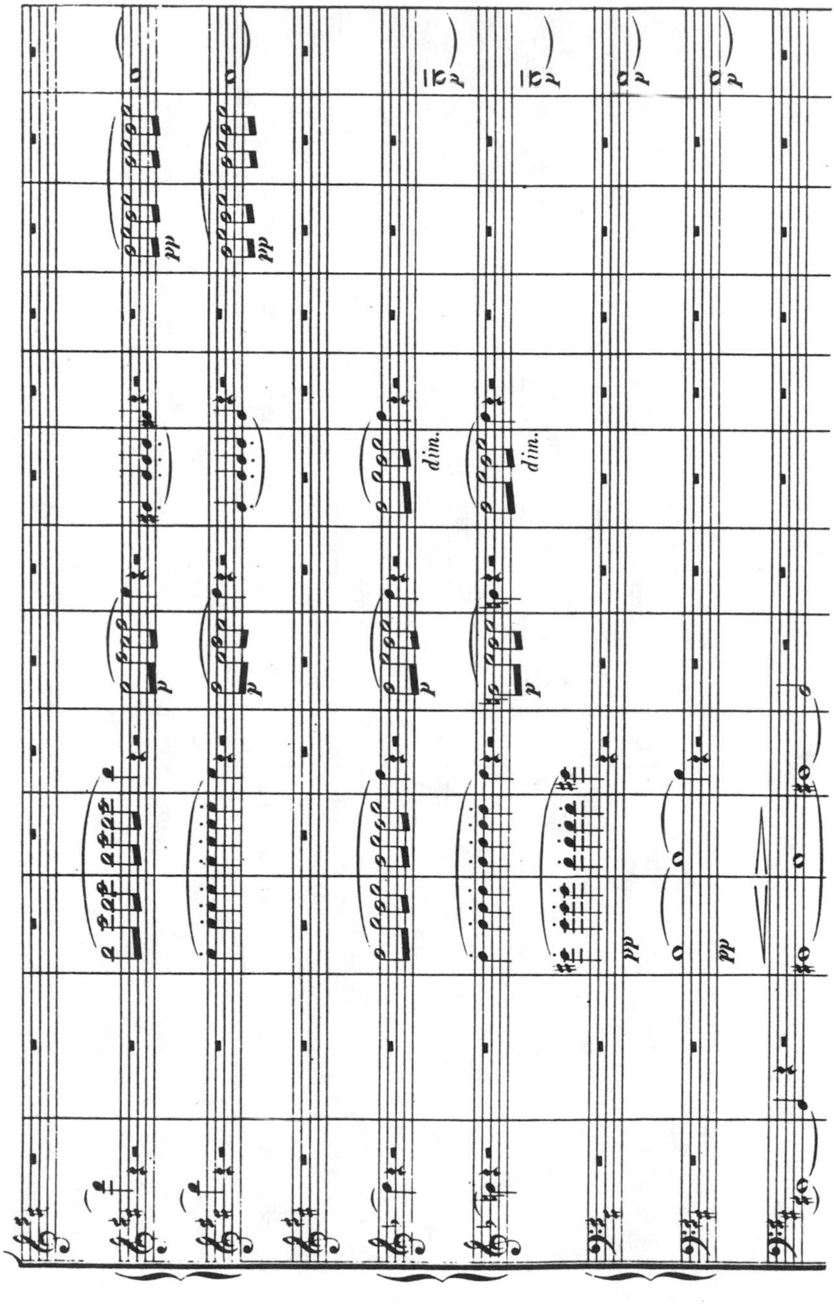

Example 43. Mendelssohn, Overture, *Calm Sea and Prosperous Voyage*, Op. 27, mm. 173–200. (Continued.)

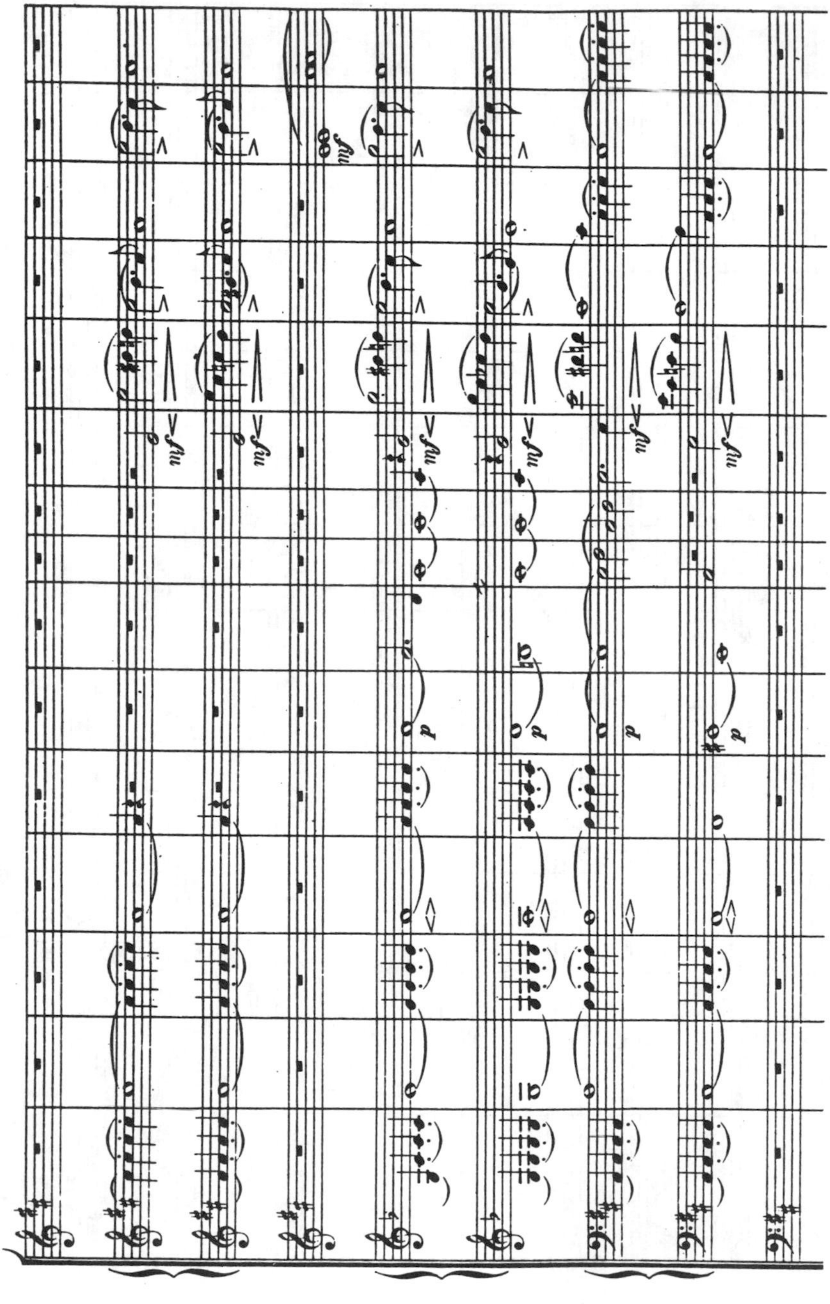

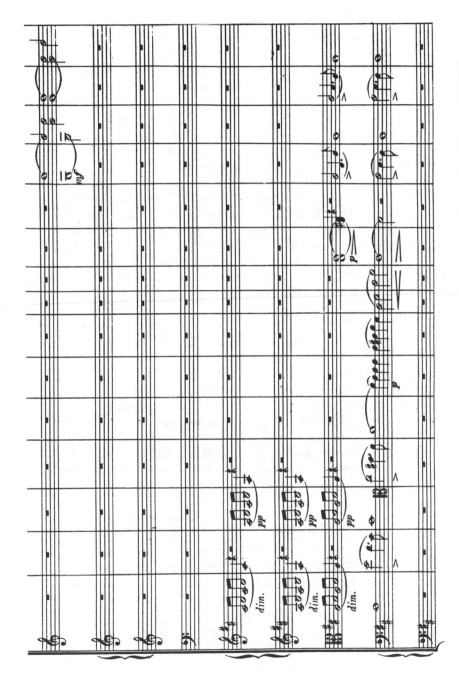

Example 43. (Continued.) Mendelssohn, Overture, *Calm Sea and Prosperous Voyage*, Op. 27, mm. 173–200.

representing the final stages of both the motivic and the programmatic proc-esses. The use of the term "developing variation," with its distinctive con-stellation of Schoenbergian associations, in connection with a composer with a reputation for timid conventionality might seem to be stretching a point, but the treatment of the motive as a separable construct of rhythmic and dias-tematic elements in this work is not particularly far removed from the motivic process concretized in Schoenberg's row technique: our critical pre-conceptions have simply obscured Mendelssohn's technique behind a mist of disinterest. Characteristically, though, Mendelssohn does not invent a new, "romantic" form in which to realize his scheme; instead, he adopts a technique derived from eighteenth-century sonata procedures.

At the end of the development section, the closing theme of the exposition returns in the tonic (mm. 379-92), but in such a way that it sounds like part of the development rather than the beginning of the recapitulation. The tonic, perched over a dominant pedal, is achieved as the goal of a steadily rising bass line that supports a chain of 5-6 progressions (mm. 355-79). But this arrival in D major does not register as an important structural event: the se-quential pattern has broadened tremendously on its penultimate step, G mi-nor, and it takes half of the entire length of the passage to accomplish the motion from G to A. This weakens the sense of continuity with the larger linear progression when the bass finally does move to A (*pp!*) (mm. 378-79), and at the same time it seems to identify D major as a dominant within the functional realm of this broadly laid out G minor rather than as a clearly established, structurally significant manifestation of the tonic. The orches-tration also weakens the articulative force of this arrival, since it recalls an identically scored passage earlier in the development section where the sec-ond theme had appeared in C major, again over a dominant pedal (mm. 335-47). And, of course, the dominant pedal that underlies the passage points on toward a cadence; the passage is both in D major and preparing D major.

Mendelssohn's treatment of the tonic at this point in the movement is simi-lar to a procedure used by Mozart at the end of the development section in the first movement of the D-major Symphony, K. 504 (mm. 189-208), where part of the second group, played in the tonic, turns out to be the beginning of the retransition leading into the opening of the recapitulation. The passage functions as part of a large-scale cadence that pushes toward a stable tonic arrival, and the final stage is marked by a restatement of the main theme itself over a dominant pedal—as Rosen puts it, "Mozart prepares the recapitulation by recapitulating, announces the tonic with the tonic."[10] But Mozart is work-ing out one of his most stately processions to the opening of the recapitula-tion, and the retransition culminates in a strongly articulated double return;

Mendelssohn manipulates his material to avoid any clear articulative break at the beginning of the recapitulation. As at the end of the exposition, it seems to be his intention—in keeping with the programmatic subject of the work—to downplay the internal articulations of the form.

The passage eventually swings around toward the dominant, initiating a clear cadential motion to D major, but the violins jump in with the main theme while the bass is still perched on A (Example 44, mm. 401ff.). The bass catches up two measures later, but as in the Scherzo of the Octet, the harmonic and thematic elements of this double return are slightly out of synchronization with one another; in fact, this shortened restatement of the main theme rushes by without establishing any solid root position tonic chord at all. Apparently, the closural process of the recapitulation will be concerned with establishing a coordination of tonic stability and thematic articulation—a process shaped on the one hand by the cadential drive that controls the thematic process itself, and on the other by the design imposed by the programmatic subject.

The transitional material is extended slightly to accommodate a turn to the subdominant, G major (mm. 413–44), and the triumphant return to the tonic in m. 445 reestablishes the f#''' that, as the initial note of the work's fundamental line, is the focus of the upper-voice cadential motion around which the recapitulation as a whole is organized. But the tonic still isn't in root position—this time it is represented by a first inversion chord—and the theme that marks this return is not the closing theme of the exposition, which presumably should show up at this point, rounding off the thematic pattern and completing—in the tonic—the upper-voice cadential motion from $\hat{3}$ to $\hat{1}$. The closing theme has already returned in the tonic at the end of the development section; we have, in both a musical and programmatic sense, left it behind.

In place of the closing theme, Mendelssohn introduces a new cadential figure that echoes faintly some of the characteristic elements of that material—an initial motion from $\hat{3}$ to $\hat{1}$ and a slight submediant coloring—while avoiding any direct melodic resemblance. And like the closing theme of the exposition, this new theme, while foreshadowing a $\hat{3}$-$\hat{1}$ descent in its initial melodic gesture, leaves the larger motion to the tonic incomplete. The leading tone, c#''', is left hanging at the end of each phrase, unresolved in register: the upper-voice line is displaced from c#''' to d'' in m. 448 and from c#''' to d in m. 456.

The evasion of a close to $\hat{1}$ is further prolonged by a statement of the head of the main theme in augmentation (mm. 457ff.). This grand gesture seems to break open the time frame of the work, expanding with breathtaking suddenness to accommodate a final cadential drive sufficiently broadly laid out to

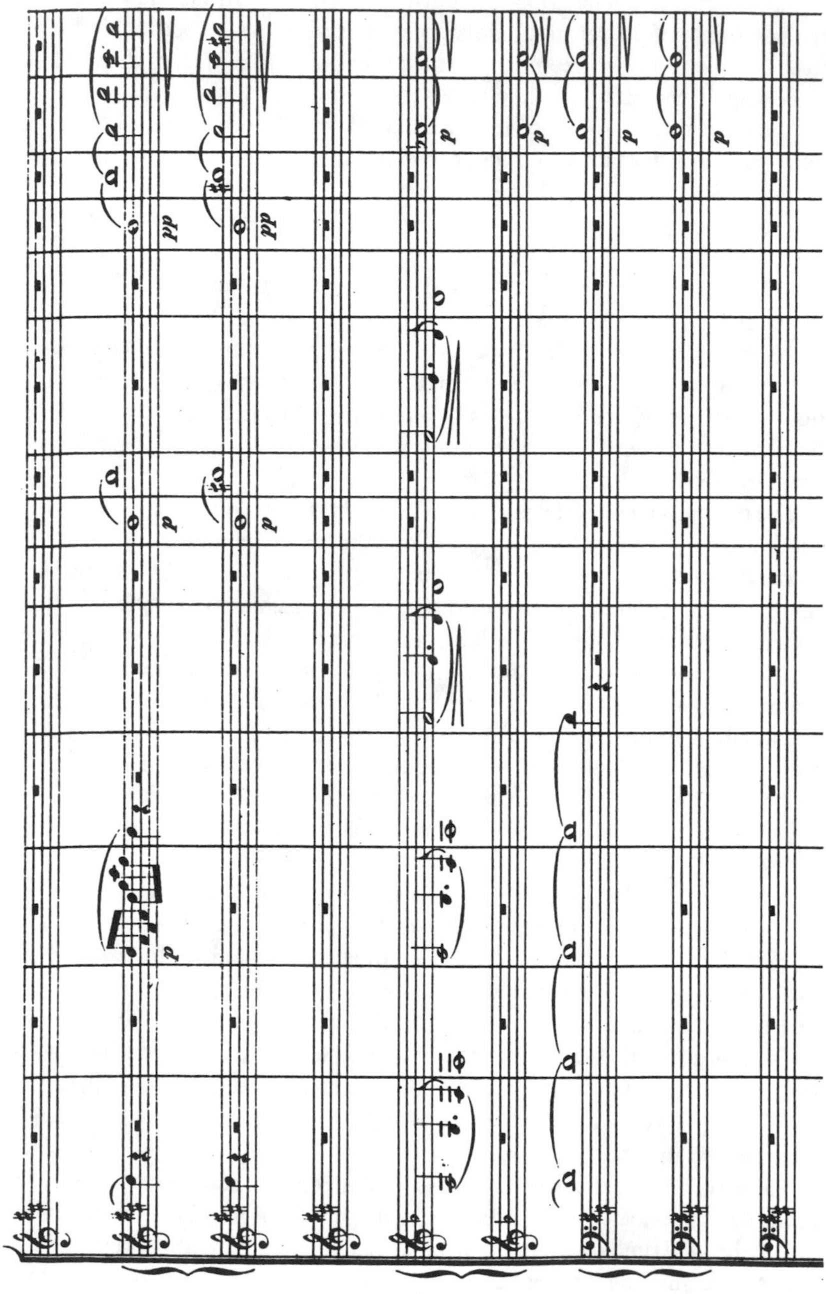

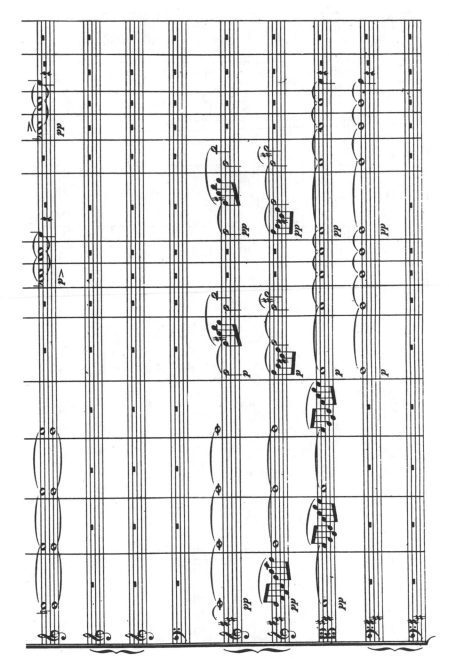

Example 44. Mendelssohn, Overture, *Calm Sea and Prosperous Voyage,* Op. 27, mm. 387–411. (Continued.)

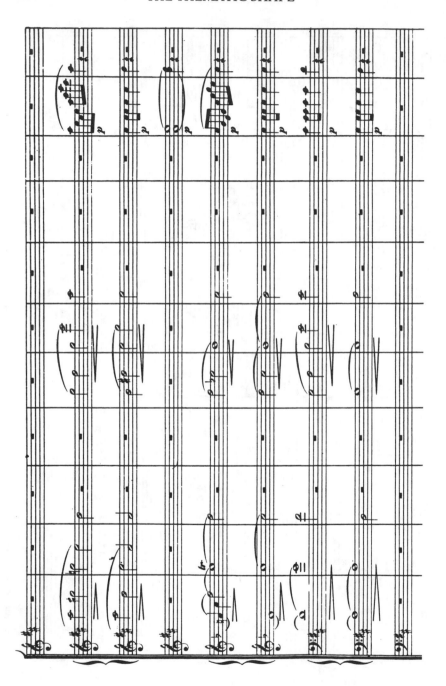

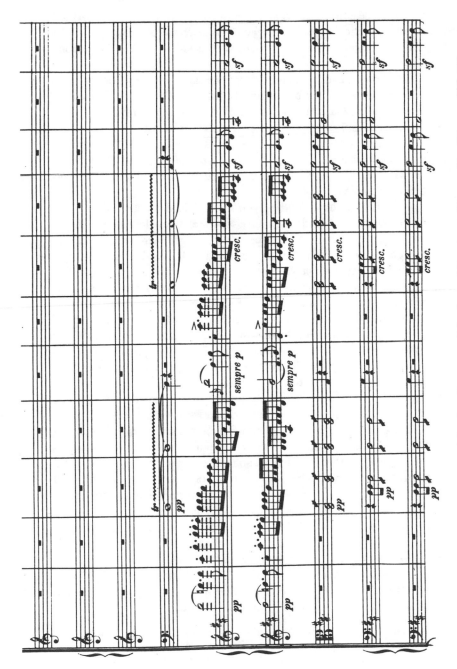

Example 44. (Continued.) Mendelssohn, Overture, *Calm Sea and Prosperous Voyage*, Op. 27, mm. 387–411.

encompass the beautifully calculated motivic process that has spanned this entire work. In particular, this new time scale places a strong emphasis on the $f\sharp''''$-$f\natural''''$-e''' motion of the theme, and on the inability of the line to complete the descent to d'''.

The arrival on $\hat{1}$—and the establishment of a stable root position tonic—is finally accomplished in the brass-band flourishes of the coda. The triumphantly repeated $\hat{3}$-$\hat{2}$-$\hat{1}$ fanfares in these closing pages are a final variant of the motive, now firmly rooted in the tonic, that completes a cadential process that has spanned the entire work. Heard in this sense these fanfares support the weight of all that has gone before, and lose some of the "Chamber of Commerce" quality with which a strictly programmatic interpretation burdens them (Example 45).

The programmatic subject of the Overture, with its distinctly linear "plot," seems to have inspired Mendelssohn to adopt a relatively loose thematic design, rejecting—at least on the surface—the balanced symmetry of exposition and recapitulation typical of the classicist style. But instead of simply turning to a potpourri style in which the themes are strung out like clothes on a line, he employed a means of organization that allowed him to retain the dramatic coherence of the sonata form while adopting its structural elements to the demands of the program. More particularly, Mendelssohn exploited the organizational clarity of the tonal design of sonata form, with its cadential imperative, while adopting this to the explicitly cadential process that animates the motivic transformations of the work. This process, abstracted from any specific thematic realization, simply represents the accomplishment of the $\hat{3}$-$\hat{2}$-$\hat{1}$ cadential descent latent in the opening measures of the Adagio and played out over the course of the work; the new material at the end of the recapitulation and in the coda represents the culmination of this process, completing a line that spans the entire course of these two juxtaposed pictures. It is revealing, then, of Mendelssohn's sensitivity to the role of recapitulation as resolution—to the "sonata principle"—that he does not simply abandon the closing theme of the exposition in favor of the final transformation of its fundamental cadential function as realized in the fanfares of the coda: the closing theme is replayed *in the tonic* at the end of the development section, its function reinterpreted, and the asymmetry of the formal design is retained. It is this control over both the formal and programmatic elements of a work—a distinctive characteristic of both the *Midsummer Night's Dream* and the *Calm Sea and Prosperous Voyage*—that sets Mendelssohn's approach to illustrative music apart from that of his contemporaries.

A fragmentary autograph of an early version of the Overture containing only the exposition and the opening of the development section, indicates that as was the case in the Octet, Mendelssohn seems to have arrived at the unusual form of this movement by chipping away at a more regular design until this one emerged.[11]

As was noted above, in this earlier version the closing theme of the exposition (beginning in m. 189) was followed by a more emphatically closed cadential theme. Todd suggests that Mendelssohn eventually eliminated this material because it sounds like a quote (in inversion) of part of the second theme from the Overture to *A Midsummer Night's Dream* (specifically, the passage beginning in m. 120 of that work).[12] I would suggest that the revision also reflects the influence of the work's programmatic subject.

As Example 46a shows, the profile of this theme traces a stepwise melodic ascent in half notes answered by a balancing descent in quarter notes. Although this does not correspond exactly to the new theme at the end of the recapitulation (beginning with the cadential preparation in m. 441, Example 46b), the general shape and rhythmic organization of the two are really very similar: in this earlier version of the Overture, the new theme in the recapitulation is actually a variant of the closing theme of the exposition.

By eliminating this material, Mendelssohn accomplishes two improvements in the design of the work. On the one hand, the earlier version maintained a more regular formal design, with a clearly defined, closed exposition that is typical of a classicist sonata movement, but which does not reflect well the programmatic character of the Overture: the revision smooths over this intrusive formal articulation. On the other hand, in foreshadowing the new theme that will appear at the end of the recapitulation, the cadential tag in the manuscript spoils the effect of the large-scale asymmetry that is essential to Mendelssohn's strategy. (Since the manuscript breaks off well before the opening of the recapitulation, it is not possible to say with any certainty that the end of this version would have been identical to the final version; the similarity of the excised theme to the closing material would suggest, perhaps, that it was.) The revision strengthens both of these moments, tightening both the musical design and the relation between the music and the poem.

In the works considered so far in this chapter, at least part of the impetus behind the formal strategies can be traced to the influence of a programmatic subject, but Mendelssohn's most radical strategy for handling the thematic structure of a sonata-form movement grows out of a singular intermingling of fugal texture and sonata form in the most remarkable movement of one of his most remarkable—and strangely neglected—works, the Scherzo from the Quintet, Op. 18 (written in 1826; revised, with the addition of a new slow movement, in 1832).[13]

In the two principal models for the use of fugal textures in a sonata-form exposition—the last movements of Mozart's G-major Quartet, K. 387, and of Beethoven's C-major Quartet, Op. 59, No. 3—fugal writing serves primarily as a special type of thematic texture that, in its strict form, breaks down relatively early in the movement. In K. 387, the textural breakdown occurs after a seventeen-measure fugal exposition; fugue returns to mark the arrival in the secondary key, however. Both of these passages function as

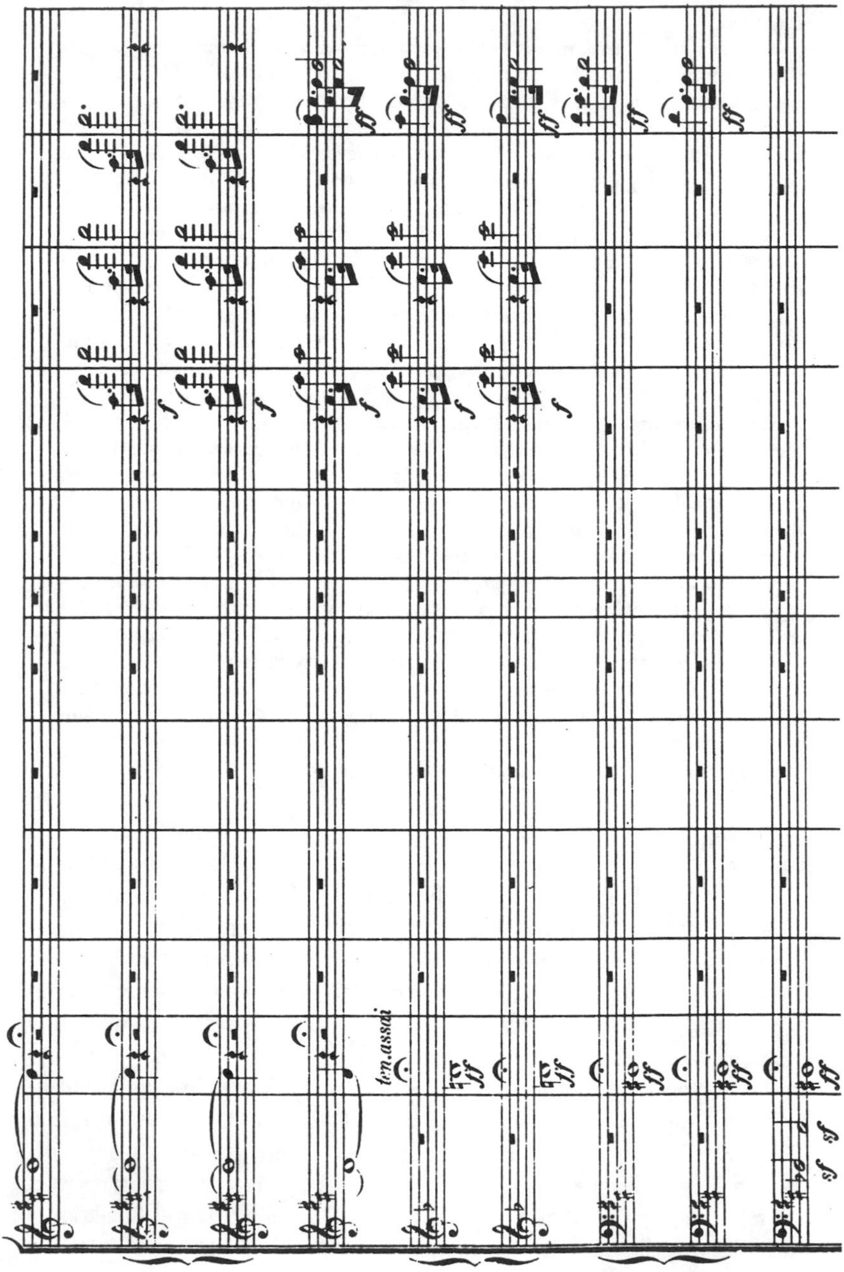
ten. assai

Example 45. Mendelssohn, Overture, *Calm Sea and Prosperous Voyage*, Op. 27, mm. 494-517. (Continued.)

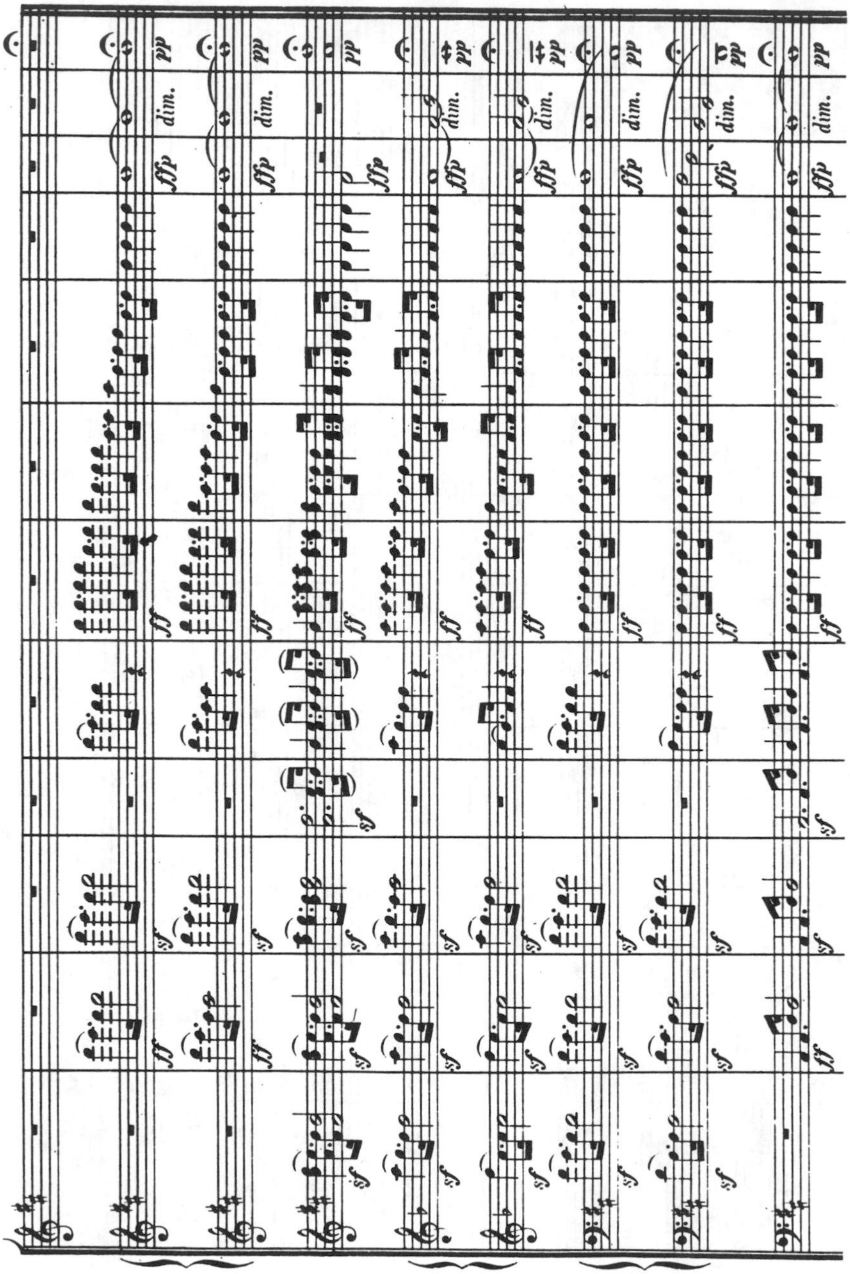
ff
sf
ff
ffp
dim.
pp

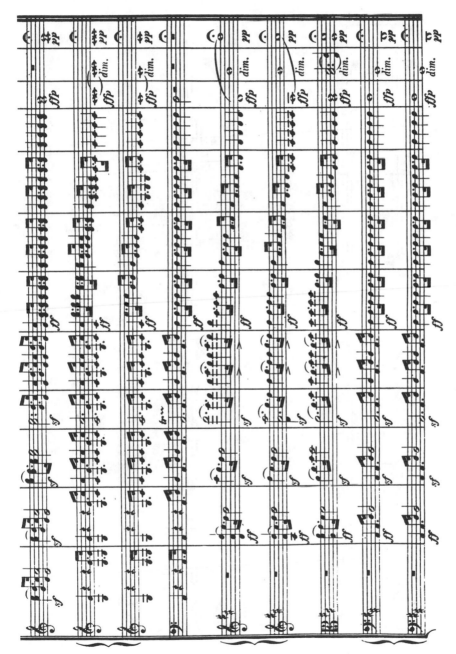

Example 45. (Continued.)   Mendelssohn, Overture, *Calm Sea and Prosperous Voyage*, Op. 27, mm. 494–517.

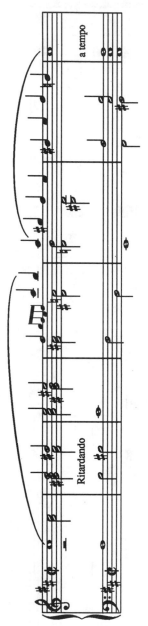

Example 46a.   Manuscript version, closing theme of exposition.

Example 46b.   Printed score, mm. 448–56.

Example 46.   Mendelssohn, Overture, *Calm Sea and Prosperous Voyage*, Op. 27.

thematic articulations within what proves to be an essentially regular sonata-form exposition that eventually closes with a blatantly Italianate theme-and-accompaniment cadential tune. In Op. 59, No. 3, the breakdown occurs somewhere between the third and fourth statements of the subject: the countersubject itself incorporates a disintegration of contrapuntal texture into simple accompanimental thumping that becomes particularly pronounced during the third statement, and the fourth entrance is doubled at the octave, further loosening the sense of independent part-writing. The ensuing transition and second group are essentially non-fugal.

Each of these movements is marked throughout by a strong contrapuntal bias, of course, and the treatment of the opening theme in each will prove to have important consequences later, but the articulation of the underlying sonata-form processes clearly takes precedence over the continuity that is one of the defining characteristics of fugue: fugue is exploited not as a generating structural principle, but as a particularly brilliant articulative texture available, under special circumstances, within a sonata-form structure.

Mendelssohn does not use fugal procedures in this way. Fugue and sonata form are pitted against one another as fundamentally incompatible methods of organizing textures in the Scherzo of Op. 18, and the friction this confrontation generates gives rise to one of the composer's most impressive formal designs.

The Scherzo opens with a skittish fugal subject similar in character to that of the finale of the Octet from the preceding year; both reveal a taste for contrapuntal irreverence that, unfortunately, the composer never again indulged. The exposition of the fugue, although regular in its overall shape, is extraordinarily fluid in phrase structure and harmony. The subject covers eight measures, but does not divide into balanced 4 + 4 phrases. Krummacher suggests a subdivision of 3 + 3 + 2, citing both the harmonic underpinning of the subject—three bars of tonic, three of dominant, and two modulating toward v—and the motivic design—three measures focused on D, three on A, and two of scalar motion (Example 47).[14] This account is essentially accurate, but the details that animate these opening measures require closer attention.

Because there is no opening downbeat accent in m. 1, the first three eighth-note d's tend to sound like an extended upbeat. But instead of providing a persuasively articulated point of arrival, the downbeat of m. 2 only sets off a slightly more agitated continuation of those repeated d's, and the downbeat of m. 3 offers nothing but another d'.

In its normal form, an extended upbeat repetition usually leads to a strongly articulated downbeat marked by an appreciably longer note than those of the upbeat figure, or by a change of pitch that registers as an arrival, or simply by a dynamic accent—each of these changes in the initial pattern serves to absorb the energy generated by the upbeat: the opening of the Beethoven Fifth Symphony combines all three devices to create a particularly spectacular effect. On the other hand, an extended opening passage of steady, rapid motion is usually initiated by a downbeat accent that acts as a springboard, generating the rhythmic impetus for what follows: the opening of the first movement of the "Waldstein" is a particularly subtle example of this procedure. Since neither of these conditions is met in the opening of the Scherzo, the entire three-measure group seems to be perched rather precariously, forming a single, extended upbeat. It is only at the move to c♯' on the downbeat of m. 4—the first change from downbeat d's, marking a shift to the dominant and setting off a distinctively new motivic figure—that an articulative break is clearly enough defined to establish a downbeat accent that can absorb the energy of this initial impulse (Example 48).

This "running start" generates an impressive rhythmic energy, but the opening provides a strong harmonic drive as well, since the tonic pitch has become, primarily through simple repetition, an appoggiatura to the leading tone. This transformation is subtly prepared in the quivering d'-c♯' figure in m. 2 and in the stepwise descent from f' toward c♯' in m. 3: the motion to c♯' develops as part of the motivic elaboration of the upbeat figure itself.

The answer-form of the subject lasts only six measures before the next statement of the subject-form breaks in (m. 15). Since the harmony has not yet swung back to the tonic when this third statement begins, the first three measures—the repeated d''s—function even more clearly as an upbeat to the harmonically stable arrival on V in the fourth measure (m. 18). This elusive treatment of the opening of the subject is continued throughout the first section of the movement, animating a continual, organic expansion that grows seamlessly from the innocuous repeated d's in m. 1.

In addition to the remarkable energy generated in this fugal exposition by placing the strongly articulated rhythmic and harmonic arrivals away from the tonic and by repeatedly breaking the symmetry of the phrase structure, the resulting ambiguity of the passage, with its clearly defined but weakly articulated tonic orientation, will have important consequences later in the movement.

There is a clear push toward the dominant latent in these opening measures, but this is not realized in the first part of the movement—the harmony drifts toward F major instead. As in Mendelssohn's early string symphonies, there is no sharp break in texture to articulate an arrival in the secondary key until late in the exposition, where a short tag leads into the first stable cadence of the movement (mm. 82–83). The texture does begin to coalesce into a cadential pattern as far back as m. 64, however, and there has been a

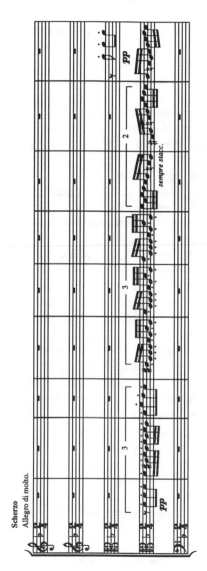

Example 47. Mendelssohn, Quintet, Op. 18, III, mm. 109.

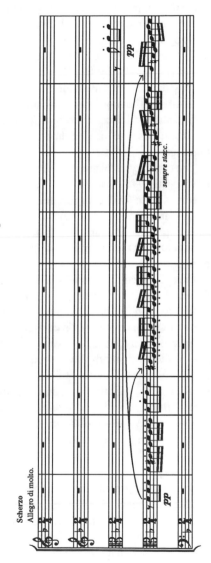

Example 48. Mendelssohn, Quintet, Op. 18, III, mm. 1–9.

gradual—almost imperceptible—thinning of the contrapuntal texture since m. 55.

After the full close to the mediant in m. 83, fugal writing is dropped abruptly, replaced by a complex, but essentially homophonic melody-and-accompaniment texture with rapid harmonic motion articulated in distinct steps by a series of open fifths in the drone bass and a melodic line consisting of fragmented motivic figures that are scattered across the upper voices. The effect is suspiciously like that of a sonata-form development section, suggesting that, despite appearances, what has happened in the first eighty-three measures of the movement might have been a sonata exposition—although an unusually thick-textured one in which the secondary key was established at the last possible moment and was articulated by a particularly flimsy second theme.

The capacity of this new texture to generate a sense of formal organization retrospectively reveals the significance of the articulative function of texture in sonata style. Unlike fugue, sonata forms depend upon a relatively specific organization of textures over the course of a movement, with particular textures appropriate to particular functions within the unfolding of the design.15 Sonata *form* is the interrelation of these textures and the coordination of the resulting pattern of relations to articulate the underlying harmonic structure of the movement. Because of the unique role of specific textures within the formal design, the appearance of this development-section texture at the appropriate point in the movement—after a relatively clearly articulated full close in a secondary key—is enough to establish (retrospectively) at least the suggestion of a sonata-form organization that would subsume the fugal texture of the first part of the movement into its web of articulative gestures.

The first part of this section (mm. 84–106), with its wonderfully hollow parallel fifths, departs from, and eventually circles back to, F major. The F root in the bass of m. 106–9 quickly proves to be an appoggiatura to E, which supports the dominant of A minor (m. 110), and the next twenty-five measures serve as an elaborate dominant preparation for that key. After the elusive harmonic side-stepping of the first part of the movement, this mass of secondary dominant, coming at a point in the formal process where we expect only fragmentation and harmonic instability, is particularly striking.

The event to which all of this dominant preparation is leading turns out to be the introduction of a rollicking square-cut tune in A major (Example, 49, mm. 138ff.), a surprise that forces yet another reorientation of formal expectations. (Notice that the bass line has not quite finished its cadence when the melody begins—this smoothing over the articulations is by now a familiar element of Mendelssohn's style; it is particularly appropriate for the tangled

Example 49. Mendelssohn, Quintet, Op. 18, III, mm. 135–50.

Example 50.   Mendelssohn, Quintet, Op. 18, III, mm. 1–138.

textures of this fugal romp, and it gently underlines the jaunty insouciance of the tune.)

It is certainly not unusual for a development section to reach the dominant eventually, but to prepare it on such a massive scale and to articulate it so strikingly is anything but normal. Both the expansiveness with which this is carried out and the strong thematic articulation tend to mark the establishment of A major as a formal event of much greater stability and significance than even the most elaborately laid out preparatory dominant would warrant.

One particularly important function of this arrival is that it realizes, finally, the move to the dominant latent in the opening measures of the movement. The clarity of its articulation and the specific machinery of its preparation, hinging on the reinterpretation of the lower-voice F in mm. 106–10, subsume the F major established in the latter stages of the exposition as a provisional arrival within a larger modulatory process that now is revealed to extend over the formal division of exposition and development implied by the textural articulation in mm. 83–84. The primary tonal opposition of the movement, mediated by this impressively gradual harmonic process and articulated by a sharp thematic contrast, is persuasively established between the D minor of the opening and this madly displaced A major. Mendelssohn appears to have concocted what is perhaps the only unarguable example of a sonata-form movement in which the second theme—the theme that articulates the establishment of the secondary key—makes its first appearance in the middle of the development section (Example 50).[16]

At this point, it might seem that the analysis of this movement in terms of sonata-form procedures is yielding rather dubious results. The relation of this presumed underlying formal design to the events of the musical surface is proving to be more delusive than regular, and, in particular, the notion of the second theme showing up for the first time in the development section would seem to contradict fundamental principles of formal logic. But it is precisely the friction between formal logic and surface gesture that animates this work, and, in contrast with the more spectacular, but less tightly coherent, formal experiments of other composers of the early romantic period, it is the heavily disguised influence of sonata-form principles that provides the coherence on which the interrelation of events depends. Mendelssohn exploits the ambiguity generated by the conflicting formal signals in the work—the juxtaposition of a seemingly independent fugal organization and a sonata-form structure formulated more by implication than by the coordination of functional elements—to disengage the thematic design of the exposition from its articulative function, allowing him to establish a remarkable long-range tonal process that withholds the establishment of the "real" secondary key area, the dominant, until the middle of the development section. The joking in this Scherzo is a matter of form, not merely of manner: the movement seems to be organizing itself as it goes along, tucking in its loose ends wherever there is room.

Obviously, all of this will have consequences for the organization of the rest of the movement if the functional coherence of sonata form is to be salvaged from the tangle of the structural design. First, the recapitulation of the opening part of the movement will have to reflect the retroactive transformation of fugue from the fundamental generating principle of the movement into an articulative texture within a more highly organized sonata-form structure.

Mozart and Beethoven, in the works considered earlier, defuse the autonomy of fugal writing early in the course of the exposition, clearly establishing it as an articulative—rather than generative—device. As a result, they do not face quite the same problem Mendelssohn does, although the special qualities of fugal writing do influence the organization of the latter stages of each movement. In K. 387, the recapitulation slips in stealthily, reflecting some of the seamless continuity characteristic of fugue. The transitional material from the exposition turns up in the middle of the development section in the subdominant; by simply continuing with a literal restatement of this material, the passage naturally leads back to the tonic, where all of the fugal material from the first and second groups is thrown together in one impressive contrapuntal tangle: the opening of the recapitulation, the climax of the tonal process, is marked by an imposing thicket that forms the climax of the fugal procedures that have colored so much of the movement as well. This combined restatement reduces the main body of the thematic design to twenty-seven measures (as opposed to ninety-two in the exposition) before rushing on to the *opera buffa* closing tune. The coda returns briefly to the contrapuntal complexities of the development section before transforming the fugal subject itself into a hilariously ordinary homophonic cadential tag to close off the entire work. The loose-limbed, sprawling design of Beethoven's Op. 59, No. 3, on the other hand, can absorb a complete restatement of the fugal exposition to mark the opening of the recapitulation. In fact, the dimensions of the movement seem to require just such a massive affirmation of the tonic at this point.

Mendelssohn's design poses another problem, as well: the second theme, which very pointedly could not be accommodated within the exposition, will require special treatment if it is to be brought into the functional processes of the recapitulation.

The first step in Mendelssohn's strategy is to recapitulate the first group—the fugal exposition—without giving more than the slightest hint that he has even returned to the tonic. After that first statement of the second theme in A major (m. 138), the tune is repeated in G major (m. 146), and a third statement, in F major, is begun in m. 154. Throughout this passage, the accompaniment figure, which consists of little more than repeated notes, has hinted quietly that it is a close relative of the fugal subject. Not surprisingly the subject does turn up eventually (in the second viola, m. 161), in the midst of the F-major statement of the second theme; but the fugal tune is perched oddly on the third degree of the F-major scale—previously, the repeated opening notes have been the tonic pitch.

As was the case in m. 110, F major turns out to be distinctly unstable, and the harmonic bias of the fugal theme, which suggests an orientation toward A minor, quickly pulls the accompanying parts into line. The bass circles around from F through E to D♯ and finally back to E in m. 164: this is the fourth measure of the fugal statement in the viola, and with the lower-voice arrival on E, the harmony settles onto the dominant of A minor, the appropriate harmony for the fourth measure of an answer-form of the fugue theme in the tonic (compare mm. 164ff. and mm. 12ff.).

Three more statements follow, beginning on d'' (second violin, m. 167), a'' (first violin, m. 173), and d'' (first viola, m. 179), establishing a thematic pattern of answer-subject-answer-subject that suggests a tonic reprise of the opening fugal exposition. But as a result of the ambiguity inherent in the harmonic structure of the subject—the tendency of the first three measures to sound like an upbeat preparation leading to the fourth measure—Mendelssohn is able to avoid any clear tonic articulation during the entire course of this thematic recapitulation. Each entrance of the subject is embedded in a harmonic context that carefully obscures its relation to D minor; and yet, each entrance eventually slides toward either D minor or its dominant, so that, although the passage clearly revolves around the tonic, there is really no specific point at which it actually arrives there. The first stage of the recapitulation acts more like a transition toward the tonic than the culmination of the motion back to the tonic, and the entire fugal exposition is recapitulated while merely seeming to point on to a decisive coordination of tonic arrival and thematic articulation. Just as the functional lines between exposition and development were blurred in the first half of the movement, the lines between development and recapitulation are obscured here; fugue is subsumed as a distinctly unstable—appropriately developmental-transitional—texture, and the reacquisition of a stable tonic becomes a matter of impressively subtle urgency.

A gradual drift toward a more secure tonic cadence begins in m. 179, but when this cadence finally does settle down, after repeated attempts by the fugal theme to reassert itself, it lands on D major, and it is marked by a return of the second theme from the middle of the development section (m. 206). Placed at this sensitized formal juncture—the seemingly unambiguous return to the tonic in a cadence that has been prepared by over forty measures of tentative and gingerly approaches—the theme takes on the primary closural function of the movement, a gesture that provides a stabilizing counterbalance to the extraordinary formal disruption created by its first appearance. To ensure that the meaning of this event—the assimilation of the second theme into the quirky sonata-form procedures of the movement—is not missed, a new transitional passage repeats the gradual move toward the tonic (with further attempts by the fugal theme to establish itself as the principal thematic articulation), and the cadence once again turns to D major at the last moment for a restatement of the second theme (mm. 222–40ff.).

But in both of these cadential preparations, and in the entire recapitulation, the tonic implied is D minor. As in the Scherzo of the Octet, the tonic major sounds like an intrusion, and, in the end, the recapitulation of the second theme only intensifies the need to return to a stable minor mode of the tonic. This return is accomplished in m. 255, marked by a stretto on the fugal theme, and D minor is confirmed in a final cadential passage. In addition to providing cadential ballast for the tonic minor, this last part of the movement finally provides a stabilization for the precarious tonic orientation of the fugal theme, neutralizing the sensitive D–C♯ relation that repeatedly propelled the opening of the subject toward the dominant. First, the opening measures of the subject are harmonized as V^7 of V (mm. 255–56, 278, and 282), making the tendency-tone relation implied in the opening measures of the movement—the sense that D was tipping over onto C♯—an explicit harmonic fact. This relation is immediately reversed, with C♯ clearly identified as the leading tone in an emphatic i$^6_4$–V–i cadence based on the head of the subject. The last loose ends seem to be tied into a knot of magical delicacy (Example 51). (The disembodied D–major shimmer in the last five measures is the final surprise in this movement, and the unexpected shift to the major third, F♯, will prove to be a subtle link to the triplet figure, e″–f♯″–e″, that sets off the work's infinitely good-natured finale.)

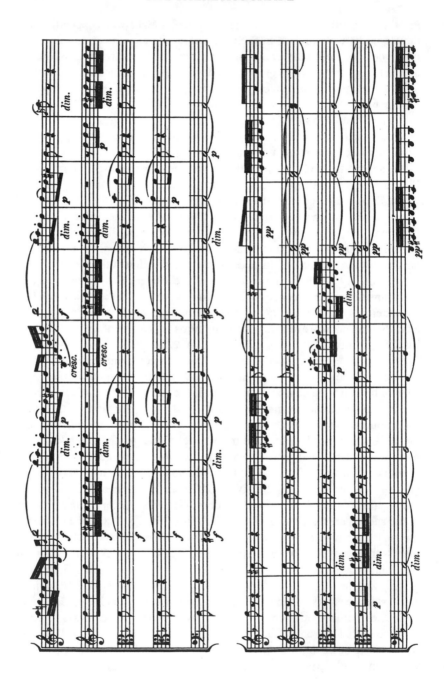

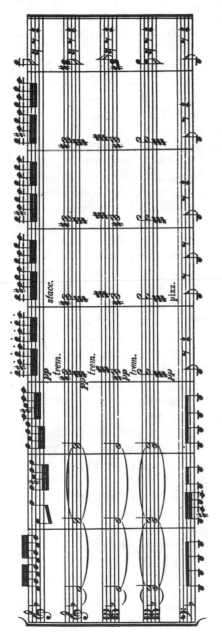

Example 51. Mendelssohn, Quintet, Op. 18, III, mm. 277–303.

It should be emphasized once again that the basic structural gestures of the Scherzo of Op. 18—the full close in mm. 82–83 followed by a sharp break in texture that suggests the opening of a development section, the thematic articulation of the establishment of the dominant key in m. 138, the return of the fugal material "in" the tonic in m. 161, and the return of the new theme in the tonic in m. 206—are the gestures of sonata form, and they reveal their significance only with reference to an underlying, if camouflaged, complex of sonata-form functions. In turn, the treatment of these gestures—the shadowy outline of the exposition as a whole, the establishment of the dominant in the middle of the development section, the obscurity of the tonic orientation at the "double return," and the emphatic double resolution of the second theme in the course of the recapitulation—reflects the unusual status of fugal texture in the first part of the movement: the refusal of the texture to coalesce into more normal sonata-style part-writing engenders a displacement of the thematic articulation of the fundamental harmonic polarity from the exposition to the development and results in a drastic reworking of the closural processes carried out in the recapitulation. If the functional identity of these paradoxically deployed sonata-form gestures is ignored, the structure of the movement disintegrates into a juxtaposition of fugal and non-fugal textures, with no particular rationale for the shift from one to the other.[17] Although the relation of the events in this movement to sonata-form procedures may seem tenuous at times, the explanatory value of an analysis that recognizes the functional significance of these events in terms of sonata form is, I think, clear enough. In particular, such an analysis helps uncover the true nature of Mendelssohn's formal innovations—innovations that exploit the functional coherence that underlies the sonata style rather than simply rearranging surface elements that have been stripped of any structural significance.

The organization of the first movement of the Quintet does not involve the wholesale displacement of structural elements that shaped the Scherzo, but its remarkable coordination of thematic and harmonic processes repays careful examination. The most unusual aspect of Mendelssohn's strategy centers on the latter stages of the second group, where there is an abrupt shift from the dominant key, E major, established by the second theme (m. 80), to F♯ minor, in which key the exposition closes.

The first theme and transition are unusually expansive, but essentially regular. The second theme begins quite normally (Example 52a), and, after a slightly obscure digression (Example 52b) leads into a lyric cadential figure in E major (Example 52c). This cadential tune intertwines a neighbor-note figure (x) that runs through both the second theme and the digression with a stepwise descending fourth, a″-g♯″-f♯″-e″, (y). This thematic shape was foreshadowed in mm. 93–99, where the neighbor-note figure and the descending fourth were superimposed upon one another as independent strands of the texture (Example 52b); in the closing theme, they are united in a single, compact gesture (Example 52c). This kind of thematic foreshadowing is by now becoming a familiar aspect of Mendelssohn's style.

In mm. 109-10, when this cadential figure seems about to close to e'' for the last time, the harmony shifts suddenly to F♯ minor: the new key is simply hung from the melodic line—again, a procedure that is by now becoming familiar. The crucial pitch in this shift is a'', the uppermost note of the cadential figure. In the preceding cadences, a'' had leaned toward g♯'', the third of the local tonic (Example 52c). The melodic figure from m. 102 is retained at the turn to F♯ minor in m. 110, but the inflectional relation of the crucial elements of the line has been reversed: a'' is now the third of the tonic triad, so there is some tendency for g♯'' to push back up to that relatively more stable pitch; the delicate shimmer that colors this theme is due, at least in part, to the conflicting inflectional impulses that reverberate in these two pitches (Example 53).

Like the D major that is draped in a similarly unexpected way over the second group of the Scherzo of the Octet, this new key simply does not go away, and the exposition closes in F♯ minor. The resulting large-scale harmonic pattern of the exposition, moving from the tonic to the minor submediant, is reminiscent, perhaps, of the first movement of Beethoven's C-major Quintet, Op. 29, in which the exposition moves from C major to A major/minor. As in the Beethoven, the descending third motion unfolded over the course of the exposition proves to be only the first step in a long chain of thirds that runs well into the development section. The tonal outline of Mendelssohn's exposition may reflect the influence of Beethoven's experiment, but the delicately romantic means through which the move from E major to F♯ minor is carried out are uniquely his own. In addition, Mendelssohn has embedded this structure within another design that accomplishes an integration of the harmonic design with the thematic process that is completely original. It is with the return of the opening theme in the repetition of the exposition that the principle underlying this process is revealed; the repeat of the exposition is, therefore, essential to the coherence of the movement.

Both the lyric cadential figure in E major (mm. 102-10) (Example 52c) and the closing theme in F♯ minor (mm. 110ff.) (Example 53) center on the sixth, c♯''-a'', with, as we have seen, a'' serving as the hinge for the shift from one key to the other. At the repeat of the exposition, this c♯''-a'' sixth reappears as the framing interval of the first phrase of the opening theme (Example 54). The outline that defines all three of these themes is the same, but the functional identity of the framing elements of that outline is continually

m. 80

m. 88

Example 52a.   Mm. 80–84 and 88–92.

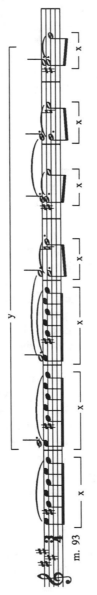

m. 93

Example 52b.   Mm. 93–99.

m. 102

Example 52c.   Mm. 102–10.

Example 52.   Mendelssohn, Quintet, Op. 18, I.

Example 53.   Mendelssohn, Quintet, Op. 18, I, mm. 110–13.

Example 54.   Mendelssohn, Quintet, Op. 18, I, mm. 1–5, mm. 102–4, and m. 110.

transformed as the harmonic context in which the frame is embedded changes. The least stable—most dissonant, structurally—context is E major—the dominant, and, appropriately, the key which at first seems to be the goal of the exposition, establishing a polar opposition to the tonic: in the cadential figure in mm. 103-10, both a'' and c#'' are dissonant to the E-major triad. The most stable configuration, on the other hand, is the opening gesture of the work, where c#'' and a'' are, of course, the third and root of the tonic triad, a stability emphatically reaffirmed with the repeat of the exposition. The F#-minor passage forms an intermediary stage between these extremes; both c#'' and a'' are part of the local tonic triad, but this triad is itself highly unstable, a kind of harmonic mirage that materializes out of thin air and quickly evaporates back into the tonic.

The formal procedure that lies in the background of Mendelssohn's strategy is related to a technique used frequently by Mozart, in which the cadential theme serves as a transition back to the beginning of the exposition. Mozart normally transforms the dominant key into a dominant chord by introducing the flatted seventh degree; the end of the exposition in the first movement of the C-major Quartet, K. 465, offers a characteristic example. Mendelssohn treats this juncture rather differently, of course; he dissolves the dominant into its opposite, a form of subdominant (see the first ending, where F# minor is linked directly to D major at the beginning of a IV–V–I cadence that effects the return to the tonic). The result is a particularly gentle transition that perfectly matches the luxuriant lyricism of the thematic material. More important, the harmonic design of the exposition as a whole, which might seem to be no more than a typically romantic exploration of colorful third relations, turns out to be only one element in the multifaceted play on the a''-c#'' motivic frame that is common to the thematic elements through which that design is realized. Again, the subtlety of Mendelssohn's thematic process must be recognized: the themes through which this process are realized exhibit almost no overt similarities to one another—the relationships are at a deeper, subcutaneous level, and resist easy detection.

The intertwining of harmonic and motivic processes through the course of the exposition poses important problems for the organization of a recapitulation that will gather these elements into a closural design.

On the one hand, the a''-c#'' framing sixth that is central to the thematic process of the exposition obviously cannot be retained without alteration in the recapitulation. But the invariant pitch structure of the frame is a fundamental element in the modulatory structure of the exposition; if the motivic frame is not preserved, much of the significance of the modulatory pivot within the second group—in the exposition, the a''-g#'' hinge in m. 110—is lost. The problem is similar to the difficulties created by the inflectional issues surrounding D♯ in the first movement of Schumann's F♯-minor Sonata examined earlier in this chapter. On the other hand, although that half-step pivot is without question the most striking event in the exposition, a recapitulation that retained literally the modulatory relation between the two elements of the second group would threaten the tonal coherence of the recapitulation as a whole. If the first part of the second group were to return in the tonic, the pizzicato closing theme would come back in B minor, while a transposition that would end in the right key would bring back the first section in G major. The first of these alternatives is not impossible—it could be integrated within a larger cadential motion to A major without particular difficulty—but neither offers a convincing analogue to the large-scale coherence of the exposition.

Mendelssohn's solution again reveals the freedom with which he approached the thematic structure of sonata form in the works of this period. It involves a double recapitulation of the pizzicato closing theme that allows the composer to weave the end of the second group into the larger cadential process of the movement's elaborate coda. This strategy centers on the half-step pivot, and it is set in motion in the latter stages of the development section, where the bass line establishes a sensitized half-step relation between F♮ and E (mm. 222ff.).

The first step in this process occurs immediately after what appears to be the double return marking the beginning of the recapitulation. The first theme returns in A major in m. 250, but it is supported by a first inversion tonic triad, obscuring slightly the sense of tonal arrival. (The shift of the bass line to an inner voice in the course of the preceding cadential preparation also contributes to the sense of elided articulation at this point: the c♯ of the cello in m. 250 is quite explicitly not part of the lower-voice motion established at the end of the development section.) The instability of this return gently undermines the tonic, and the harmony begins to drift toward the subdominant beneath a long-held a″ in the third and fourth measures of the theme (mm. 252–53). But as Example 55 shows, when the bass leaps from c♯ to D in m. 254, regaining the lower register abandoned earlier, the harmony does not move to D major; instead, it jumps abruptly to G minor, where the pizzicato theme appears to mark the materialization of yet another unexpected key.

The important point here is that although the juxtaposition of A major and G minor does not parallel the E-major–F♯-minor shift at the end of the exposition, the upper voice does retain a version of the half-step relation on which that earlier passage had hinged. The b♭″–a″–b♭″ of the G-minor version of the pizzicato theme in m. 254 does not link back explicitly to a figure planted in the preceding material, as the pivotal a″–g♯″–a″ in m. 110 did; but the shift from A major to G minor establishes a new inflectional identity for a″,

Example 55. Mendelssohn, Quintet, Op. 18, I, mm. 243-63.

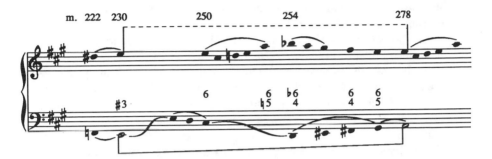

Example 56. Mendelssohn, Quintet, Op. 18, I, mm. 222–79.

the note which has just been established as the tonic pitch and the high point of the melodic line—it is now the lower neighbor to bb'' and at the level of the phrase, it is a passing note between bb'' and g''. The functional significance of the earlier passage as an inflectional pivot is retained but the crucial melodic half-step relation is reinterpreted, disengaged from the specific harmonic structure—the shift from tonic to supertonic—of its original presentation. (The "mirror image" quality of this harmonic shift, substituting a descent of one step—from A major to G minor—for the original rise of one step—from E major to F# minor—might seem to suggest a resolution of the original presentation, analogous to Beethoven's procedure in the "Waldstein," for example, of balancing a tonic-mediant opposition in an exposition with a tonic-submediant recapitulation; the context in which Mendelssohn places this reappearance of the pizzicato theme hardly suggests stabilization and resolution, however.)

As Example 56 shows, the G-minor statement of the pizzicato theme eventually merges into a new dominant preparation that carries the lower-voice line through a stepwise ascent to A, leading to a stable root position tonic for a decisive return of the main theme and explicitly closing the gap created at the end of the development section (m. 278). This lower-voice registral gap establishes a "parenthesis" around a subsidiary process at the beginning of the recapitulation in a manner that recalls the analogous place in the first movement of Haydn's Op. 33, No. 1, but which creates a parenthetical tangle—part recapitulation, part transition, part development, and part secondary development—that obscures the opening of the recapitulation even more completely than Haydn did.

As a result of the disengagement of the harmonic and melodic aspects of the pizzicato theme in this passage lying on the vague border between development and recapitulation, Mendelssohn can reinterpret the half-step relation when the theme returns in the course of the second group without endangering the coherence of the formal design.

Instead of tying the closing theme to the d'''-c#'''-d''' figure established in the recapitulation of the second theme—which returns in the tonic—Mendelssohn establishes a new half-step relation, bringing back the pizzicato theme in A minor (the minor tonic). This entails no change of key at the return of the theme, of course—the end of the recapitulation is kept in the tonic, after all—but it hinges on a new, and persuasive, analogue to the sensitive half-step interplays that have characterized every appearance of this material, generating an expansive cadential drive that overflows into the coda. This time, the join between the second theme and the pizzicato theme hinges on the confrontation between c#'''' and c♮'''' inherent in the juxtaposition of A major and A minor (m. 237).

The reacquisition of c#'''' occupies the movement's luxurious coda, which gradually works its way through a climactic upper-voice ascent from a'' (m. 262) to b'' (m. 295) to c#''' (m. 305). In m. 312, the upper voice begins a delicate cadential gesture descending in dotted half notes from c#'''' to b'' but then slipping past a'', falling to e''. The reacquisition of a'' is accomplished in the last measures of the movement, when the head of the main theme returns as a final cadence, closing off the upper-voice motion by absorbing it back into the gesture from which the entire movement emerged.

One particularly beautiful detail in this passage must be noted. The coda is built out of little more than repeated waves of gradually expanding cadential progressions. At first, these are based on the main theme, reestablishing the c#''-a'' frame; the first expansion introduces a triad on F#—the harmony that had disrupted the closing group in the exposition by reinterpreting the elements of that frame. But this time the chord is a dominant seventh on F#—V of V of V; as Example 57 shows, it is easily subsumed within a particularly warm cadential progression in A major. The upper voice leads down from f#'' through f♮'' to e'', explicitly reversing the inflectional relation established at the end of the exposition: even in this most luxuriously lyric of the early works, every detail seems to have its place in the articulative design.

(As we have seen, in the finale, an e''-f#''-e'' upbeat figure provides the initial impetus for what is perhaps Mendelssohn's most ingratiatingly jolly inspiration—a rondo designed along Mozartean lines that is nonetheless as completely original and characteristic as any of the masterpieces from this period. The brief cadential expansion on f#''-e'' in the final measures of the coda of that movement proves to be another link in what is perhaps the most delicate and the most persuasive cyclic gesture in his entire output.)

Mendelssohn's coordination of a delicately fluid, romantic sense of tonal structure, an extensively worked-out process of motivic transformation, and

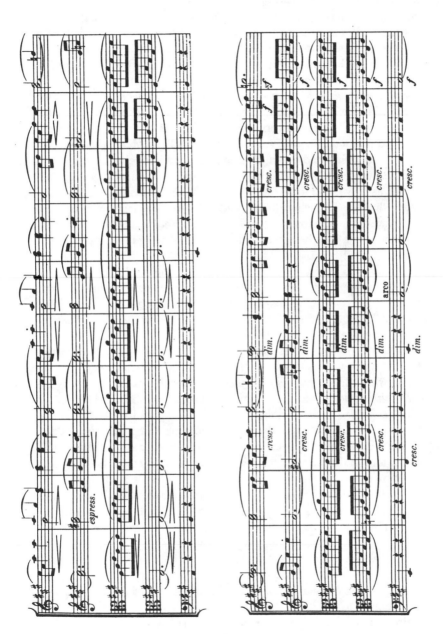

Example 57.   Mendelssohn, Quintet, Op. 18, I, mm. 262ff.

a beautifully balanced network of sonata-form processes in the first movement of the Quintet shows him to be in no sense an unthinking classicist,
borrowing ready-made formal schemes in order to save himself the bother of
being original. In this movement, no less clearly than in the more obviously
"progressive" and experimental treatment of form in the Scherzo from this
same Quintet, or in the realization of programmatic implications in the *Calm
Sea and Prosperous Voyage* or *Midsummer Night's Dream* Overtures, the
suppleness of detail—the coordination of form and process—reveals that
through the late 1820s sonata form remained for Mendelssohn a living complex of compositional alternatives rather than a jellymold inherited—with a
mixture of reverence and despair—by a timid and unworthy heir. In Mendelssohn's finest works from this period, even a comparatively "regular"
form will usually prove to be the vehicle of great originality.

The truth of this is nowhere more vividly apparent than in what is unquestionably one of the composer's finest works, the *Hebrides* Overture, Op. 26.
In this tone poem, Mendelssohn employs a formal design that appears to be
the most regular of any of his important early works in the realization of the
most impressive of his large musical designs. Once again, the subtlety of this
realization has apparently obscured the fact that anything of interest is going
on beneath the beguiling instrumental surface. (And, again, this work only
took on its final shape after a long period of revision; some of the most important changes will be considered below.)[18]

From the opening measures, with their aura of mystery and distance, this
work creates a new musical world. Of course, the evocation of watery undu-
lation on which the opening is built is not a particularly difficult trick—familiar examples would include the aria "Che puro ciel," from the second act
of Gluck's *Orfeo ed Euridice*, the terzettino "Soave sia il vento," from the
first act of *Così fan tutte*, and the second movement of Beethoven's Sixth
Symphony. But Mendelssohn creates a sense of immense spatial depth that is
almost unique in the music of the period—the only comparable example is
the opening of the last movement of, again, Beethoven's Sixth Symphony,
where the stylized shepherd's song in the horn seems to echo from a distant
hillside. (This sense of spatial recession, accomplished by essentially the
same techniques Mendelssohn and Beethoven employ, becomes a characteristic feature of the turn of the century style, with examples ranging from the
vast canvases of Mahler's Symphonies to the exoticism of Stravinsky's early
ballets.)

The spatial sense evoked in these works invariably relates to a programmatic reference to nature. Carl Dahlhaus pointed out that there seem to be
two primary musical metaphors for the depiction of nature. The first involves
the creation of a stationary, but internally active musical texture:

In terms of compositional technique, the most striking examples of the musical depiction of nature—in the "Forest Murmurs" from *Siegfried*, in the Nile scene from *Aida*, or the scene at the river in Gounod's *Mireille*—are almost always based on a principle that in the new music of the 20th century has been taken to extremes, becoming the fundamental formal idea from which entire works are developed: the principle of an almost motionless, but internally active tonal field. It makes no difference whether it is an idyll or a storm (as in the Prelude to the first act of *Walküre*): the music—no matter how agitated or relaxed the rhythmic activity—remains harmonically and motivically motionless.[19]

This combination of an immobile tonal background—or at least of a very slow rate of harmonic motion—with an internal shimmer of motivic detail is, of course, the normal metaphor for the motion of waves, and is the common characteristic of almost all of the examples mentioned above. In the opening of the *Hebrides* Overture, the wave-like undulations of the main theme in the middle voices are framed by complexes of pedal tones in the outer voices.

The second technical resource Dahlhaus identified involves the treatment of dissonance within this static harmonic field.[20] Non-harmonic tones are neither prepared nor resolved in the normal sense, but are simply superimposed against the unchanging background. The model for this is, of course, once again the opening of the last movement of the *Pastorale*, where the horn's slightly distorted echo of the shepherd-horn figure in the clarinet floats over the superimposed C-G and F-C fifths of the lower voices. Although the eventual shift from the C major of the clarinet figure to the F major at the opening of the finale suggests a normal progression from dominant to tonic, the effect of the passage is less that of a resolution from V to I than of the emergence of F major out of an obscure tonal haze at the moment when the C-major elements of the harmonic texture are pulled out and replaced by F-major elements.

Dahlhaus suggested that the sense of nature evoked by this harmonic technique is expressed in the contradiction of the laws of musical logic, which represent the principles of art—and therefore of urbanized society. I would suggest that the effect has somewhat simpler origins. The superimposition of non-functionally interconnected harmonies creates a slight blurring that suggests music heard from a distance—that is, by implication, out of doors. The actual (or, rather, expected) progression from note to note or chord to chord is obscured by faintness and the interference of reverberating echoes. This is certainly the effect implied by the horn call in the *Pastorale* or the gradually receding posthorn figures in the coda of the first movement—"Das Lebewohl"—of Beethoven's Eb-major Sonata, Op. 81a.

Mendelssohn's realization of this technique in the *Hebrides* Overture is characteristically refined. The first six measures of the Overture comprise three statements of the wave-motive, in B minor, D major, and F# minor. As

Example 58.   Mendelssohn, *Hebrides* Overture, Op. 26, opening.

Example 58 shows, with each statement a new line is added to the upper-voice frame of the harmonic background: each of these new lines doubles the fifth of the new chord-center (which is also the first note of the new statement of the motive), while the fifth of each previous chord-center is retained in the voice immediately below.

Obviously, these superimposed lines are not dissonant to one another, nor are they dissonant to their harmonic surroundings; but each new pitch in the upper-voice frame is dissonant to the harmony of the preceding statement of the motive. The natural acoustic blurring caused by the momentary resonance of the old harmony at the moment the new harmony and new upper-voice line enter creates a fleeting impression of the superimposition of a dissonant pitch over the old harmony. This impression is subtly reinforced by the doubling of the old upper-voice fifth by the last, and lowest pitch of each of the wave-motives, which causes the old harmony to seem to reverberate even more clearly in the held-over upper-voice line. The result is a peculiarly delicate illusion of dissonant harmonies that not only do not resolve from one to another, but simply vanish just as we become aware of their existence.

At the same time, the held-over pitches in the upper voice, although dissonant neither in their original surroundings nor within each new harmonic context, are strangely unstable. Normally a pedal serves to anchor transitory harmonic progressions to an underlying fundamental harmony. Indeed, in the present case, the f♯'' pedal of the violins would seem, at first, to encompass this entire opening within the tonic, B minor. But with the addition of each new voice to the pedal—and the function of the upper-voice structure is made clear by the segregation of the passage into lower-voice harmonic foundation, middle-voice thematic statements, and upper-voice pedal—the functional identity of the pedal changes: the fifth of the B-minor pedal, F♯, becomes the third of the D-major pedal in m. 3, and in mm. 5–6 it is the root of the F♯-minor cloud shimmering over the waves. The implied stability of the pedal is contradicted by exploiting the common-tone relations between the successive, non-functionally related chord-centers, paradoxically rendering these common tones unstable as a consequence of a sequence of chords that carefully avoids dissonant relations between its elements. This treatment of common tone relations—and the delicate D♮–D♯ friction set up in the cadence through V of iv at the end of the phrase—will prove to be central to the organization of both the transitional material and the secondary key area of the exposition and recapitulation.

The second theme, in D major, is approached through an unusual process for which the term "modulation" in its normal sense hardly seems appropriate. Instead of working through a gradual transition from B minor to D major, Mendelssohn abruptly replaces the dominant of B minor with the dominant of D major, and the old tonic simply melts into the new key. This remarkable effect was the focus of a major revision at one stage of the work's tangled history (this revision will be considered later); in the final version, the harmonic pivot is quietly prepared by a process in which elements of the tonic triad are rendered unstable within the course of a series of cadences to the tonic itself.

As the opening section of the movement progresses, the third and fifth of the tonic, D and F♯, are continually treated as dissonances in the course of upper-voice cadential motions to B. The first step in this process occurs in mm. 27ff. This is almost certainly the moment Wagner is reported to have singled out for special praise in discussing the Overture: "The place where the oboes' lament rises out of the other instruments like the wind over the water is extraordinarily beautiful."[21] (Wagner—or von Wolzogen, who reported the comment—seems to have misremembered the score: the first oboe is doubled by the flute and bassoon—there is no other place in the movement that would fit his description more closely.)

The haunting quality of this passage can be traced to two particularly Mendelssohnian characteristics. The first is the strange impression that we have heard the oboe theme before, although this is its first appearance in the work. The explanation lies, once again, in the composer's sadly underrated sophistication in handling thematic transformations. On the one hand, the new theme bears an obvious, though generalized, relation to the triadic outline of the wave-motive of the opening measures of the work. This naturally creates a straightforward sense of familiarity, but the particularly striking effect of this moment has a more specific, though less obvious, origin.

The cadence immediately preceding m. 27 has introduced a new figure in the first violin that is itself clearly a variant of the wave-motive. Example 59 shows that the new theme in the oboe is simply a retrograde form of the first half of this cadential figure. Since both are played in the same register, the oboe theme reverberates within the remembered echo of the violin line, both new and a reminiscence.

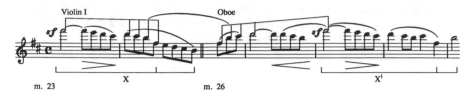

Example 59.   Mendelssohn, *Hebrides* Overture, Op. 26, mm. 23–24, 26–30.

Example 60.   Mendelssohn, *Hebrides* Overture, Op. 26, mm. 26–30.

The second element that contributes to the striking quality of the passage involves the harmonic implications it unfolds. The theme outlines the profile of a B–minor tonic triad, but in such a way that the third and fifth of the triad are never treated as consonances. The third, d''', is presented as an appoggiatura to the implied root in m. 27, C♯, and f♯''' interrupts the implied resolution of that d''' to c♯''', functioning, on the local level, as an ornament to the underlying structure of the passage, which is simply a $\hat{3}$–$\hat{2}$–$\hat{1}$ cadential descent (Example 60).

The cadential impulse of this figure is rendered increasingly urgent in the following measures, where the motion to $\hat{1}$ is strongly implied but left pointedly uncompleted. In m. 35, an arrival on B is suddenly shunted to C♮, which acts as an appoggiatura (that never resolves) to the root of V$^6_5$ of iv (E minor). (This in turn further sensitizes the third of B minor, D♮, by opposing it to the temporary leading tone, D♯, in the bass of mm. 35–36.) The d'''–c♯'''–b'' motion is expanded in mm. 37–41, with each of the first two steps taking two measures, suggesting a final, decisive cadential drive. But Mendelssohn handles the orchestration of this passage in such a way that although the descent to b'' is completed in the woodwinds (m. 41), the c♯''' of the first violins in mm. 39–40 is carried back up to d''' in m. 41, where the beginning of a repetition of this cadential passage is dovetailed into the completion of the first statement.

This repetition never completes the motion to b'': the c#''' of mm. 43–44 is held over into m. 45 while the harmony shifts beneath it from V of B minor to V of D major, leading into a cadence in this new key for the beginning of the second theme. But the crucial c#''' is left hanging, unresolved in register, and the functional status of d''' is becoming a crucial issue in the tonal structure of this exposition.

The modulation in mm. 44–45 is prepared, then, by an elaborate play on D and F# (and more particularly d''' and f#'''), the members of the tonic triad common to B minor and D major—a relation first exploited in the opening measures of the work. This process begins with the treatment of these pitches as passing dissonances in the course of a cadential motion toward the tonic, but the integrity of the cadential motion itself is soon undermined in a series of transitory digressions that culminate in the upper-voice overlap in m. 41. This last event replaces the implied, and only covertly accomplished, motion from d''' through c#''' to b'' with a return from d''' through c#''' to d''', and it is from the delicate uncertainty surrounding the functional identity of c#''' and d''' within the tonic that Mendelssohn suspends the sudden shift to D major—a shift that still leaves c#''' hanging unresolved. Nonetheless, the secondary key seems to provide a stabilizing context for this cluster of sensitized pitches; the emergence of D major is like the sudden dispersal of an obscuring mist.

Tovey called the second theme "quite the greatest melody Mendelssohn ever wrote."[22] The theme is remarkable, and almost unique in the composer's output, for its serene breadth and for its iridescent harmony; much of the particularly touching quality of the harmonic design derives from lingering echoes of the play on D and F# that emerge over the course of the theme.

By the third measure, F# has become a leading tone to G (mm. 49–51); a few measures later, D is taken as the third of a temporarily established B minor, reopening the play on C# and D that generated the modulation away from the tonic just moments before. At the end of the first phrase (mm. 56–57), the theme finally closes back to D major with a melodic descent from F# through E to D in the cellos and bassoons—a figure that recalls faintly the increasingly troubled cadences of the first group.

The return of the upper-voice line to d''', linking back to the unresolved c#''' of m. 45, is accomplished in the course of the restatement of the theme in the violins, but it occurs just as the harmony shifts suddenly to B minor (m. 63), reopening the play on this acutely sensitized pitch. At the end of the counterstatement of the theme (m. 66), the cadential descent, now in the violins, is interrupted, only reaching e'' in a motion that is repeated in each of the next three measures. When the cadential descent is finally completed in m. 70, after an anticipation on the last quarter of m. 69, the upper voice is shunted to d''', rather than d'', and at the same instant the bass suddenly moves to E♯. This shift reintroduces—just at the moment when the second theme had seemed, finally, to be rounding itself off with a solid tonic cadence—the diminished seventh chord that had initiated the cadential destabilization of d''' at the beginning of the oboe melody in m. 27: even the spacing of the two chords (although not the scoring) is the same. To strengthen the reference to that earlier event, the flutes bring back the wave-motive from which the oboe line was derived, underlining the tinges of B minor that have suddenly reappeared.

After a noisy return to D major (mm. 77ff.), the upper voice begins a chromatic ascent from d''' toward f♯''' supported by a cadential progression that would seem to be stabilizing these two delicate pitches within the secondary key (mm. 81ff.). But the penultimate step, e♯''' (m. 84), is supported by G in the bass, forming an augmented sixth that pushes hard toward the dominant of, once again, B minor; the f♯''' that is the goal of the passage is wrenched out of D major and thrown back into that insistently obtrusive tonic key. This outburst is quickly absorbed within the cadence to D major in m. 89, but it is clear that the second group, for all its smooth lyricism, has not really been able to resolve the inflectional uncertainty surrounding F♯ and D. On the contrary, the play on these sensitized pitches has been intensified throughout the later stages of the exposition. In the end, it is both inevitable and surprising that when D major is finally established in the triumphant flourishes of the brasses in mm. 89–96, the third, D–F♯, that rings through that cadence dissolves instantly back into B minor when the strings add a quivering B to the harmony in m. 96.

The second theme, which at first seems to provide a stabilizing context for the D–F♯ third, but which actually continues the disorienting play on these pitches, does not, in the end, so much articulate a key of its own as suspend a harmonic complex—centering, to be sure, on D major—from the D–F♯ thread that is woven through the entire course of the exposition, a thread that is spun out from the mysterious common-tone relations propounded in the opening measures of the first theme.

The unusual complex of tensions and relations that animates the second group of the exposition, linked as it is to the structure of the first group, clearly does not lend itself to an orthodox recapitulation. The problem is by now a familiar one: since the second group sustains the inflectional ambiguity of D and F♯ introduced within the tonic group, a literal recapitulation with the necessary changes to produce a transposition of the second theme into the tonic major would presumably threaten the sense of this larger structural process: the play on B and D♯ that would naturally result from this transposition (corresponding to, but not resolving the D–F♯ interplay of the exposition) would raise new issues rather than resolve old ones.

Mendelssohn's solution to this problem does, in fact, hinge on a recapitulation of the second theme—or at least a part of it—in the tonic major. Through a careful balance of harmonic relations, this most regular of formal procedures is made to yield a functional ambiguity surrounding B and D♯ that recaptures the iridescent beauty of the play on D and F♯ in the exposition.

The crucial element in this design is the stability with which the major third, D♯, is introduced. It first appears in the bass, in m. 190, as the leading tone to iv, corresponding to its function in the cadence at the end of the first statement of the main theme in the opening measures of the exposition. In the following measures, this move toward the subdominant is intensified, and a cadence to iv is fleetingly accomplished in m. 196. The harmony swings back toward B minor in the following measures, and the tonic *major* is identified as a functionally subordinate element, tightly bound to this momentary shift to iv. By linking the tonic major to this purely local event, Mendelssohn identifies the major mode as a cadential coloring within a prevailing tonic minor rather than as a resolution of the inflectional instability normally associated with a minor tonic. As a result, the appearance of the second theme in B major, following on the heels of this passage (mm. 202ff.), sounds like an elaborate melodic prolongation of this cadential chromaticism. This impression is strengthened by the tendency of the theme itself to lean toward the subdominant—a tendency enlarged upon by a strong emphasis on iv (and IV) in this version of the theme, which corresponds to the original only through the first four measures (see mm. 206–10). In fact, this cadential implication spills over past the dissolution of the theme: the final B-major chord (m. 217) proves unambiguously to be V of iv and leads into the opening of the coda, which is essentially an enormous iv–V–i cadence in B minor.

This treatment of the tonic major in the recapitulation of the second theme sounds a faint reverberation of the shimmering cadential B-major chord in the seventh measure of the Overture. In fact, the overall tonal plan of the work represents an expansive elaboration of the progression plotted out in the opening measures of the exposition. As Figure 12 shows, the initial succession of chords forms the basis for the succession of the principal key areas of the entire work. This method of developing the structure of a movement out of the structure of its opening phrase is similar, of course, to the organizational principle we have already seen worked out with impressive thoroughness in the exposition in the first movement of the Octet. The dexterity—and poetry—with which the process is made to span the entire course of Op. 26 is

Structure of the opening theme

B minor	i	–	III	–	v		V/iv	–	iv	–	i
Measure:	1		3		5		7		8		9

Structure of the Overture

B minor:	i	III		V	(i)	V/iv		iv	(V)	i	
		Exposition	Development		Recapitulation			Coda			
Measure:	1	47			180	202		217		268	

Figure 12. Mendelssohn, *Hebrides* Overture, Op. 26, mm. 1–9 and 1–268.

a measure of the continual refinement of Mendelssohn's technique through the first years of the 1830s. In one of the rare instance in which the composer explicitly described his conception of musical structure, Mendelssohn discussed the central position of this kind of large-scale organizational principle for his work. (The extract is from an 1828 letter to a friend, Adolf Fredrik Lindblad; the music under discussion is the second movement of Beethoven's recently published Quartet in C♯ minor, Op. 131.)

> You see, that is one of my points! The relation of all 4 or 3 or 2 or 1 movements of a sonata to the others and to the parts, so that from the very beginning, and throughout the work, one knows its secret (so when the unadorned D major reappears, the 2 notes go straight to my heart); it must be so in music.[23]

In light of this concern for the relation of detail and structure, it is worth noting that the *Hebrides* Overture, with its air of spontaneous inevitability, went through numerous stages of revision in the three years between August 1829, when, during his first trip to Scotland, Mendelssohn jotted down a version of the opening measures in a letter to his family, and June 1832, when the autograph score of the final version of the work was completed. Characteristically, although the thematic content of the work as we know it was set in the second completed version of the score, dated 16 December 1830, the tight interrelation of structural processes that animated the final version was achieved only later, in connection with revisions to the transitional and cadential passages of the exposition.[24]

The first of these revisions concerns the shift from B minor to D major (mm. 27–47 of the printed score; a summary sketch of the manuscript version of the passage is given in Example 61). In the 1830 version, after the first statement of the oboe-flute melody (corresponding to mm. 27–31 of the printed score), the counterstatement is diverted after one measure, leading into a bridge passage that establishes V of F♯ minor—the minor dominant. The thematic material of this bridge is derived from the ascending arpeggio of the oboe-flute line, expanded to quarter notes, with an accompaniment consisting of the wave-motive of the main theme. The principal link between the first and second themes

Example 61. Mendelssohn, *Hebrides Overture, transitional theme in the 1830 manuscript version.*

in this earlier version of the passage, then, is thematic: the ascending quarter-note figure both recalls the main theme and foreshadows the opening of the second theme. It is particularly interesting that the modulation from F♯ minor to D major pivots on common tones, just as the final version does—but the pivot tones are F♯ and A rather than F♯ and D. The effect in the final version is both smoother and less obvious than the carefully worked out thematic links in this earlier one, and the play on the D-F♯ pair knits the structural web of the entire work more tightly.

The second theme itself is identical in these two versions, and the continuation from the cadence of the second phrase in the 1830 version does center on D and F♯, but in a much less rigorously controlled way than in the printed score. And in the 1830 version, as in the final version, the closing cadence of the restatement of the second theme is diverted from D major; but in the 1830 version the chord under the violin's d''' (corresponding to m. 70 of the printed score) is simply a G-minor triad: the allusion to the diminished seventh chord that links this digression to the pivotal d''' of m. 27 is not part of the original plan.

The continuation from this point to the end of the exposition is also less cogently worked out in the 1830 version. As we have seen, the final version of this material, which covers twenty-seven measures, centers continually on upper-voice cadential motions around D and F♯ that are subverted by lingering traces of B minor. This culminates in a deceptively sturdy cadence on the D-F♯ third at the end of the exposition that melts back into B minor one measure later. In the earlier version, this closing passage, which covers thirty-nine measures, makes no allusion to B minor, but leans instead toward the minor subdominant, the G minor first introduced at the end of the second theme. This subdominant bias does generate a certain inflectional ambiguity concerning F♯ (as the temporary leading tone), but it does so without relating this to any structural subcurrent of references to B minor. As a result, the surprising return to the tonic at the opening of the development section does not have the sense of inevitability it has acquired in the final version. Even the join between D major and B minor at this point is handled with considerably less finesse in the earlier version. The exposition closes with a fully scored cadence to D major that ends on octave Ds—without F♯: as a result, the emergence of the B-minor triad from beneath this cadence lacks an important element of the magical common tone reverberation that colors this moment in the final version.

The revisions serve, then, to sharpen the realization of structural principles that are already discernible in the early version of the work. As was the case in the revisions of the first and second movements of the Octet and of the *Calm Sea and Prosperous Voyage*, this is accomplished primarily through the replacement of conventional formal gestures typical of the classicist sonata style—the clever, but somewhat unfocused, passage of thematic transformation that links the first and second groups in the 1830 version of the *Hebrides* Overture, for example—with material that more clearly reflects the workings of the fundamental structural processes of the form, and which more cogently interweaves its harmonic and thematic thread.

The last work to be considered in this chapter, the "Reformation" Symphony (1832), raises the issue of cyclic form—of the relation between individual movements in a multi-movement work. This matter, which will be considered in more detail in chapter 5, is introduced here because the cyclic design of the Symphony hinges on the treatment of the second theme of the first movement.

The transition in the exposition of the first movement (mm. 60–96) prepares an arrival in the minor dominant, A minor. As Example 62 shows, the second theme itself, however, is harmonized insistently around A major, although the use of the minor subdominant in the opening measures of the theme places this major tonic on a disconcertingly precarious footing: the major mode (mm. 97ff.) functions more as a cadential chromatic alteration of the minor mode than as an independent key. In m. 117, this first section of the theme is finally reharmonized around A minor, setting off a string of cadential themes to close the exposition in that key.

Taken by itself, the uncertainty of focus in the initial harmonization of the theme seems to be something of a miscalculation—an example of what Tovey claimed was Mendelssohn's inability to tell the difference between major and minor.[25] The conflict between the insistent major mode of the second theme, maintained in spite of the strong minor-mode preparation and the pull exerted by the minor subdominant, is, admittedly, rather hard to decipher: the first C♯ of the melodic line (in the third measure of the theme) is particularly unsettling, as it places a conspicuous metric accent on what would have seemed to be a purely transient chromatic alteration.

In the recapitulation, the instability of the major mode is intensified even further: the initial D–major chord of the second theme (m. 376) is explicitly presented as V_5^6 of iv. As a result, the continuation of the theme in the tonic major registers unambiguously as a prolongation of this cadential inflection, and the turn back to D minor functions even more clearly as the resolution of this distinctly unstable D major. Within the first movement, then, the tonic major never does establish itself as a stable key—or more precisely, the stability normally associated with the tonic major is repeatedly undermined at crucial points in the course of the movement. It is this sense of a resolution offered and yet withheld that Mendelssohn exploits in establishing the programmatic and cyclic designs of the work.

The third movement, an Andante in G minor, is one of the composer's most successful serious slow movements. The melodic line is clearly vocal throughout, and the doleful anxiety that shapes it almost attains explicit expression in a short outburst of recitative that forms the climax of this impressive miniature. At the end of the movement, the antiphonal closing cadence seems to be settling to G minor, but the final tonic chord is shunted to G major, and it ushers in a statement of the head of the second theme from the *first* movement—through the troubling major chord on the downbeat of its third measure (Example 63). But now this fragment functions as a *tierce de Picardie* cadence for the whole of the Andante: the unsettling pull of the minor mode is assimilated as a reverberation of the whole of the movement, and the precarious major mode is stabilized within this beautifully expressive cadential gesture. Since this consoling turn leads directly into the pointedly ecclesiastical presentation of the chorale tune, "Ein' feste Burg," that serves as the introduction—and later reappears as the climax—to the finale, the cyclic return, and in particular the reinterpretation of the major mode that is the focus of that return, is invested with a relatively clear programmatic significance: the uncertainty and agitation of the first movement, which had prevented the stabilization of the major mode, and the anxious yearning of the Andante are swept away by the exultant chorale, with its message of the triumph of faith over weakness and doubt.

That message is couched in sharply sectarian terms. The opening of the cyclic theme echoes the first measures of the slow introduction to the first movement, a figure that bears some relation to the canticle *Nunc dimittis*, and which is presented in a polyphonic setting that evokes an *a cappella* "Palestrina" style, while the introduction closes with the "Dresden Amen," from which the main theme of the first movement is developed;[26] the leanings of the finale are, of course, unmistakable. The thematic material of the work as a whole seems, therefore, to be organized into "Catholic" and "Protestant" groups, with the final victory falling to the Protestant themes—a fitting programmatic gesture for this pointedly partisan work.

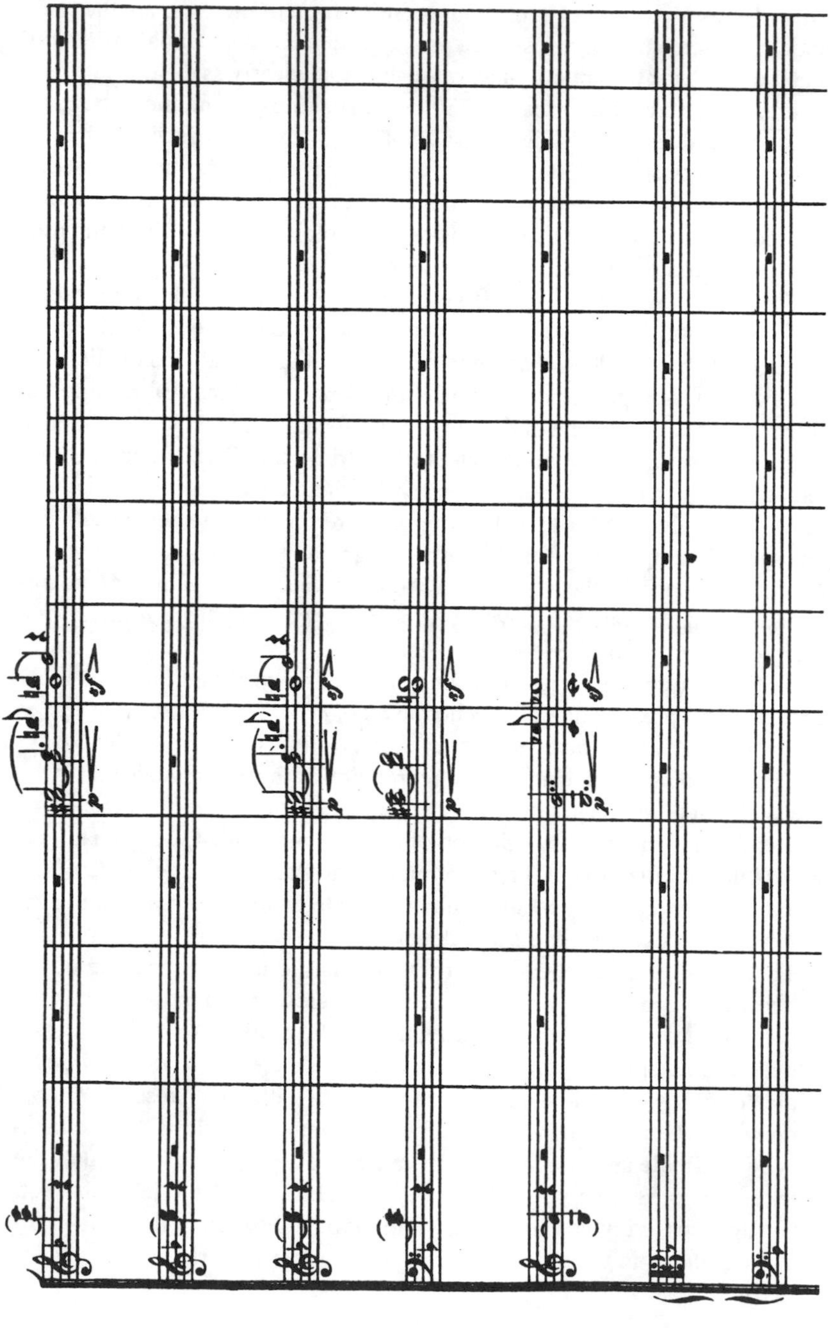

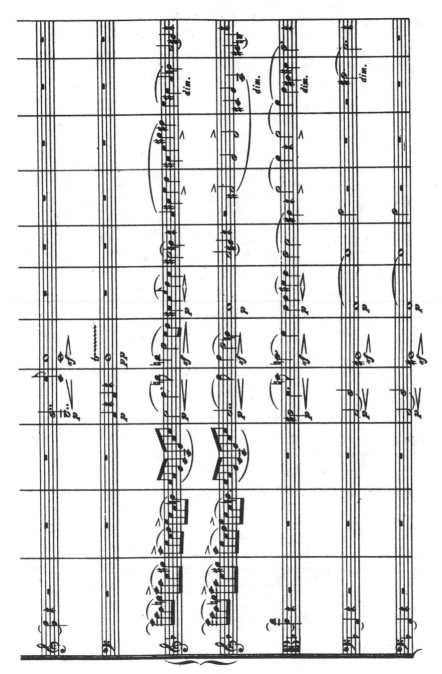

Example 62. Mendelssohn, "Reformation" Symphony, Op. 105, I, mm. 94–119. (Continued.)

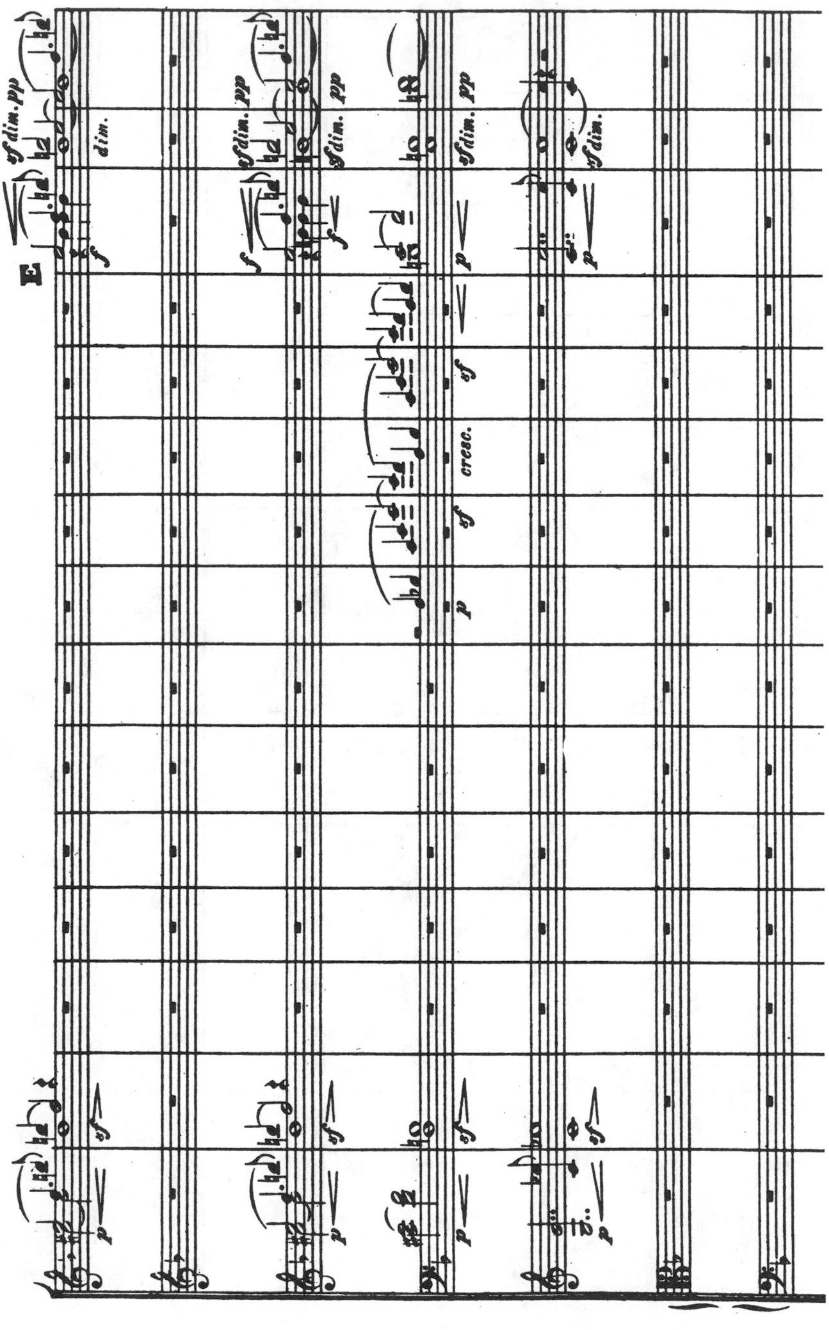
E
sf dim. pp
dim.
cresc.

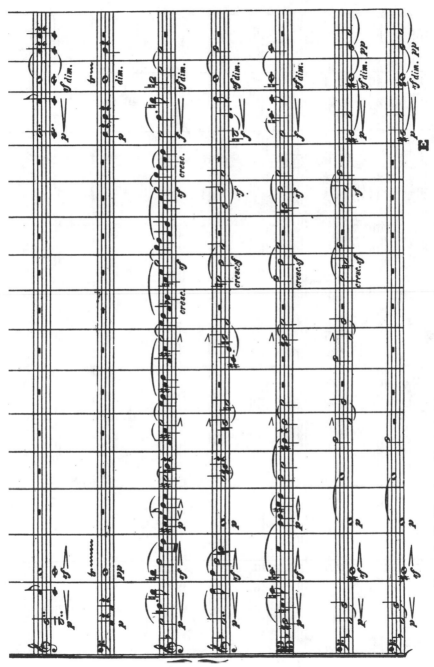

Example 62. (Continued.)   Mendelssohn, "Reformation" Symphony, Op. 105, I, mm. 94–119.

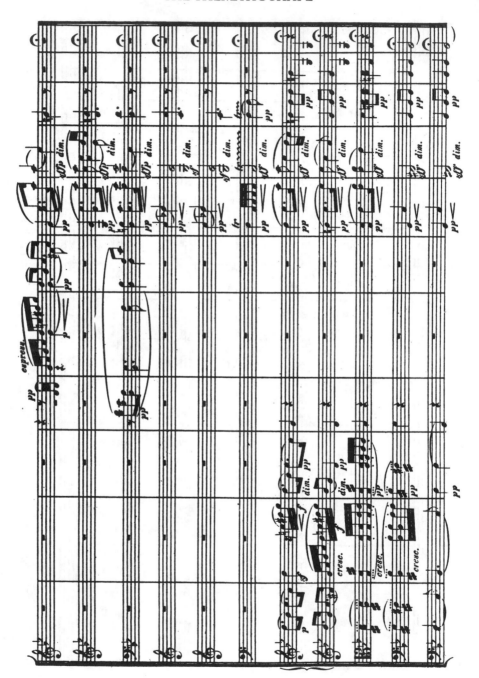

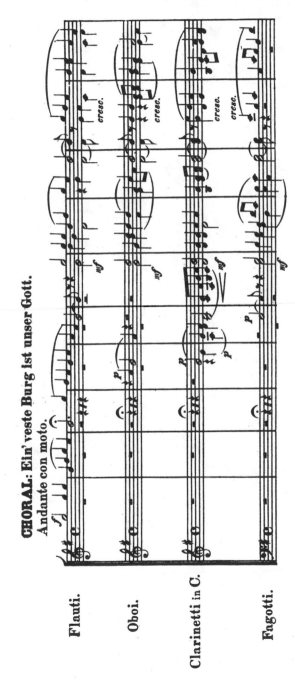

Example 63. Mendelssohn, "Reformation" Symphony, Op. 105, III, mm. 44–54 and IV, 1–10 (winds only).

CHAPTER 5

THEMATIC PROCESS AND CYCLIC FORM

The use of the same material in different sections of a large work is an important element of structural coherence in some of the earliest multi-section pieces in the western musical tradition, and the principle of unity in diversity that underlies this procedure is one of the oldest elements of aesthetic theory. But cyclic procedures—either the explicit reappearance of material from one movement in the course of another, as, for example, in the "Reformation" Symphony, or the establishment of implicit, but relatively unambiguous, thematic relations between different movements—are particularly characteristic of the music of the mid-nineteenth century. Across the range of Mendelssohn's output, the treatment of large-scale cyclic designs offers an important measure of his accommodation of romantic formal conceptions and classical sonata-form procedures.

Rosen has noted that the use of implicit cyclic relations already had a long history by the end of the eighteenth century.[1] The similarity of melodic gestures, harmonic progressions, or textures in different parts of a classical sonata-form work—whether by Haydn, Clementi, or Galuppi—is a fundamental premise of the style. What is less clear is the functional significance of these similarities—the point at which they become *relations*. As we have seen in chapter 2, Mendelssohn had developed a masterful control of this type of thematic manipulation in his earliest published chamber works and in the C-minor Symphony, Op. 11—works written, for the most part, before the composer's fourteenth birthday. Within individual movements in these works—the first movement of the F-minor Piano Quartet, for example—thematic similarities do, in fact, reflect functional relations: in the transformation of the nervous gestures of the main theme into the flowing lyricism of the second theme, the exposition traces the history of a complex of motivic gestures—a history that proceeds from tension to resolution—articulating a progression that, unfortunately, contradicts the increased tension generated by the establishment of the tonal polarity that animates the dynamic of sonata form.

Overt cyclic references from one movement to another, on the other hand, are relatively rare in the classical sonata style.[2] The fundamental premises of the style depend on the closed, self-generated structural integrity of the individual movements of a work: the animating processes of tension and resolution run their course within the single movement, and one movement does not normally carry on the work of another. Cyclic procedures by their very nature obscure the boundaries between the individual movements that articulate this internal formal coherence.

This structural integrity is crucial for the sonata style because it is the clarity with which the formal processes are articulated and realized that establishes the aesthetic basis for the dramatic—but non-referential—significance of the form. In Carl Dahlhaus's formulation, "the self-contained nature of the form is the correlate to the autonomy of the work."[3]

Beethoven, however, did employ explicit cyclic procedures in a number of his most dramatic sonata-form designs—the two most spectacular examples, the Fifth and Ninth Symphonies, are perhaps the most "Beethovenian" of all his works. A consideration of the means by which he overcame—indeed exploited—the apparent formal contradictions this entails will help lay the groundwork for the study of Mendelssohn's cyclic experiments.

The cyclic design in the Ninth Symphony, for example, is only one element in a larger complex of gestures: the recall—and immediate dismissal—of the earlier movements at the beginning of the finale is part of a process that demolishes the non-referential autonomy of the work in order to set the stage for the translation of the torrent of instrumental recitative into explicitly vocal terms and for the intertwining of sonata, concerto, variation, and opera in the setting of Schiller's text.[4] And all of this is part of an overarching process in which the vision of brotherhood that illuminates that text provides the resolution for the entire work, the victory over the turmoil that ravaged those earlier movements.

On the other hand, the cyclic element in the Fifth Symphony, the return of material from the Scherzo in the finale, performs a rather different function—both within the finale and in relation to the design of the entire work.

Beethoven establishes in a number of ways that the opening of the finale is to be understood as a resolution for the entire work. As an example of the generalized sense of resolution basic to the classical style, Rosen has cited the main theme as "a model of the difference in phrasing and the emphasis on the tonic that were necessary for the firm sense of ending indispensable in a finale."[5] On a more specific level, the opening of the finale triumphantly reestablishes the C major that had apparently been achieved in the later stages of the first movement—apparently, that is, before it was battered back to C minor in the coda.

On the most immediate level, the opening chord of the finale serves as the long-delayed tonic cadence that should have come at the end of the third movement (m. 324); in a very real sense, then, the opening of the finale explicitly provides the resolution for an earlier event. At the same time, the enormous gulf that separates that evaded cadence from its resolution—fifty measures of "great darkness" as Tovey called it—and the shattering incommensurability of the eerie C-minor hush at the end of the third movement and the blazing C major unleashed at the beginning of the finale make it clear that the functional role of this opening tonic downbeat extends far beyond any purely local relations. By dissolving the boundary between the beginning of the finale and what has gone immediately before, Beethoven has opened the finale to everything that has gone before; it is this larger relation that is established in the mysterious transition between the third and fourth movements.

The crucial event in that transition is the initial motion in the lowest voice from G to A♭ at the (deceptive) cadence in m. 324 of the third movement. A♭ leans heavily on the dominant root throughout the first part of the passage, and finally, as the bass of an augmented sixth chord in m. 349, it presses back to G, touching off the massive dominant preparation that leads into the opening of the finale. In turn, this large-scale G–A♭–G bass motion recalls a number of striking events from earlier movements, invoking a shadowy network of reminiscences that reinforces the sense that we are witnessing a formal process that extends far beyond its immediate context.

In the first movement, the A♭–G pair is an inflectionally sensitive pivot around the dominant of C minor; echoes of this half step throb through the entire movement. More specifically, in the recapitulation the second group, ostensibly in C major, is stalked by a persistent shadow of the minor subdominant, F minor (with its third, A♭). This elusive companion continually undercuts the functional stability of C major, which, as V of iv, lacks the inflectional major-mode stability this painstakingly "normal" recapitulation would seem to be celebrating. The crisis begins to intensify in the weirdly forced resolution of ab'' to a♮'' in m. 330, and it is clinched in m. 376, when the final cadence of the recapitulation, a triumphant blaze of C major, finally topples over into F minor—with A♭ in the bass—wrenching the coda into C minor.

In the course of the second movement, the Andante con moto in A♭ major, there are three luminous passages in C major. The third of these is approached through a sudden modulatory shift, but the first two arrivals in C major grow out of elaborate transitions that hinge on the transformation of a lower-voice A♭ from tonic root to the bass of an augmented sixth chord, resolving to the dominant of C major (mm. 23–31 and 72–80). Of course these C–major episodes are markedly unstable within the structure of the movement, and, despite their ponderous brilliance, they dissolve in an instant, restoring A♭ as the tonic root.

At the join between the second and third movements, the lower-voice A♭ of the last measure of the second movement, which has been the focus of a carefully drawn-out cadence (mm. 229–47), is transformed once again—retroactively and by implication—into an appoggiatura to the ghostly upbeat G of the third movement.

The transition at the end of the third movement reverberates with these earlier events, funneling them into the preparations for the triumphant C–major eruption at the first chord of the finale. As a result of there non-thematic, subcutaneous functional interrelations, the transition stands—in a very real sense—for these earlier movements, and the opening of the finale, scored with a brilliance and power new even to Beethoven's symphonic style, registers as a resolution not just of the deceptive cadence that set the transition in motion, but of everything that has preceded it.

But if the opening theme of the last movement functions as a resolution for the entire work, that theme has obviously taken on a significance that reaches far beyond its role within the movement. The meaning of the theme is not determined solely by its function within the structure of the finale, but is derived from the accumulated weight of the first three movements toppling over into its first chord. It is in its relation to this double meaning of the main theme that the functional significance of the explicit return of material from the Scherzo at the end of the development section of the finale can be best understood.

Simply stated, the problem in dealing with the return of this theme is that it is difficult to imagine any sort of dominant preparation for the opening of the recapitulation that could recapture the tremendous power of the first appearance of the theme without grotesquely overextending the formal proportions of the movement, expansive as those proportions are; any plausibly normal return would seem to be doomed to anticlimax.

Beethoven's solution is to superimpose the two functions of the main theme—as an element within the formal design of the finale and as a gesture that acquires its full significance only in relation to the entire work—at the climax of the finale, using the cadential focus of the opening of the recapitulation to reaffirm the triumph of the C-major resolution achieved in the opening of the movement.

The return of the Scherzo material (mm. 153–206) comes on the heels of a remarkably noisy passage of dominant preparation (extending back to m. 132) that had seemed to be leading to the decisive reacquisition of the tonic. Within this formal process, the sudden intrusion of the Scherzo, bringing C minor in place of C major, breaking the integrity of both tempo and meter within the finale, and introducing material from outside the movement in place of the anticipated return of the main theme, acts as an enormous deceptive cadence, intensifying the tension of the dominant preparation by derailing its expected resolution at the last possible moment. It is the specific mechanism of this intensification—not simply the reappearance of the Scherzo theme, but the recollection of the larger process that was spun out of the transition from the Scherzo to the finale, and in particular the wide-ranging associations embedded in the lower-voice motion from G through Ab and back to G which shaped that transition—that establishes the link between this approach to C major and the stupendous resolution provided at the opening of the movement, and it is the intertwining of formal processes generated by the structure of the finale itself with this larger gesture of resolution that integrates the two functional roles of the main theme at this crucial juncture.

The point is that the explicit cyclic return—the reappearance of the Scherzo within the finale—is not itself the primary agent of unification in the Symphony. The larger coherence of the work is a function of a dynamic of tension and resolution that spans all four movements, culminating in the triumphant affirmation of C major in the first measure of the finale: the cyclic return articulates the final stage of that progression, identifying the decisive closural moment of the entire structure—the convergence of the processes that span the four-movement structure and the internally generated processes of the finale—with intense dramatic clarity. Similarly, the many implicit motivic relations that permeate the thematic surface of the Symphony are better understood as manifestations of that larger dynamic than as, in themselves, the source of unity: they are the inescapable reverberations of the fundamental tensions that shape the entire work.

The Fifth Symphony is exceptional—although, paradoxically, it is quintessentially Beethovenian in its explicit dramatic power. In a number of other works Beethoven establishes large-scale processive relations between movements without deploying any explicit thematic relations. In the C-major Piano Sonata, Op. 53, the "Waldstein," for example, the overarching design hinges on the continually shifting inflectional tendencies that accrue to one note, F, and in particular, to f'''.

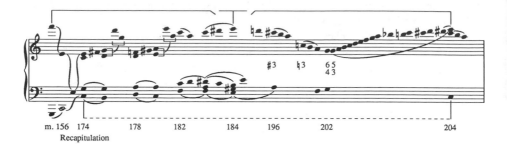

Example 64. Beethoven, Piano Sonata in C major, Op. 53, I, mm. 152–204.

Just before the opening of the recapitulation in the first movement, f''' is insisted upon strenuously as the seventh in the home dominant seventh, forming the climax of a long passage of dominant preparation (mm. 152–55). But f''' is left hanging, unresolved in register, when the upper-voice line plunges three octaves in little more than one measure to regain the original register of the main theme, marking the beginning of the recapitulation (mm. 155–56). The upper-voice line only establishes a completely stable e''' in m. 204, where the second theme—which has just been played in A major (with a counterstatement in A minor)—is restated in the tonic—beginning on e''', and explicitly resolving, in register, the f''' (and the massive V7 of C major) of m. 155. The registral connection from the f''' of mm. 152–55 to the e''' of m. 204 has the effect of bridging over the restatement of the first theme, transferring the weight of resolution to the tonic statement of the second theme while retaining the imposing stability of a symmetrical thematic balance between the exposition and recapitulation (and a harmonic structure in which the initial motion from the tonic to the mediant is counterbalanced by motion from the tonic through the submediant and back to the tonic).

As Example 64 shows, the preparation for this redistribution of formal balances is worked out with particular care. In the passage of dominant preparation preceding the statement of the second theme in A major, there has been a strong emphasis on e''' (mm. 181–95), but this e''' is harmonically unstable—it is part of the preparation for a digression away from the tonic within the recapitulation—and it is registrally unstable—approached through a leap from the middle register that echoes one of the basic instrumental gestures of the movement—the sudden shift from low to high registers in the right hand. This line gradually descends from the three-line register (beginning on c♯''', m. 196) to f', as the harmony shifts from A major and A minor toward C major. A single measure leads into the C–major

Example 65.   Beethoven, Piano Sonata in C major, Op. 53, II, mm. 1–9.

counterstatement of the second theme through an ascending scale whose final steps subsume the secondary chromatic details of A major and its dominant, c♯''' and d♯''', into the conclusive reacquisition of the tonic and its third, e'''. (In particular, the motion through d♯''' recovers the grace-note d♯''' that had introduced e''' in m. 181.) The play on e''' over the first part of the recapitulation functions, then, as an anticipation of the return to the tonic—and the explicit resolution of the dominant at the end of the development—accomplished by the C–major version of the second theme in mm. 204ff.

The double recapitulation of the second theme seems to absorb f''' into the closural processes of the movement, resolving its inflectional tendencies by emphasizing the gradual stabilization of e'''. But the play on f''' returns at the end of the movement, first in the cadenza-like preparation for a last reference to the second theme, now firmly settled in the tonic (mm. 282ff.), and then in a repetition of the precipitous descent from f''' that marked the end of the development section, which again leaves f''' dangling, unresolved, at the final cadence. As the repetition of a gesture prominently resolved earlier in the recapitulation, this might seem more stable than at its first appearance—to at least a certain extent, we have come to accept registral disjunction as part of the language of the movement. But Beethoven seizes upon the vague sense of incompleteness left by this cadence to forge an explicit link from the first movement through the Introduzione and into the finale.

The two pages of the Introduzione are almost completely preoccupied with shifting relations between F and E in various registers and various harmonic settings. In the first two measures, the tonic root, F, is transformed into an appoggiatura to E—a transformation the transience of which is emphasized both by a pyramid of crossing voices in the upper parts and by a striking registral shift in the bass, lifting the E of m. 2 to an inner voice and only returning to the lowest register in m. 9, at the return to F major (Example 65).[6]

The shifting relations between E and F are played upon throughout this short movement, culminating in the reacquisition of f''' in m. 23 as part of a diminished seventh, Ab–B–D–F, that immediately tips over to V7 of C major. This event marks the return to the tonic key of the Sonata and would seem to reestablish the primary inflectional identity of f'''—as an upper neighbor to e'''—that had been so carefully explored in the first movement. But once again f''' is left hanging as the upper voice is led through a broad descending arpeggiation of the dominant seventh; in the closing measures of the Introduzione, the upper voice only manages to regain f'' (m. 26). After a last flicker of the shifting inflectional play on the F–E relation (with F resolving to E, but within a cadence to the submediant), f'' is shunted *up* to g''—which will be taken up as the first note of the Rondo theme. This marks a fundamental change in the expressive character of the work—an almost physical sense of expansion and a fundamental change of sonority that is central to the sense of luminous resolution that glows throughout the finale.

Rosen has pointed out that the characteristic sound and propulsive energy of the first movement of the "Waldstein" reflect the pervasiveness of dominant sevenths in the harmonic structure of the thematic material: every other chord of each of the main themes is a dominant seventh.[7] The continual inflectional play around F, the seventh of V7 of the tonic key, represents the most prominent and structurally significant exploration of the generative energy latent in this fundamental sonority.

But the opening of the finale clearly establishes G as the principal upper-voice pitch, replacing the cramped inflectional reversals around F and E that have driven so much of the music with the shining purity of a remarkably spacious—and sonorous—C–G fifth. This complex of pitches, inflectional ambiguities, and registers—and registral disjunctions—was initially set in place in the opening measures of the first movement (mm. 1–13); the new clarity with which these elements are unfolded and subsumed within the sweeping gestures of the finale identifies the sense of resolution that illuminates the opening of the finale as the surface manifestation of a closural process that encompasses everything that has happened in the work. (Notice, for example, how the play on F–E and F–Eb in the consequent phrase of the Rondo theme (mm. 14ff.) recalls and reinterprets the e'''–f'''–eb''' figure of mm. 9ff. of the first movement, drawing Eb back into the tonic and grounding the enharmonic modulatory impulse on which the initial stages of the tonal process in the first movement had pivoted; in turn, this delicate chromaticism prepares the turbulent flat-side excursions later in the finale.)

The establishment (or reestablishment) of the fifth scale degree—opening the cramped intensity of the preceding movements into the bell-like reverberations that characterize the finale—first takes place outside the originally sensitized register: the Rondo theme begins on g''—the register first staked out by G in m. 4 of the first movement. G''' is first introduced in m. 31, initiating an upper-octave embellishment of the theme, and the upper register is stabilized with increasing firmness at each restatement of the theme. A direct registral connection linking f''' to g''' is finally made over the course of a sweeping upper-voice motion that spans the dominant preparation for the final return to the main theme, with the g''' achieved in m. 279 linking forward to the climactic g''' at the return of the main theme in m. 313.

In this last statement of the theme, g''' is, therefore, no longer an embellishment to the principal line, but is itself established as the primary structural note of the theme. Following this return to the principal upper-voice register of the entire work, g''' blazes throughout the enormous coda, which saturates the registral space with a delirious fabric of cadential descents from G to C. The finale serves as a conclusion to the work neither simply as the result of a generalized lowering of tensions and increase in virtuoso brilliance nor of a process of explicit cyclic thematic recall, but through a processive design that spans the entire work, resolving, in its final stages, inflectional and registral issues that shaped the earlier movements.

This suggests a fundamental principle concerning the sense of large-scale coherence in Beethoven's sonata-form works. Both Rosen and Tovey have pointed out that the sense of inter-relation between the various movements in the classical sonata style is normally the function of a generalized progression of intensity and complexity of texture over the entire course of the work—usually from greater complexity in the first movement to simpler textures and a lower level of intensity in the finale.[8] The looser texture and more regular phrase structure typical of a sonata finale provide a relaxation of tension—a sense of expressive resolution—for the entire work without compromising the integrity of the individual movements. This overall dynamic even operates in an exceptional work like Mozart's G-major String Quartet, K. 387, where the finale bristles with complex fugal part-writing. As we have seen, fugal texture quickly merges into expanses of brilliant passage-work and rollicking Italianate lyricism; at the end of the coda the fugal subject itself is transformed into a tidily homophonic cadential turn—the complexities of fugue are assimilated as a form of the virtuosity appropriate to a brilliant finale.

In works like the "Waldstein," this loose dynamic progression is transformed into a structural process that spans the entire course of the work, linking the individual movements into a single gesture shaped by an enormous expansion of the effective range of large-scale dissonance and resolution. The cyclic procedures in the Fifth and Ninth Symphonies represent special cases of this same procedure, dramatizing the larger progression by explicitly identifying the nodes of tension and the decisive resolution within a clearly articulated design. The cyclic returns are articulative devices, then, just as, within a movement, the thematic pattern serves to articulate the underlying tonal process. Recognizing this functional hierarchy in Beethoven's works is essential for an understanding of romantic cyclic designs, which often seem to be based more or less directly on those works.

The organization of three of Mendelssohn's most elaborate cyclic designs, for example, clearly suggest the influence of the Fifth Symphony. In the earliest of these works, the Sextet for Piano and Strings, Op. 110 (1824), Mendelssohn even goes Beethoven one better, introducing a restatement of the entire main body of the third movement, a Minuet in D minor marked *Agitato*, to interrupt the closing cadences of the D–major finale; this cyclic return grows out of a delicate minor-mode coloring in the complex of cadential themes at the end of the second group of the finale. The effect is delightful—the interruption eventually dissolves into a torrent of brilliant cadential figure-work that only manages to scramble back to D major in the final three measures of the work. Like the return in the Fifth Symphony, the cyclic return functions as a special articulative texture—a deceptive cadence that intensifies the drive to the tonic. But this interruption does not interweave the return and the central climax of the movement itself—the return to the tonic at the beginning of the recapitulation; rather, it intensifies the final cadence. The difference is revealing: in contrast to the close structural focus in Beethoven's Symphony, there is no clear functional relation between the various movements of Mendelssohn's sprawling work, and consequently the return does not serve to integrate large-scale processes with the internally generated structure of the finale. The return is a type of terminal modification that affirms, with extravagant superfluousness, the impending conclusion of what is essentially a paratactic structure.

The cyclic return in the finale of the Octet (considered in chapter 3) is at least superficially reminiscent of the Fifth Symphony as well—there are, however, profound differences that will be considered below. The last movement of one of Mendelssohn's finest "later" works, the "Italian" Symphony, also follows a similar plan, but the cyclic references are more elusively managed. The result is one of the composer's most impressive achievements, and once again, the unusual shape of the movement emerged gradually from a more regular, balanced design that has been preserved in a manuscript version of the Symphony.9

As in the Octet, the treatment of the exposition sets up conditions that allow the final stages of the movement to accommodate a cadential expansion that embraces—implicitly and explicitly—the entire work. Mendelssohn's strategy centers on the organization of the second theme, which subtly fore-

Example 66.   Mendelssohn, "Italian" Symphony, Op. 90, IV.
a. Mm. 6–8   *b.* Mm. 52–54.

stalls the emphatic formal articulation it seems to be providing. The melodic line of the second theme is new and memorable, but as Example 66 shows, its rhythm is exactly the same as that of the first theme. Furthermore, instead of marking a stable arrival in the secondary key, this theme threads itself around a (local) dominant pedal (horns, mm. 53ff.), and cadential arrivals within the continuation of the second group are repeatedly undercut by increasingly colorful harmonic digressions (mm. 62, 88, etc.). Indeed, the entire second group, although full of memorable thematic fragments, never seems to coalesce, and at the end of the exposition the E major/minor around which the second group has hovered instantly drops back into the tonic (mm. 103–5).

The development section begins with a striking new theme (m. 122), but, as we should by now have come to expect, this "new" theme is actually a close relative—elaborately disguised—of material presented earlier in the movement. Its triplet rhythm has permeated almost every measure of the exposition, its rushing scalewise ascent was introduced in a short developmental passage within the second group (mm. 71–76), and the minor seventh that sets the range of the new theme is taken from the cadence figure at the end of the first group (mm. 45–48).

Elements of the cyclic design begin to materialize almost immediately: first in the pizzicato bass line under the new theme, which is almost a literal quotation of the principal accompanimental figure of the second movement, and later in an outbreak of repeated chords in quick staccato triplets in the winds, recalling the opening of the first movement (mm. 156–65). Rather than standing out clearly, however, these brief allusions are almost completely assimilated into the kaleidoscopic flow of the movement, flashing by almost before they can be identified.

The return to the tonic at the end of the development is heralded by a rousing *fortissimo* passage of dominant preparation (mm. 175–94). At this point in the manuscript version of the movement the second theme was recapitulated "in" the tonic—that is, perched on V of A minor. The passage corresponded, roughly, to mm. 53–70, followed by an expansion of mm. 71–75, and merging, finally, into what is m. 196 of the printed score, where the "new" theme from the development section shows up in the tonic. In its original shape, then, the opening of the recapitulation served both to resolve the second theme and to prolong the cadential drive toward the tonic set in motion over the course of the development section. There are, I think, several reasons behind the revision of this impressive formal design. First, the accompanimental material for the second theme and for this restatement of the "new" theme are essentially identical. This does not seem to represent an element of the process of thematic transformations in the work—the revelation of an unexpected relation through the superimposition of elements of one theme onto elements of the other—however; it is, rather, simply a means of articulating the large-scale cadential tension that animates the entire passage, exploiting the dominant pedal embedded in the accompanimental material. One part of the problem may have been simply that the novelty of the new combination of elements was jeopardized by the repetitiousness of this dual presentation of that accompanimental figure. A more important issue, I think, involves the larger formal strategy that is being worked out in these closing pages of the Symphony.

As in the last movement of the Octet, Mendelssohn gradually filters out thematic elements of the finale, replacing them with elements from earlier movements in order to identify the tonic affirmation of the recapitulation— actually a massive cadential drive toward the tonic—as a concluding gesture for the entire work. When the main theme of the finale does manage to reappear in the course of the recapitulation in the Symphony (mm. 210ff.), for example, it flashes by as part of the general cadential rush and never has a chance to reestablish a stable articulative function for itself. The only other material from the exposition that returns in this last part of the movement is a wisp of a cadential progression from the second group (mm. 84–86), and all that is retained is part of the harmonic skeleton (see mm. 237–38). Within this design, the careful recapitulation of the second theme found in the original version of the movement places too much emphasis on the internally generated formal processes of the finale—processes that Mendelssohn is systematically sifting out of the structure of the last stages of the movement. In the final version, the pointedly elusive thematic articulation of the opening of the recapitulation better reflects the special role of these final pages of the movement within the larger structure. The logic of Mendelssohn's procedure is reinforced, in turn, by the underlying rhythmic identity of the first and second themes of the exposition; as in the last movement of the Octet, there is, in a sense, no new material associated with the establishment of the secondary key area, and consequently, there is, strictly speaking, nothing to recapitulate. Instead, the closing pages of the movement are given over to the new

Example 67.   Mendelssohn, "Italian" Symphony, Op. 90.
   a. IV, Mm. 6–8   *b.* I, Mm. 60–62.

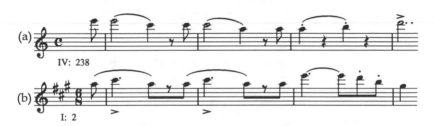

Example 68.   Mendelssohn, "Italian" Symphony, Op. 90.
   a. IV, mm. 239–41.   *b.* I, mm. 2–5.

thematic fragments that color this expanse of tonic affirmation with shadowy references to the first movement.

When the dominant pedal supporting the recapitulation of the "new" theme from the development section resolves (m. 214), it is to A major, as V of iv, further prolonging the drive toward a stable tonic cadence. The first strongly marked cadence to A minor, in mm. 234–36, bears a distant relation to a figure from the second group, as was mentioned above, but as Example 67 shows, it also introduces a faint reverberation of a cadential detail from the first movement—specifically from the counterstatement of the main theme in the exposition. The allusion is shadowy, perhaps, but it is immediately reinforced by another, more explicit reference that strengthens the sense of cyclic interconnection. In m. 239 the distinctive rhythm of the main theme of the first movement—a rhythm that contrasts sharply with the pervasive triplets of the finale—reappears in conjunction with an upper-voice descent through the A-minor triad which echoes that theme without actually quoting it (Example 68).

Certainly, neither of these cyclic references is exceptionally striking; indeed, I would suggest that they are not meant to be striking. They set off delicate reverberations, familiar, but so subtly altered that they make their effect and vanish before we can register their identity. The closing pages of the finale seem to reverberate with echoes of the earlier movements, rounding off the work while avoiding any trace of the emotional machinery an explicit cyclic design might suggest.

If the cyclic designs in the Octet and the "Italian" Symphony do seem to suggest the influence of Beethoven's procedures in the Fifth Symphony, there are important differences of detail that bear on central issues concerning the functional coherence of a multimovement work. In the Octet, for example, the most obvious of these differences involves the placement of the return of the Scherzo material and its relation to the formal processes of the finale. I have suggested that the cyclic return in the Fifth Symphony can be understood, in one sense, as a special articulative texture that is exploited to intensify the preparation for the central climax of the finale; in large part, the persuasiveness of the cyclic design of the entire work derives from the tightness with which the return is assimilated within the structure of the movement. In turn, this close intertwining of elements reflects the pervasive influence of carefully circumscribed musical relations—primarily the pivotal (in many senses) role of the G-Ab half step—at crucial junctures throughout the work.

In contrast, the return of the Scherzo material in the last movement of the Octet *disrupts* the formal processes of the finale just as the development section seems to be leading toward the opening of the recapitulation. The return derails the preparation for that climax rather than reinforcing it; indeed, in a very real sense, there is no recapitulation at all in this movement. On the one hand, this is a marvelous realization of the quicksilver good humor of the work as a whole; the tonic reaffirmation at the end of the Octet has never been accused of being the musical expression of Men's Triumph Over Fate. On the other hand, this disjunction of cyclic process and formal structure points up the absence of the kind of underlying musical processes that generate the formal organization of the Symphony. The explicit thematic return in the last movement of the Octet does not stand for an interconnected series of events in the way the return in the Symphony did—it does not summarize and complete musical relations central to the structure of the entire work. As a result, the closural process of the finale cannot be explicitly identified as the resolution of some larger network of relations, encompassing, by extension, the entire work; Mendelssohn simply replaces that internally generated closural process with an elaborately expanded cadence, and he identifies this massive tonic affirmation as the conclusion for the entire work by drawing in thematic elements from the other movements. In the "Italian" Symphony, the approach to the tonic is less devious—while the tissue of thematic allusions is considerably more ephemeral—but the disruption of the internal processes of the recapitulation engendered by the larger significance of the final tonic expanse of the work is similar. In comparison to Beethoven's procedures in the Fifth and Ninth Symphonies on the one hand and the "Waldstein" on the other, the looseness of the cyclic processes in the Octet and the "Italian" Symphony—and the loosening effect these processes have on the structure of the movements in which they occur—reflects the essentially paratactic relation between the various movements of these works. Mendelssohn's procedures stand somewhere between the generalized progression of movements characteristic of the eighteenth-century sonata style and the closely interwoven processes of Beethoven's implicit and explicit cyclic designs: they represent a compromise that succeeds brilliantly in part because the expressive stakes are not particularly high.

Of course, for Beethoven the stakes were high indeed. Cyclic procedures by their very nature imply the working out of processes that are too powerful to be contained within the structural dynamic of tension and resolution that shapes a single movement; the playing out of a cyclic design seems to point, however inscrutably, to the influence of intensely dramatic forces that transcend the balance inherent in that dynamic. The Ninth Symphony, for example, is the work in which the urge to explicit vocal expression that marks so much of the late music can no longer be contained. The confrontation of cyclic recall and instrumental recitative renders the normal processes of resolution and integration meaningless; the complex designs that have brought us to this crisis can only be transcended through the intercession of the human voice, which can clarify and complete Beethoven's message of the triumph of brotherhood and joy. The formal crisis—the disintegration of the system of internal balances and resolutions—is touched off by the cataclysmic dissonance at the opening of the finale, an event that is itself the culmination of a processive design that ranges over the entire work. The half-step simultaneity, A–B♭, that racks the opening is an elemental compression of the A–B♭ pairings that have marked pivotal moments throughout the work.[10] Properly heard (and performed) the b♭'' in the flute completes the upper-voice cadential line of the third movement—but the overlap is disastrous, touching off a grotesque eruption that instantly sweeps away the vision of solace unfolded in the astonishing timeless arabesques of the Adagio molto e cantabile.

Even in the Fifth Symphony, where there is no trace of explicit (or implicit) vocal intervention, the emotional power embodied in the cyclic process overshadows the mechanism of its realization, and even a critic like Tovey, for whom programmatic explications were anathema, could not discuss the work without coming surprisingly close to resorting to the terminology of a program—a program involving "terror," and "the security of the present triumph," and even "a note of self-pity for which we had no leisure when the terror was upon our souls."[11] The emotional power of Beethoven's design is obvious, of course, but a fundamental element of that power is that it is expressed completely within the terms of the formal processes of the work: a detailed programmatic explication of the significance of those processes necessarily seems insipid because the drama of the design is so completely assimilated into the drama of the form.

These two symphonies loom over the history of nineteenth-century music in a way no other works do: the combination of intense, immediately communicative power on the one hand and an obvious unity that seemed, at least, to be the product of thematic continuities over the entire course of a work on the other was particularly significant for composers attempting to reconcile romantic conceptions of formal coherence and a concern for direct expressivity with the seemingly intractable, and decidedly conservative, formalism that they took to be the essence of sonata form. But the organization of Beethoven's designs depends on an intricately calculated control of form and texture that simply was not readily available within the terms of the romantic musical language: neither the clarity of harmony and texture nor the careful isolation of registral events from which Beethoven shapes the elements of his larger designs were normal attributes of that language. On the other hand, for the composers of the early romantic generation, motivic relations and cyclic form seem to have fulfilled somewhat different purposes from those considered so far—expressive and rhetorical purposes that are, in fact, well served by a disjunction of surface and structure.

Among the early romantic composers, Berlioz seems to have been most fascinated with the rhetorical—essentially narrative—significance of cyclic procedures. In works like the *Symphonie fantastique* or *Harold en Italie*, the relation of cyclic procedures to a "poetic"—that is to say, programmatic—subject is central to the coherence of the musical design, and the relation between technical means and expressive ends is particularly striking. Berlioz himself explained that the cyclic procedures in these works are poetic devices that disrupt the internal organization of the individual movements rather than agents of large-scale structural unification—they segregate the various elements of the musical design in order to reflect the sense of isolation that is such a fundamentally romantic characteristic of the program's "hero":

> the theme of the *Symphonie fantastique*, the *idée fixe*, interposes itself obstinately, like an episodic, passionate figure, into scenes which are foreign to it, and within which it acts as an interruption, while the melody of Harold superimposes itself on the melodies of the orchestra, with which it contrasts in movement and character, without interrupting the course of their development.[12]

The reappearance of the cyclic element—the *idée fixe* in the *Symphonie fantastique* or the principal viola theme in *Harold*—is carefully segregated from the flow of events within the particular movement, and it is this isolation that gives the theme a poetic, programmatic significance. The second movement of the *Symphonie fantastique*, "Un bal," offers a striking illustration. The glittering A–major waltz—the "tumult of a brilliant party [*tumulte d'une fête brillante*]"—reaches a noisy climax on the dominant (m. 115), but collapses in an instant to a shivering F major, *ppp*, when the beloved, identified, as always, by the *idée fixe*, appears. To the dismay of the young artist, she joins in the dance—the theme is taken up in the waltz rhythm—but quickly vanishes into the throng—after the dynamic once again collapses to *pp*, the tumult of the A–major waltz is resumed at the point it had broken off (m. 174—note the return to the dominant of A major, *fortissimo*, scored to link back to the cadence in m. 115; note also the hesitant disruption of the surface rhythm in mm. 163–73 as the vision fades). The effect of the harmonic and dynamic disjunctions in this passage are very much like the cinematic trick of opening a crowd scene to reveal a fateful confrontation between the main characters. Indeed, the synesthetic quality of the passage is central to its poetic meaning and is a principal source of its vivid expressive power. The effect, and similar ones both in this work and in *Harold*, depend on the extent to which the cyclic element resists assimilation into the purely musical structure of the movement.

This technique is admirably suited to the programmatic effects Berlioz is pursuing, but it is not particularly relevant to the closely knit structural premises of sonata form. Indeed, the movements through which Berlioz scatters his cyclic effects generally have nothing to do with sonata forms at all. [13] The formal organization of these movements is of considerably less significance than the fact that they are without exception genre pieces that evoke a programmatic space—a ballroom, a mountain field, a path over which the pilgrims pass—in which these narrative-cyclic juxtapositions might conceivably occur.

The disjunction of formal and poetic processes is central to the rhetorical function of these cyclic gestures. In works that more clearly aspire to a position within the German symphonic tradition—in contrast to the tangential relation of Berlioz's music to that tradition—the integration of cyclic procedures within a sonata-form design is distinctly problematic. Schumann, for example, found the program of the *Symphonie fantastique* particularly unpalatable: "such signposts always have something unworthy and charlatanlike about them!"[14] Supported by neither an explicit program on the one hand nor a clearly traced processive structure on the other, Schumann's cyclic designs nonetheless tend to make particularly strong demands on the suggestive powers of vocal music. In the F♯-minor Piano Sonata, for example, the various restatements of material from the introduction over the course of the work are carefully designated *basso parlando* or, with wonderfully Schumannesque reticence, *Aria—senza passione, ma espressivo*. In his C-major Symphony, Op. 61, the complex intertwining of implicit and explicit cyclic designs and sonata-form procedures culminates in a "recapitulation" in the finale that is concerned almost exclusively with the opening phrase of the last song of Beethoven's *An die ferne Geliebte*. In his discussion of this extraordinary example of the "Finale Problem" that seems to have plagued every nineteenth-century composer, Carl Dahlhaus observed that

> Schumann's idea of joining the movements of the cycle to one another through citation and reminiscence is a "poetic" notion, that at the same time represents a compensation for formal weakness: the richness of associative relations replaces tectonic strength, which the work lacks.[15]

Here again, expressive coherence is less a function of an internally generated formal integrity than it is of the "poetic" meaning of the work—a meaning that is embedded in the explicit quotation of Beethoven's song. For any non-Philistine, this fragment would instantly bring the touchingly self-referential opening line of the song to mind—"Nimm sie hin denn, diese Lieder (die ich dir, Geliebte, sang)." This phrase obviously had a special meaning for Schumann; it is the "leiser Ton" that runs secretly through the first movement of his C-major Fantasie, Op. 17—emerging in an explicit quotation only in the last page of the movement, when the harmony finally settles to a tonic cadence.[16] (In the original, unpublished version of the Fantasie the quotation returns at the end of the last movement as well, closing off the entire work.) The phrase is also woven into the last movement of the F-major String Quartet, Op. 41, No. 2. In each instance, its meaning must be comprehended as a functional element in the design of the entire work; but in each case that meaning must be brought to the work by the listener: it is only accessible to the extent that the quotation is recognized as such—to the extent that it functions as an interpolation that remains unassimilated by the formal processes of the movement.

Dramatic expressivity that strains the limits of formal coherence seems to be the normal condition for the music of Berlioz or, to only a slightly lesser degree, Schumann; it is certainly not the emotional climate we expect to encounter in Mendelssohn's scores. But his most elaborate essay in both explicit and implicit cyclic organization, the A–minor String Quartet, Op. 13 (1827, published in 1830), approaches extremes of romantic expressivity not unlike those explored by these more conspicuously adventurous composers; indeed, much of the difficulty of this uncharacteristically difficult work arises from the friction between a curiously unsupple formal frame on the one hand and a cyclic design that is realized in overtly rhetorical—and explicitly poetic—terms, on the other. In addition, there is another remarkable aspect of this unusual work that directly shapes Mendelssohn's compositional strategies: an extraordinary relation, on almost a moment-to-moment basis, between Op. 13 and Beethoven's only A–minor Quartet, Op. 132 (1825, published in 1827)—a work that must rank as one of the most elaborately, and mysteriously, unified of his creations. Mendelssohn's Quartet is usually cited as evidence of brilliantly progressive tendencies inexplicably not pursued in later works. I would suggest, however, that the conflicting requirements of the fundamentally irreconcilable conceptions of cyclic form that animate Op. 13—the poetic, non-integrative effects of the romantic style on the one hand and Beethoven's powerfully integrated structures on the other—result in unavoidable structural problems that seriously flaw this strange work.

The similarity—often to the point of confusion—between the themes and formal gestures of Op. 13 and those of the Beethoven Quartet (and a number of other late works as well) has been noted in most studies of Mendelssohn's chamber works. In fact, Op. 13 is only one of a number of works from the late 1820s in which the influence of Beethoven is continually, and quite openly, in evidence. The E–major Piano Sonata, Op. 6, from 1826, for example, is a beautiful reminiscence of Beethoven's Op. 101 (with, as has been pointed out, touches of Op. 90 thrown in for good measure).[17] The B♭–major Sonata (1827)—which Mendelssohn did not publish—is a discouragingly uninspired parody of Beethoven's Op. 106, while Op. 13 is a bewildering collage of the late-period quartets, and the first movement of the E♭–major Quartet, Op. 12 (1829), contains a number of conspicuous references to Beethoven's Quartet, Op. 74—also, of course, in E♭ major.

The clarity of the references in these works can be understood, on the one hand, as a symptom of the brashness of youth—the last of the works in which explicit quotations are found, the E♭–major Quartet, was written when the composer was all of twenty. But they offer evidence of specific compositional problems as well. In particular, in Op. 13 Mendelssohn seems both to be trying to come to grips with the overwhelming stature of Beethoven—whose death in March of 1827 seems particularly significant in view of the probable composition of the Quartet between July and October of that year—and to be working out certain problems of large scale coherence that are central to the master's last works.[18] The relation of Op. 13 to those works is meant to be heard—in fact, some elements of Mendelssohn's design simply cannot be understood fully if that relation is not recognized. It will be useful, therefore, to begin with a close examination of certain aspects of the structural principles that shape the work on which Mendelssohn modeled his Quartet.

Dahlhaus demonstrated that the role of the primary motivic cell in Op. 132 can be most profitably explored when that cell is recognized as a "subthematic" complex consisting of two ascending or descending half steps separated by a variable interval.[19] The motive is "subthematic" in that it can be realized either in specific thematic configurations—as it is unfolded in the exploratory, almost pre-musical opening measures of the work or in the graceful, but obsessive, contrapuntal manipulations of the second movement—or in less immediately tangible ways—as in the main body of the first movement, where half-step relations permeate the texture without actually coalescing into themes, generating, for example, the eruption on the Neapolitan in mm. 18–19. At this subthematic level, the motive is no longer confined to realizations that reflect easily recognizable processes of thematic transformation. In fact, at this level, the functional role of the motivic cell is more clearly understood if it is abstracted even further—to a single half step. Over the course of the Quartet as a whole, the processive design focuses with increasing urgency on shifting inflectional relations between one central half-step pairing—F♮ and E, the flatted sixth and fifth scale degrees of the tonic, A minor.

The various themes of the movement do not overtly resemble one another—they are not spun out from a complex of interrelated figures engendered by this fundamental motivic unit; but each of the principal themes pivots around prominent half-step pairings, and the modulatory scheme of the exposition—moving from A minor through D minor to F major—is controlled by a chain of sensitive half-step inflectional hinges.

The persistent F♮s of the opening page of the Quartet eventually attract a stray B♭, which soon erupts in the fanfare on the Neapolitan, B♭ major, and then initiates a modulation toward F (mm. 30ff.), that carries with it, of course, the implication of a reversal of the inflectional relation between F and E. A nervous march in D minor, elaborated in canon, interrupts this modulation almost immediately (mm. 40ff.). Although the new tune vaguely recalls the general rise and fall of the opening Allegro theme, it bears no obvious relation to the fundamental motive. But the composite profile outlined by the canonic entries is defined by the two half-step pairs around which so much of the music has already been shaped: E-F (the first and lowest notes of the successive entries) and A-Bb (the second and highest notes of each). This strange interruption quickly stumbles on toward F major, and the arrival in that key is marked by the astonishing lyricism of the second theme (mm. 48ff.). Joseph Kerman has observed that the contrast provided by this new theme is both drastic and "magically" appropriate.[20] Part of the magic derives from the way this theme recalls and subsumes its troubled past.

The new theme emerges from the same intervallic space as that outlined by the second statement of the march theme—the fourth, F-Bb; the two thematic shapes even occupy the same registral space. But in the canon, that fourth staked out what was essentially a double chromatic upper neighbor to E and A (representing the dominant of D minor), an acutely sensitized inflectional relation prolonged within an intricate—and strangely destabilized—thematic articulation. In the F-major theme, F is stabilized as the (local) tonic to which E♮ resolves, the initial leap of the march is replaced by a gentle stepwise ascent in the anacrusis of the theme, and when the melody twice turns back on itself around Bb and A, it redefines once again the relation between these two pitches, absorbing their inflectional energy within a gesture of immeasurable lyric grace.

As a response to this subtly woven design, the recapitulation is surely the most unusual in Beethoven's output. The recapitulation retraces the general thematic outline of the exposition—with innumerable changes of detail—but it begins in E minor (m. 103), moves through A minor (mm. 151ff.), and leads into a restatement of the lyric second theme in C major (mm. 159ff.); it is only in the coda that all of the primary thematic material is restated in the tonic.

Indeed, recapitulation and coda might seem to be troublesomely inappropriate terms for the latter stages of this design, but the significance of these formal elements becomes clearer if the relation of motive and form is recognized.

In the recapitulation, each of the themes returns in a key that places its half-step pivot on E and F♯: the Neapolitan outburst in the E minor of the first group is, of course, F major (mm. 128-29); the upper edge of the canonic presentation of the march theme in A minor is E-F♯-E (mm. 151ff.); and the delicate transformation of that figure in the C major of the lyric theme hinges, of course, on F♯ and E (mm. 160ff.—note the elaborate echoes of this figure in the first violin). This unobtrusive, but persistent, circling back to the fundamental form of the motive pulls inevitably to the tonic, transforming this "thematic recapitulation" into a massive drive toward the tonic—a cadential thrust controlled by the interpenetration of unchanging thematic succession and motivic immutability.[21]

In the coda, when the closing theme returns in A major, it is yet another half-step hinge that pulls the movement into its grim A–minor conclusion. The continuation of the theme has, at each appearance, passed through a beautiful chromatic descent that seems to be leading into a closing cadence (mm. 53ff. and 163ff.); the cadence is left uncompleted, however, sliding on into more animated closing material. In this final statement, that line circles from g♮″ to f♯″ and then through e♯″ and back to f♯″ (mm. 227ff.). In the past, this gentle chromaticism has melted back into the local tonic. But E♯ is F♮, and all the tendentious play on F that has run through the movement resonates in this momentary chromatic glimmer; the past which reverberates in this last, most luminously consoling statement of the second theme is the inflectional tension that has driven the entire movement, channeled into this acutely ambiguous enharmonic confrontation. Burdened with this history, the E♯ in m. 228 must register as F♮—the flatted sixth of A minor—and must resolve back to E, and with that resolution, the circle of the movement is completed, and A major must collapse into A minor.

As in many of the late works, the second movement reexamines issues raised in the first, but the focus is less intense, the tone almost parodistic. The mysterious, groping half steps of the opening of the first movement reappear in the pointedly offhand accompanimental vamp that opens the second, and as Kerman, among others, has pointed out, the entire melodic substance of the main section of the movement consists of repetitions of a two-measure cell first presented in mm. 5–6[22]—a cell that turns out to be little more than two versions of the motivic half-step pairs played against one another.

In spite of its elegant refinement, there is an obsessive quality about the second movement that suggests less the normal procedures of thematic manipulation than a crystalization of the motive in this just-barely-melodic fragment, which is then displayed from every possible angle. The intense concentration of this investigation seems intended to exhaust the purely thematic potential of the motive, while the hypnotically repetitious symmetrical balance of the dance form in which it is realized seems to isolate these overtly thematic processes from the rest of the work.

If the second movement explores the possibilities of a thematic realization of the motivic cell with a singlemindedness that is at least slightly disconcerting, the third movement, the "Heiliger Dankgesang eines Genesenen an die Gottheit," explores fundamental tensions within that motivic material with an abstract expansiveness that is distinctly otherworldly.

Much has been written about Beethoven's exploration of the Lydian mode in this movement, but the larger functional significance of the acute tonal ambiguity this entails has not been directly addressed.[23] As every commentator has noted, the raised fourth of the Lydian mode—B♮ in place of B♭—skews the harmony of the chorale, making a normal V–I cadence to F impossible and creating a strong bias toward the dominant, C major; but it is less in this substitution itself than in the troubled inflectional relation between—once again—F♮ and E, the "tonic" and "leading tone," that the generative frictions inherent in this bias are concentrated. Throughout the course of the "Dankgesang," the background centrality of F major, in which E would resolve to F, is undermined by the pull toward C major (generated by the leading-tone quality of B♮ in this white-note Lydian/tonal scale), in which F resolves to E. In fact, the only functional non-triadic sonorities in the first thirty-seven measures of the movement are the repeated dominant sevenths of C major, which explicitly pull F down to E (mm. 7–8, 11, 13, 14, 19, 21–22, 23, 26, and 27). It should be clear from this pervasive insistence on F as a dissonance resolving to E that Beethoven is not simply submitting to textbook rules dictated by a capricious decision to employ the Lydian mode: the ambiguities inherent in the modal-tonal friction he has carefully nurtured allow him to weave a particularly subtle web of inflectional instability around F and E, the principal elements of the fundamental motivic cell of the work as a whole.

It is significant, in this respect, that the establishment of an ambiguous inflectional relation between F and E seems to have been an element of Beethoven's strategy from the first. Sieghard Brandenburg has shown that the early sketches for Op. 132 indicate that the slow movement was originally planned around a chorale-like theme in F major.[24] There is no hint of the intense ambiguities that characterize the final Lydian-tonal conflict in this earlier version of the movement, of course, but the melodic line circles continually around F and E, worrying the inflectional relation between them at almost every cadence. Strictly speaking, the final version of the movement simply intensifies the effect of this interplay.

Kerman has suggested that the establishment of D major for the two contrasting episodes identified as "Neue Kraft fühlend" can be explained as an extension of modal harmonic practice, according to which the pivotal chord of the modulation, A major, is available as a cadential goal in F–Lydian.[25] For Brandenburg, on the other hand, the decision to use D major fulfills the need for "harmonic diversity," introducing a key not previously heard in the cadential pattern of the chorale.[26] But it is important to note that the remarkable—and characteristically Beethovenian—disjunction between a highly equivocal F–Lydian and this gloriously normal D major hinges once again on the F–E half step. The end of each statement of the "Dankgesang" pushes hard toward C major, with a strong emphasis on an upper-voice motion in which F resolves to E (mm. 25–30, and later, 108–14); the measures leading into these cadences are saturated with F♮s, intensifying the drive toward E. But it is precisely the point of the modal-tonal confrontation in this movement that a close to C is as implausible as a close to F is impossible. When the first violin finally settles onto the acutely sensitized E (m. 30), Beethoven nonchalantly hangs an A-major chord from it. A major proves to be V of D major, and the tendentious ambiguity surrounding F♮ is simply wiped away by the unshakable stability of D major, with its third, F♯. This displacement will prove to be a distant foreshadowing of the turn to A major at the end of the finale, an event that will be considered below. Again, the sketches indicate that a confrontation between F♮ and F♯ was present in the earliest plans for this stage of the work: the end of the slow movement, turning, apparently, to F minor, closes abruptly into a recitative in F♯ minor, which in turn leads into what Brandenburg rightly describes as "a fairly lightweight Allegro in A major."[27]

At the end of the movement, the cadential pull toward C major exerted by the white-note Lydian scale seems irresistible, and the final pages hover around that key from m. 185 on. A stable close to C major is carefully avoided in the ensuing passage, but this only gives the eventual arrival—which sets off a cascade of F–E resolutions—a particularly serene stability (mm. 196–201). The pull of C major is so compelling, in fact, that when the harmony swings around to F major in m. 202, this registers as the cadential subdominant typical of a coda rather than as the reacquisition of the tonic. The sense of cadential affirmation (of C major!) is intensified by a new chain of F–E resolutions that leads into the luminous cadence to C major five measures from the end of the movement (m. 202, cello; m. 203, viola; m. 204, viola; m. 205, second violin; m. 206, first violin).

After all this, when the upper voice moves from e''' to f''' in mm. 208–9, it sounds at first as though Beethoven is embarking on a remarkably banal IV–V⁷–I cadence in C major—and the banality only underlines the clarity with which the F–E relation has been stabilized around E rather than F: the massive, almost motionless elaboration of C major in this closing section of the movement has erased any tendency of E to act as a leading tone to F. That the movement does, in fact, end on an ethereal F-major chord represents less a resolution—or even a stable arrival—than a final compression of the inflectional ambiguity surrounding these two pitches. This time the upper-voice F does not fall back to E—but we have not *really* heard E resolve to F. The movement simply ends, and these two pitches are left hovering in a functionally undefined juxtaposition to one another; they mark the point at which the tonal and modal implications of the movement collide, and the seemingly willful imposition of Lydian inflections within a shadowy F-major context proves to be a uniquely Beethovenian exploration of the constructive potential of his motivic material.

The precarious F major of the final cadence tips over with jarring abruptness into the perky A major of the fourth movement, the Alla Marcia. Once again, the shift hinges on a reversal of the F-E relation, with the final F of the "Dankgesang" resolving—in retrospect, and over a sharp registral break— back to E, the first note of the Alla Marcia tune. The totally inappropriate character of this "resolution" of the inflectional crisis, bursting in on the unearthly stillness of the "Dankgesang," undermines the stability of this garish A major from the outset, and the impassioned recitative that follows seems less an "ambush," as Kerman would have it,[28] than an inevitable—though nonetheless shocking—consequence of this latest manifestation of the almost schizophrenic contrast of tone that seems to rack every gesture of this work.

The recitative, too, hinges on a whirlwind of E-F reversals and reaches a jarring climax on a wrenching f''' in the first violin (mm. 39–40), recalling, as in a nightmare, the breathlessly poised f''' of the last measure of the "Dankgesang." But this time f''' is part of a shrill diminished seventh chord: it is unambiguously an appoggiatura to E, and it is forced to resolve into the dominant of A minor, ushering in the opening of the last movement.

Echoes of the fall from F to E permeate the texture of the finale. They are woven through the accompaniment of much of the main theme—beginning with the throbbing vamp in the opening measures of the movement—and the cadential extension of the theme that leads to the second group. The F-E pair even turns up within the E-minor second group in a fleeting Neapolitan shimmer, and the entire movement is racked by harsh chromatic excursions. Near the end of the movement, this seemingly inescapable half-step throb erupts in a frenzied hammering on f'''-e''' that leads into a final statement of the main theme (mm. 271ff.): Mason noted that this is the first time in the movement that the F is placed squarely on the downbeat, a detail that sharpens the pounding intensity of this climactic presentation of the central motive of the entire work.[29]

The sudden turn to A major at the cadence of this statement (m. 296) is distinctly uncanny, but its role as a reaction to—and resolution of—the accumulated tension of the entire work is unmistakable: like everything else, it hinges on the F-E half step. The cadence is hung from an e''' in the first violin that, in Kerman's words, "freezes" just short of a decisive cadence to A minor (mm. 293ff.—note the consistent registral control of the motive throughout the latter stages of the work).[30] This pivot into A major through an (extended) upper-voice motion from F to E carries a distant reverberation of the shift to D major in the "Dankgesang." Of course, A major is the tonic now, but here, as in the ethereal arabesques of the "Neue Kraft fühlend" music, the shift from F♮ to F♯ is central to the sense of inflectional clarification. The introduction of A major simply wipes away the inflectional instability of the half-step motive, absorbing E into the bright clarity of the tonic major and eliminating F♮ altogether, replacing it with the less tendency-laden major sixth, F♯.

The central importance of this alteration is reemphasized in the course of the extraordinary cadence to A major that makes up the body of the first half of the coda. Just as this cadence seems to be completing itself (mm. 336–50), f♮''' suddenly reappears in the first violin, and the ensuing play on f♮'''–e''' must be explicitly led back to f♯'''–e''' before the cadence can be accomplished (mm. 339–44). The inflectional friction embedded in the F–E relation, which has animated every gesture of the entire work, is finally exorcised within the diatonic clarity of the tonic major, assimilated as a cadential coloration that only reinforces the stability of its resolution. In the second half of the coda, the entire A–major celebration is repeated with numerous changes of detail. One of these, a jagged octave doubling of the cadential f'''–e''', *forte*, in mm. 388–90, briefly superimposes F and E before f''' is pulled up to f♯''' over the course of the *diminuendo* that follows; the motive, and the propulsive energy it embodied, simply dissolve, leaving no trace, in a last blurred echo before the final cadence.

It is because the motivic element in Op. 132 is subthematic that Beethoven can generate a sense of processive unity over the course of the astonishing range of contrasts that characterize this work. The multifarious realizations of the motive are not simply different melodic patterns drawn from a common source; they are reinterpretations of fundamental relations between the elements of the motive—centering with increasing urgency on the F–E pairing—that reflect and intensify one another both within each movement and across the entire course of the work. The almost pre-musical half steps deployed in the opening measures of the Quartet, the multitude of textural and structural references to the motive in the events of the first movement, the obsessive melodic realizations of the motive in the second movement, the precariously balanced F–E ambiguity played out in the "Heiliger Dankgesang," and the dramatically charged interplay between this mystic vision, the perky A major of the Alla Marcia, and the recitative that grows out of it—all of these can be refocused into the throbbing F–E figures that permeate the finale, reverberating in the f'''–e''' frenzy of the last restatement of the rondo theme and finally in the f'''–e''' twitches in the coda: every strand of the musical fabric is drawn along this thread into the work's fantastic resolution.

Given his sensitivity to the issues surrounding the large-scale coherence of a multi-movement work—that "from the very beginning and throughout the course of a work, one knows its secret"—it seems unquestionable that it was the sense of an almost palpable organic elaboration in Op. 132 that attracted Mendelssohn to Beethoven's Quartet.

As Example 69 shows, the relation between Op. 13 and Op. 132 is established early in the first movement of Mendelssohn's work. Indeed, the main theme of Op. 13 is simply an amalgam of two themes from the first movement of Op. 132. (Example 69b is the march-theme; for ease of comparison it is given in A minor, as it appears in both of the "recapitulations" in the second half of the movement.)

The E-F♮-E neighbor-note motion that is outlined by the successive entrances of the viola, second violin, and first violin in the opening measures of Mendelssohn's theme is generally not mentioned in discussions of the thematic organization of the Quartet: it will prove, however, to be the primary cyclic element of the entire work. That this figure explicitly recalls the F♮-E half step of Op. 132 is obvious, but the profound difference in the structural role of the motive in these two works requires some consideration.

All of the thematic material in Op. 13 is derived from a brief quotation of Mendelssohn's song, "Frage," Op. 9, No. 1 (see Example 70), embedded in the A-major Adagio at the beginning of the work (mm. 12-15). This relatively explicit reference to another work, and specifically to a vocal work, is in itself unusual, and points, on the one hand, to the possible influence of yet another of Beethoven's late works, the finale of the Quartet in F major, Op. 135, with its laconic mottos, and, on the other, to the explicitly poetic impulse that characterizes the works by Schumann considered earlier in this chapter (works that date from the 1830s and 1840s). The clear derivation of Mendelssohn's themes from his tiny motive—the repeated question, "Ist es wahr?" from the song (which traces a profile almost identical to Beethoven's "Muss es sein?" in Op. 135) argues for the former, and the composer himself revealed the poetic significance of the reference with totally uncharacteristic explicitness in a letter to his friend Lindblad:

> The song which I sent with the quartet is its theme. You will hear it—with its own notes—in the first and last movements, and in all four movements you will hear its emotions expressed. If at first it doesn't please you—which might happen, then play it again, and if you still find something "Minuetish," then think of your stiff and formal Felix with his cravat and valet. I think I express the song well, and it all sounds like music to me.[31]

The title page of the manuscript identifies the work as *"Quartetto . . . sopra il tema:"* and then gives the fragment of the song shown in Example 70. But the phrase from the song—"il tema"—is never quoted directly within

Example 69a.   Beethoven, Quartet in A minor, Op. 132, I, mm. 17–29.

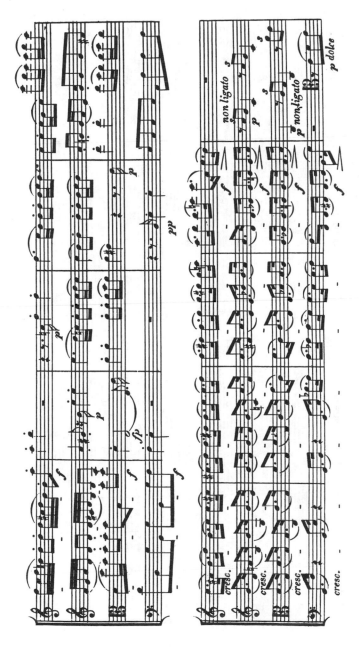

Example 69b.   Beethoven, Quartet in A minor, Op. 132, I, mm. 150–59.

Example 69c.   Mendelssohn, Quartet in A minor, Op. 13, I, mm. 19–32.

Example 70.   Mendelssohn, "Frage," Op. 9, No. 1, beginning.

the Quartet itself: after its first presentation in the introduction to the first movement it is not heard again until the postlude to the finale, where it appears as part of an extended quotation that encompasses over half of the entire song. Within the body of the quartet the intervallic constituents of this motivic cell—half step, whole step, and third—are abstracted from the melodic and harmonic context of the phrase and recombined in a kaleidoscopic succession of new shapes.

In the first movement each of the three principal themes is developed through the replication of a distinctive arrangement of the intervallic elements of the motive, much in the way a baroque theme is spun out from the pattern established by its initial figure (Example 71). The rhythmic homogeneity within each of these themes is also reminiscent of the baroque style, but the repetitious plainness of rhythm is probably modeled on Beethoven's late style, although Mendelssohn combines it with a square-cut rigidity of phrase structure rarely found in Beethoven.

The overarching design of the first movement—and of the work as a whole—is centered, then, on a dense network of explicit thematic relations spun out from permutations of the "Ist es wahr" motive, while Beethoven's motive functions at a deeper, "subthematic" level, controlling large-scale tonal processes that shape the entire course of the work. Mendelssohn's realization of the thematic design is ingenious; Op. 13 is the most thoroughgoing example of continual motivic transformation in his entire output, but it represents a translation of the fundamental structural principles of the model on which it is based, and the consequences of this translation are far-reaching.

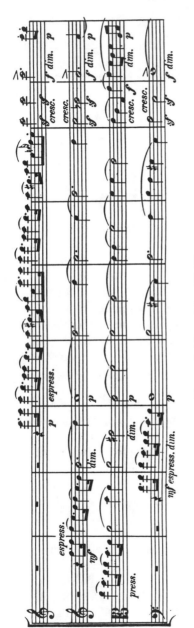

Example 71a.   Mm. 24-32.

Example 71b.   Mm. 56-63.

Example 71c.   Mm. 71-84.

Example 71.   Mendelssohn, Quartet in A minor, Op. 13, I.

This distinction is important because themes tend, by their nature, to register as relatively self-sufficient entities—it is crucial to the individuality that defines a theme that it form an internally coherent articulative unit. Locally, this means that the generative impulse of the fundamental motive tends to be more or less fully realized within the unfolding of each particular theme. By embedding his motivic process in a network of explicitly thematic realizations, Mendelssohn drains the larger structural potential Beethoven exploited over the course of Op. 132 from the inflectional energy of his half-step pair. In the first and second themes of the first movement of Op. 13, for example, the ♭6–5 figure simply provides an extended upbeat impetus that sets the melodic line in motion; the generative power of the motive is expended within the unfolding of that line—it does not spill over beyond the boundaries of the theme itself. Deprived of this larger structural significance, the persistent reappearance of the motive, each time initiating a new, but quickly familiar, process of thematic generation, seems merely repetitious and fitful.

The structural correlate of this thematic process is the carefully rounded designs that shape every level of structure in Op. 13. These stand in sharp contrast to the disturbingly unbalanced forms Beethoven explored in Op. 132, and they point to one of the most serious problems Mendelssohn faced in attempting to retrace his predecessor's hazardous path. The deployment of themes in Mendelssohn's first movement articulates a large-scale process that illuminates the nature of the problem. As the exposition progresses from theme to theme, the upper-voice line circles more and more narrowly around the (local) tonic pitch, a tightening of focus that culminates in the cadential theme, which is devoted almost exclusively to a series of descents from the third to the tonic (Example 71c). In itself, this formal organization is persuasive—and characteristically Mendelssohnian in its logical clarity—but it seems too patly controlled—too explicitly comprehensible—for the expressive purport of the music; much of the power of Beethoven's design, after all, lies precisely in the mystical incoherence of the surface disjunctions through which he realizes his underlying design. The effect of Mendelssohn's neatly delimited design, unfortunately, is that of a tempest raging in a finely wrought teacup—an example of the emotional primness that led Tovey to complain in despair that Mendelssohn "could not distinguish [tragedy] from the agonies of a lost purse or missed railway-train."[32]

More important for the structural organization of the Quartet as a whole, the thematic process generated in the first movement is pointedly completed within the course of the movement—the thematic sequence of the exposition is duly recapitulated in the tonic, and the cadential design embedded within the thematic succession of first theme—second theme—closing theme is channeled into a fully stabilized close to the tonic. This would seem to leave very little for the coda to do, but, unfortunately, the coda—the astonishing return to the tonic at the end of the first movement of Op. 132—is one of the most memorable events in the structure of Mendelssohn's model. Mendelssohn duly produces a coda that mimics this model with delightful enthusiasm and dexterity, but the gestures are empty, reaffirming a cadential stability that has already been established with almost too much clarity.

And when the last notes of Beethoven's coda are pounded out, the almost schizophrenic expressive discontinuities that rack the movement have barely been framed in coherent terms—certainly nothing has been resolved.[33] This expressive conflict is, of course, one of the fundamental generating principles of the work as a whole, played out repeatedly, and at every level of structure, within movements and between them; it is the disconcerting refusal of the first movement to subsume its contrasts that generates the continual exploration of these issues over the course of this uncanny work. In contrast, Mendelssohn's coda only confirms that at the highest level of structure, just as at the level of motive, theme, texture, and tonal process, no issues remain unresolved—nothing spills over past the emphatically punctual cadence that closes off the first movement.

This, then, is the fundamental difference between Beethoven's exploitation of a subthematic motive and Mendelssohn's ingenious network of thematic transformation. Mendelssohn's thematic design simply cannot yield the fundamental tensions that engender a processive, multi-movement structure like that of Op. 132. The consequences of this difference are particularly clear in the slow movement of Op. 13, which, like the slow movement of Op. 132, forms the hub of the larger design of the work.

The point of the "Heiliger Dankgesang" is that the friction between modal and tonal tendencies makes it impossible for the F–E motive to be assimilated into a coherent thematic line: the power of Beethoven's design lies precisely in an unrelenting focus on that impossibility, and it is the continual reverberation of this inflectional crisis that unifies the last three movements of the Quartet so persuasively. This almost anti-thematic realization of the motive obviously presents a problem for Mendelssohn's modeling process, which is based primarily on thematic similarities. His response offers an instructive illustration of his overall strategy.

The second movement of Op. 13, Adagio non lento, is centered, like the "Dankgesang," around F. But Mendelssohn's F major is untroubled by any of the ambiguities of inflection that racked the tonal-modal confrontation of Beethoven's remarkable vision. In fact, the overall design of the movement—two statements of a lyric theme framing an intensely chromatic fugue—suggests a completely different model, the Allegretto ma non troppo of Beethoven's F–minor Quartet, Op. 95. Once again, the reference is clearly meant to be heard—the fugal subjects of the two movements are similar to the point of almost total confusion. Indeed, the issue of thematic generation would seem to have been the decisive factor in this shift of allegiance from one model to another. While the "Dankgesang" offers no striking thematic presentations of the half-step neighbor-note figure that forms the principal point of reference between the first movements of Op. 13 and Op. 132, the fugal theme in Op. 95 is organized around a chain of descending thirds with chromatic ornamentation that can be recreated effortlessly from the motivic particles of the "Ist es wahr" fragment (Example 72). As Example 73 shows, Mendelssohn even managed to weave a reference to the "Neue Kraft fühlend" music from Op. 132 into this thematic web.

Once again, though, Mendelssohn seems to have mastered only the surface gestures of his model while the deeper structural issues eluded him. The D major of Beethoven's lyric opening theme is racked by chromatic inflections that repeatedly pull toward the minor mode (Example 74). The constant wavering from D major to D minor and back again over the course of this gentle melody places an intense expressive emphasis on the relation between F♯ and F♮ (and secondarily on B♭). Of course, F♯ and F♮ already have a history in this work. In the first movement, it was the juxtaposition of the Neapolitan and tonic—F and G♭—that set the grim tone of this *Quartetto serioso*, and the play on this half-step pairing runs through every level of the work in much the same way the F–E pair winds through Op. 132.

In the fugue, the expressive ambiguity surrounding these pitches is exploited in a gesture of inexorable despair. The opening of the subject winds repeatedly around the flatted sixth degree of D, B♭. The answer introduces a momentary glimpse of the major third, F♯, at the corresponding point (Example 75, mm. 37 and 40), but the strict melodic correspondences inherent in fugue immediately force this back to the minor third, F♮ (m. 41).

The emotional power of the fugue derives, at least in part, then, from an intensification of the friction between F♯ and F♮ established in the first part of the movement—an intensification that is an inescapable consequence of the relation between subject and answer inherent in the structure of fugue itself: form and content are, in a very real sense, the same thing.

In contrast, each of the two elements of Mendelssohn's design—the lyric theme in F major and the chromatic fugue in D minor—are closely woven into the thematic web of the Quartet, but they retain nothing of the structural significance, either within the movement or on a larger scale, that animate his model: unlike either the "Heiliger Dankgesang" or the opening section of the slow movement of Op. 95, the F major of Mendelssohn's lyric material is free of inflectional ambiguities, while the fugue—again, in contrast to Op.

95—exhibits neither thematic nor harmonic ties to that lyric material; it is simply the fugue that follows the lyric opening tune—"just like the Beethoven." Mendelssohn has recreated the gestures of Op. 95 with awesome skill, but the confrontation between lyricism and fugue has been drained of both the structural and emotional significance it had in his model. And while the virtuosity with which he juggles his collection of thematic references in this movement is astonishing, the conflicting influences of his various models undercut the expressive power of the resulting design even further.

Near the end of the Allegretto in Op. 95, the half step, bb''-a'', (first violin—mm. 149-54) is coaxed out of the chromatic thicket at the head of the fugue theme and made to flow into the serene cadences of the coda. These cadences place a strong emphasis on the tonic major—with its F♯—but this is a D major that is still strongly colored by B♭, hinting at D minor and preparing the final F♯-F♮ confrontation in the transition to the next movement. The apparent cadential stability of the first part of the coda actually serves to undermine the closural process of the movement, intensifying the push from F♯ to F♮, in which the close to F♮ registers, paradoxically, as a resolution—a last fulfillment of this difficult half-step relation. (It is only in the whirlwind coda of the finale that F♯ is assimilated as a cadential element—in F major—when the fall from F♯ to F♮ is reversed as part of a giddy ascent beginning with a move from F♮ through F♯ to G in mm. 132-33ff.).

Mendelssohn, too, writes a beautiful coda for his slow movement—an expansion of the final cadence of the F-major tune that gathers the opening B♭-A half step of this fugal subject into the gentle arabesques that wind through these closing measures. But as Example 76 indicates, Mendelssohn's coda established a fully stabilized tonic cadence—it nurtures no substrata of inflectional conflict.

On the other hand, the last two measures of the movement—the conclusion of his coda—are an almost exact counterfeit of the mysterious final cadence of the "Heiliger Dankgesang"—they lack only mystery. Mendelssohn's ethereal F-major triad is the afterglow of the stabilization of the tonic in the closing portion of the movement; it embodies none of the inflectional ambiguity that toppled Beethoven's visionary cadence onto the jauntily irrelevant Alla Marcia.

Mendelssohn's careful rounding of the formal design is not accidental, of course. On the one hand, it is a magnified reflection, at the structural level, of the closed structure of the themes that are the principal generative agents of the form. On the other hand, it seems to be a necessary condition of cyclic processes in the romantic style that the individual movements be fully rounded and self-contained. In the *Symphonie fantastique*, for example, each

Example 72a.   Mendelssohn, Quartet in A minor, Op. 13, II, mm. 13–30.

Example 72b. Beethoven, Quartet in F minor, Op. 95, II, mm. 30–47.

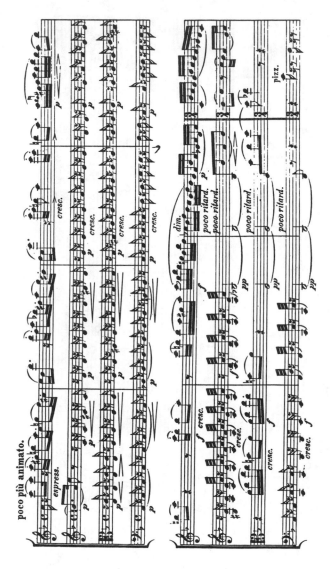

Example 73a.   Mendelssohn, Quartet in A minor, Op. 13, II, mm. 46–53.

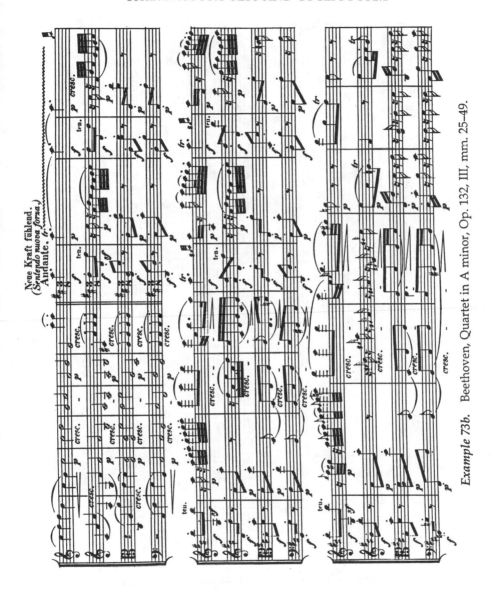

Example 73b. Beethoven, Quartet in A minor, Op. 132, III, mm. 25–49.

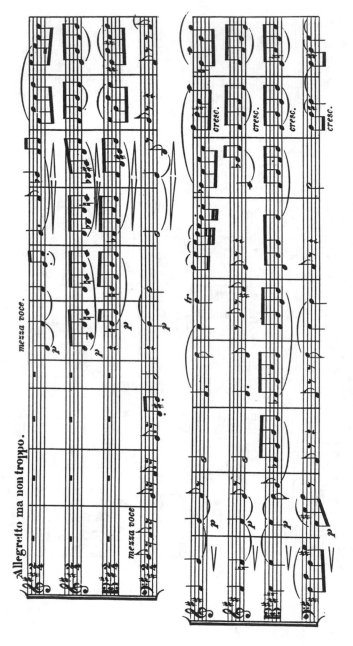

Example 74. Beethoven, Quartet in F minor, Op. 95, II, mm. 1–19.

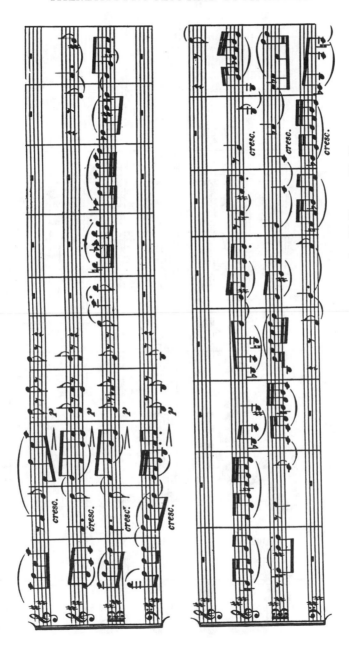

Example 75. Beethoven, Quartet in F minor, Op. 95, II, mm. 30–47.

Example 76. Mendelssohn, Quartet in A minor, Op. 13, II, mm. 92–125.

vignette is complete within itself, and it is the unassimilable quality of the genre pieces themselves that controls the structure of the work: the artist flees from the tumult of the ballroom to the isolated beauty of the open fields, but wherever he finds himself, the beloved image haunts him. The slow movement of Op. 13 is, in a peculiar sense, a genre piece: by draining the confrontation of lyricism and fugue in Op. 95 of its structural significance, Mendelssohn has created a character-piece in which the coherence of the movement does not derive from the unfolding of an internal logic, but from the evocation of a distinctive and recognizable network of conventions and connotations borrowed from a readily identifiable external source. His procedure is unusual primarily in that the genre evoked does not suggest a "programmatic space"—the ballroom or the shepherd's lonely fields that support the narrative design of the *Symphonie fantastique*, for example. Instead, Mendelssohn evokes chamber music itself; and perhaps even more pointedly than in the first movement of Op. 13, chamber music of the most esoteric—"serioso"—variety. This procedure is expressively problematic, since the peculiar nature of the genre-style evocation in this character piece does not, in itself, establish—or contribute to—an overarching programmatic narrative into which this self-contained structure can be assimilated. As a result, neither the poetic nor processive issues Mendelssohn seems to be dealing with generate problems that flow over the double bar into the movements that follow.

The third movement of Op. 13 is a lyric Intermezzo in A minor with a central episode in A major in a faster tempo. The main theme is spun out from yet another transformation of the E-F♮-E motive, and, once again, the final section of the movement carefully draws the motive into an elaborately rounded cadential design, with a strong emphasis on the minor subdominant.

The succession of closed forms in the first three movements of the Quartet makes the sudden outbreak of recitative at the beginning of the finale particularly difficult to understand—until, of course, it is recognized as a reference to the corresponding place in Op. 132. But in Beethoven's design the recitative presented a particularly intense play on the F-E relation, reflecting the crisis engendered by the juxtaposition of the "Heiliger Dankgesang" and the Alla Marcia and preparing the climactic half-step conflicts that course through the finale. Mendelssohn's recitative materializes out of thin air, and all that comes of it is the half-step upbeat figure of the main theme of the finale (Example 77); as in the first movement, the generative impulse of the motive is absorbed into the initial downbeat of the theme—no further implications are posited.

It is instructive to compare this with Beethoven's treatment of the F-E motive at the corresponding point in his design. In the finale of Op. 132, the half step is carefully segregated from the theme itself: in fact, the sketches indicate that the F–E "curtain" preceding the theme was a late addition, appearing only when the theme had been transferred from the sketches for the finale of the D–minor Symphony to those for the Quartet.[34] It is because the half-step figure is isolated from the melodic line that the tension of the motive is not simply absorbed into the opening of the theme—it pulses, unresolved, through the entire movement. This is not a trivial distinction. An attempt to whip Mendelssohn's upbeat figure into the frenzy Beethoven achieves at the end of his finale, for example, would be absurd; the implications of Mendelssohn's figure are simply too closely circumscribed to support this kind of expressive (and structural) transformation.

One impressive aspect of Mendelssohn's introductory gambit should be noted, however. Over the course of the last three movements, a shadowy, but continually intensifying emphasis on D minor has emerged: the fugue of the second movement is centered in D minor; the coda of the third movement leans heavily to the minor subdominant, again D minor; and the impassioned recitative that opens the fourth movement begins in D minor. In each of these instances, the turn to D minor is marked by a particularly striking reference to the half-step neighbor-note figure. We shall encounter traces of this intertwining of motivic and harmonic references through the course of the finale—its consequences will prove to be the most persuasive element in Mendelssohn's cyclic design.

The gathering of thematic threads in the finale is handled with impressive skill. The half-step neighbor motion is established as a primary thematic gesture from the outset, of course; but in addition, the main theme is almost identical in outline and intervallic content with the main theme of the first movement, and as Example 78 shows, the transitional material between the first and second groups is lifted almost verbatim from the corresponding passage in the first movement.

The interesting thing is that this does not readily register as a direct quotation: the thematic web of the Quartet is so finely woven that this one episode does not stand out from the multitude of more covertly deployed references—the passage simply sounds vaguely familiar. The remaining themes of the movement are built from chains of thirds and naturally recall similar gestures from the first movement. The technique of thematic generation is, once again, handled with complete mastery, but this endless succession of related melodies seems static—primarily, I would suggest, because it embodies no sense of dramatic structural progression. The themes of the finale differ only in details from those earlier tunes, neither intensifying nor resolving the bustling agitation that was their primary characteristic. As a result, the continual reworking of the same profiles and turns of phrase

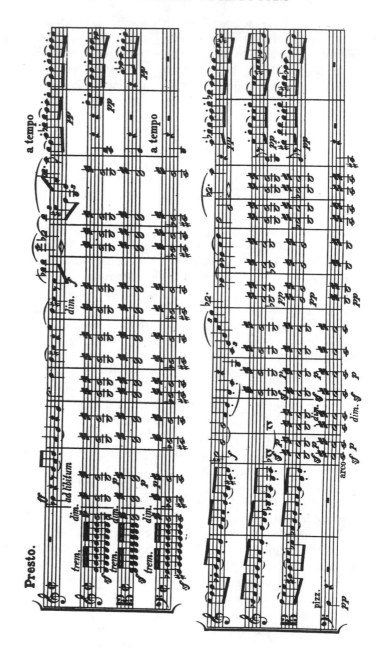

Example 77. Mendelssohn, Quartet in A minor, Op. 13, IV, mm. 1–38.

Example 78a.   I, mm. 42–55.

Example 78b.   IV, mm. 64–79.

Example 78.   Mendelssohn, Quartet in A minor, Op. 13.

comes to sound repetitious rather than processive, and begins to be at least slightly monotonous. This seems, however, almost unavoidable, given Mendelssohn's conception of the work as being "*sopra il thema*": the quartet is really a set of variations—essentially a paratactic succession rather than a dramatic progression.

The second group in Mendelssohn's finale is divided into two parts by a statement of the recitative theme in fugato that reinforces the latent similarity between this material and the fugue theme from the second movement (mm. 107-15). At the end of the exposition, after the movement suddenly comes to a dead halt, the fugue theme itself reappears, moving quickly from E minor to its native D minor. The similarity between the fugal material and the themes of the finale has already been established, of course, but the sharp articulative break—the shift from the rushing *fortissimo* octaves of the final cadence of the exposition to the faceless, strictly graduated unfolding of the fugue theme, *piano*, in a single voice—sets the return into particularly high relief: it is meant to be heard as an intrusion that disrupts the internally generated structure of the finale.

The fugue is confined to the upper three voices; the cello does not take part in the exposition, but eventually it begins insisting, very quietly, on the upbeat figure of the main theme of the finale (mm. 177ff.). The effect is reminiscent of the E-major Presto in Beethoven's C♯-minor Quartet, Op. 131, where the cello repeatedly forces the other instruments back to the main theme. As in that work, the cello has its way in Op. 13—the fugal episode is abruptly replaced by a more "normal" development that focuses primarily on the main theme of the finale. There is a rather half-hearted attempt to combine this with the fugue theme (mm. 190-98), but the project involves so many alterations to the intervallic and rhythmic structure of the fugue that this *reunion des deux themes* quickly dies out—from sheer irrelevance, it would seem.

It is particularly striking that Mendelssohn chooses material from the slow movement to articulate his cyclic design: it was in the slow movement of Op. 132 (the movement he was not able to mimic) that the central processive issue of the latter stages of that work—the inflectional crisis surrounding F and E—was most impressively developed. But Mendelssohn's procedure seems curiously stiff—curious in light of the remarkable dexterity in dealing with cyclic gestures he had already achieved in the finale of the Octet, and would recapture in the "Italian" Symphony (or in the decidedly lightweight G-minor Piano Concerto, Op. 25, for that matter). This can be traced, in part, to the material itself: fugue naturally sets its own well-regulated pace, and its identity as fugue requires a distinctive organization of textures, but there is a more fundamental problem at the heart of Mendelssohn's design.

On the one hand, the cyclic return embodies no clearly defined programmatic function. It is neither a recollection that acquires meaning from its new surroundings—"a memory which we know for a fact but can no longer understand," as Tovey called the return in the Beethoven Fifth[35]—nor a transformation of earlier material that reflects either an implied, "poetic," meaning, like the vigorous new version of the theme from the slow movement that soars into the second group in the finale of Schumann's Second Symphony, or an explicit narrative significance, like the various reincarnations of the *idée fixe* in the *Symphonie fantastique*. The anxious expressivity of Mendelssohn's fugue has already been persuasively resolved within the lyric final close of the second movement—after the seraphic F-major cadence at the end of that movement the problems of the fugue are over and done with; and, indeed, nothing new emerges from its reappearance within the last movement, which, as a result, seems less a reexamination of vital expressive issues than a display of contrapuntal combinations that somehow were missed the first time around. On the other hand, the return does not seem to play any particular functional role within the structure of the finale itself. In the end, it neither breaks open the formal processes of the finale, as happens in the Octet and the "Italian" Symphony, nor does it reinforce those processes by widening their scope, as in the Beethoven Fifth: after the fugue has been discussed for a while, it just stops being there, and the "real" development section of the movement, which is a relatively unexceptional sonata-form finale, continues. Like the recitative at the beginning of the finale, the cyclic return is extraneous to the movement, and, as a result, both of these gestures seem too calculated—they depict rather than express emotion. Neither processive nor programmatic ends are served by this elaborate stage machinery, and it is this breakdown of both structural and expressive coherence that is reflected in the way the movement grinds to a halt in order to accommodate them.

It seems remarkable, then, that Mendelssohn manages—quite persuasively—to pull many of the threads of his design together in the final page of the Quartet.

After the initial disruption by the fugue theme, the development continues along essentially regular lines, and leads into a shortened, but essentially regular, recapitulation. This time, however, the *fortissimo* cadential rush at the end of the second group leads to a hushed A-major chord, marked by the quivering accompanimental figures of the opening recitative. But now it is the fugue theme that soars above them, and the effect is electrifying. This might be attributed to the explicit revelation of the relation between the recitative and the fugue theme, but that is hardly news anymore. I would suggest that it is the interaction of more fundamental relations that invests this moment with its special power.

On the one hand, placing the fugue theme and the accompanimental texture of the recitative within the context of a final cadential move to V of iv finally brings the theme into the structural organization of the movement—these troublingly unassimilable gestures become a special articulative texture that marks this particularly significant formal event; in turn, this new functional identity is reflected in a transformation of the material itself. The theme is no longer merely a citation: the fugue theme is stripped of its fugal texture, and it is reharmonized to intensify the cadential drive it articulates. At the same time, the turn to V of iv brings the D-minor bias that has colored so many of the references to the half-step motive in the last three movements of the Quartet into the final cadential gesture of the work. There is even a momentary, consoling hint of the major subdominant, D major; the effect is particularly poignant, given the overwhelming minor-mode orientation of the entire work, and it is through this fleeting D major that Mendelssohn closes the circle of his design.

The coda gradually expires to almost total stillness as fragments of other themes drift by, leading to another statement of the fugue theme, again in D minor. This subsides into a passage explicitly identified as recitative that places a strong emphasis on F♮ as the ♭6th degree of A minor and seems to lead toward a final cadence in that key (Example 79). But in place of a final A-minor tonic, the music turns to A major—marked by the return of the introduction from the first movement, transformed, now, into a retrospective epilogue. The delicate poignancy of the return hinges on the way the opening measures of the introduction lean heavily toward D major—the *major* subdominant (Example 80).

All of the D-minor emphasis that has colored every movement of the Quartet and all the grating E-F♮-E half-step figures that define A minor throughout the work reverberate in this moment and are resolved by the strength of the connection between the A-major and D-major triads encapsulated in this tiny cadential cell from the opening measure of the work: "from the beginning and throughout the course of a work, one knows its secret." What is most remarkable about this passage is that A major emerges so gradually—it is itself the pivot on which the modulation hinges, stabilized by the shift from the D minor that has colored all four movements to the D major that is now revealed to have been at the center of the work's "secret."

This return to the beginning is the most original element in the design of Op. 13. The sense of wholeness it creates would seem to be clear—in many ways clearer than the powerful, but elusive design of his model: the entire work is quite literally encircled by the A-major frame. The device apparently

fascinated Mendelssohn: in a letter to his friend, Karl Klingemann, concerning details of a projected opera on Kotzebue's *Pervonte*, he refers to a symmetrical framing device they had devised for the work as fulfilling "our
beloved idea of the snake biting its own tail."[36]

But the function of a framing device is considerably less straightforward
than it might appear, and from the first, Mendelssohn was frustrated by the
almost universal inability of the work's first hearers to recognize the unity he
felt was central to the design. In the letter to his friend Adolf Lindblad cited
earlier, he complains that

> many people have already heard it, but has it ever occurred to any of them (my
> sister excepted, along with Rietz and also Marx) to see a whole in it? One
> praises the Intermezzo, another this, another that. Pfui to all of them![37]

Once again, a comparison with Beethoven's procedures will help to clarify the problem Mendelssohn faced. Over the course of Op. 132, the inflectional crisis surrounding F and E becomes increasingly urgent; in the first
two movements, manifestations of that crisis control both structural and surface elements, and in the second half of the work the tensions generated between these pitches spill over from one movement into the next, propelling
the work toward the eruption at the end of the finale and into the A major of
the coda. The self-sufficient wholeness of the parts is explicitly subordinated
to the processes that flow over the entire course of the work, and it is the
interpenetration of local and overarching designs—made possible by an
avoidance of realizations of the motive solely in terms of thematic processes—that allows the coda of the finale to function as a resolution for the
entire work.

The quantity of connective tissue—thematic recollections, outbursts of
recitative, and expressively gradual dying falls—Mendelssohn felt compelled to supply in the passage leading into the epilogue in Op. 13 is in itself
evidence of the lack of a clearly defined structural relation between the
events of the finale—and of the preceding movements—and the magical
pivot to A major at the end of the work. In contrast to Op. 132, the individual
movements in Op. 13, in spite of—in fact, because of—the multitude of
motivic references laced through them, remain tightly self-contained; the
half-step motives that cover the surface of the work are firmly embedded
within the various themes to which they are attached, and the turns to D minor that color the middle movements are carefully encased in elaborate structural cadences that emphatically close off each movement. No generative
tensions spill over from movement to movement, and no larger processive
flow is established.

Example 79.   Mendelssohn, Quartet in A minor, Op. 13, IV, mm. 332–72.

Example 80.   Mendelssohn, Quartet in A minor, Op. 13, IV, mm. 373–97.

The frame actually reinforces this disjunction, since, if it is to be recognized as a frame, it must stand apart from the thing it frames. As Barbara Herrnstein Smith points out, the frame "achieves its closural effect by separating itself from the . . . structure . . . and making a generalized or in some way stable comment on it from 'outside'."[38] The significance of a frame derives from the fact that it is segregated from the processes of the work: the virtuoso effect of painting the frame into a picture, for example, depends precisely on the way this blurs the crucial division between work and frame.

As a result, the turn to A major at the end of Op. 13 simply cannot function as a resolution in the way the superficially corresponding turn in Op. 132 did. The events referred to in Mendelssohn's coda are over, completed within their own carefully closed contexts. The epilogue has a gentle—and wonderfully romantic—retrospective quality, but this, too, is a symptom of the essentially paratactic structure of the entire work: as Smith has observed, a frame is "most often found as a special closural device when the structure of the work does not itself adequately determine a conclusion."[39] The frame imposes—rather than reflects—unity.

Perhaps this is not in itself a failure in the organization of the work. The explicit avoidance of structural integration is, I have suggested, a fundamental element of "poetic" cyclic form, while the framing device—the notion of a "story within a story"—is so obviously literary in nature that the impression of a narrative design lurking behind work is simply unavoidable[40]—and, of course, the use of the "Ist es wahr?" motive as both motto and frame almost necessitates an interpretation of the work in terms of the song from which it is fashioned: "you will hear it [the song]—with its own notes—in the first and last movements, and in all four movements you will hear its emotion expressed." However, Mendelssohn treats the programmatic element with a reticence that is certainly characteristic, but which renders any clear sense of a narrative design hopelessly obscure. Except for those within his immediate circle, the song would not have the associative power of, say, the Beethoven quotation in Schumann's C-major Symphony; without reading the program notes, it would be possible to remain completely unaware of this explicitly poetic and expressive aspect of the work. In addition, the notion of embedding the expressive core of the Quartet in a fugue—and a fugue that is most notable for the virtuosity with which it mimics another fugue—burdens the emotional content of the work to the point where it is difficult to tell what sort of response might be appropriate: form and content, rather than merging, as they do so impressively in the slow movement of Op. 95, undermine one another.

I would suggest that when Mendelssohn's seemingly unappreciative listeners singled out individual movements for praise, they were simply responding to the paratactic organization of the work—to a dissociation of elements that was reinforced rather than assimilated by the curious mix of cyclic gestures of the work. The apparent failure of this ambitious and elaborate project seems to have troubled the composer for a remarkably long time. Five years after its composition he was roused to a totally uncharacteristic outburst when his father expressed bewilderment over the meaning of the Quartet's design:

> You seem to mock me about my A-minor Quartet, when you say that you have had to rack your brain trying to figure out what the composer was thinking about in some works, and it turned out that he hadn't been thinking about anything at all. I must defend the work, since it is very dear to me; its effect depends too much on the performance, though.[41]

Mendelssohn had appealed to problems of performance as a barrier to understanding this work in his letter to Lindblad as well, offering relatively detailed interpretive instructions, but he may have come to realize that the fundamental problem was structural rather than expressive; in his next chamber work, the Quartet in Eb major, Op. 12, (1829) he addressed the issue of unifying a multi-movement work in a remarkable and completely original way. (Although this work was written two years after Op. 13, it was published one year earlier, accounting for the reversed numbering.)

The relation between Op. 12 and Beethoven's Eb-major Quartet, Op. 74, was mentioned earlier in this chapter. The opening measures of the introductory Adagio non troppo of Op. 12 juxtapose the two principal thematic gestures of Beethoven's Quartet—the inversion of the initial leap hardly disguises the quotation (Example 81). This reference, and another at the end of the recapitulation, do not, however, reflect stages of a thoroughgoing process of modeling like that in the relation between Op. 13 and Op. 132. For the most part, the themes of the two works are related only in their lyricism, and the organization of Mendelssohn's Quartet owes relatively little to the influence of Beethoven's.

The cyclic design in Op. 12 hinges on a subtle ambiguity surrounding the relation between the tonic, Eb major, and the submediant, C minor, first touched upon in the opening measures of the main theme (Example 82). Since this has important consequences for the organization of every aspect of the work, it will be useful to trace the various manifestations of this relation in some detail.

As Example 82 shows, although the dominant seventh of Eb at the end of the introduction seems clear enough, it is perched on an F in the bass rather than Bb, softening the cadential drive toward the tonic slightly. The melodic line of the main theme, beginning in the next measure, also appears to be

Example 81a. Beethoven, Quartet in Eb major, Op. 74, I, mm. 1–17.

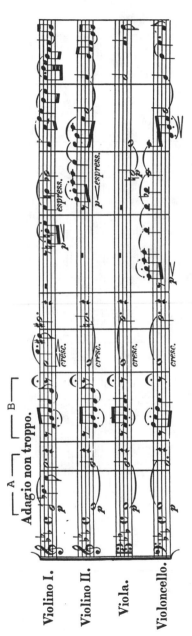

Example 81b. Mendelssohn, Quartet in Eb major, Op. 12, I, mm. 1–9.

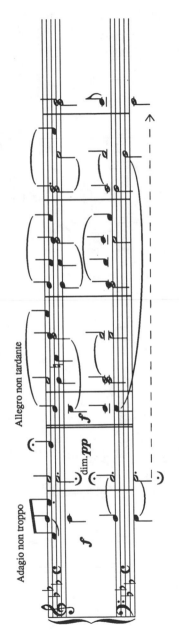

Example 82. Mendelssohn, Quartet in Eb major, Op. 12, I, mm. 17–21.

Example 83a.   Mm. 94–115.

Example 83b.   Mm. 18–30.

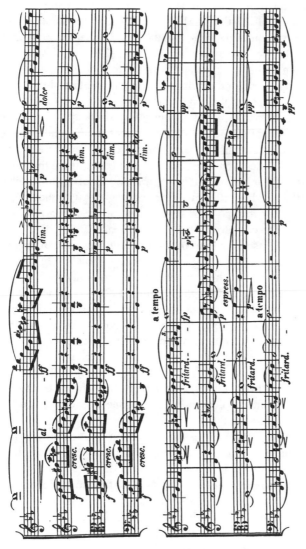

Example 83c.   Mm. 51–72.

Example 83.   Mendelssohn, Quartet in Eb major, Op. 12, I.

firmly rooted in the tonic, but its harmonic support has gone quietly awry. Continuing from the F in m. 17, the bass line moves to g—in an inner voice— under the initial bb' upbeat of the tune, and the chord under the eb'' on the downbeat of m. 18 is a root-position C-minor triad. The bass-line motion over the join between the introduction and the Allegro non tardante suggests a iv–V–i progression in C minor that reinforces this submediant turn by gently playing against the sense of the progression as V–I–vi in Eb major; this latter progression is, of course, itself an unusually fluid opening gambit. There is a friction between the bass line as implied root-motion and the chord grammar of the passage that blurs the harmonic sense in these first moments of the theme, giving a delicate emphasis to the submediant tinge that colors its opening measures. (This lyric excursion is carefully set off by the registral shift in the cello—the bass line returns to the lowest register with the Eb in m. 21 that supports the first root-position tonic chord of the Allegro, linking back to the F of m. 17 to complete, finally, the cadence to the tonic.)

The development begins with a return of the opening measures of the main theme in the tonic (m. 94). As at the corresponding point in Op. 74, this sounds at first like a repeat of the exposition, but it quickly leads to new things. The consequent phrase of the theme (mm. 102ff.) is drawn into the submediant; the harmony circles around to C, which is taken as a dominant, leading abruptly to a new theme in F minor—of course, as Example 83 shows, the "new" theme is actually a transformation of elements of the second theme, which in turn were derived from the rhythm and general contour of the main theme.

The new theme—eventually joined by other material—forms the basis of a large-scale sequential linear progression that pushes steadily toward the dominant, Bb major (Example 84).

The penultimate step of this progression, centering on A minor, a tritone from the tonic key, is enormously expanded, leading to an agitated climax that seems to press toward the decisive move to the dominant and, presumably, a retransition leading into the recapitulation. At the crucial join from A minor through F major to Bb major, however, the harmony is unexpectedly shifted from F7 to a dominant seventh on D (mm. 150–51).

This derailing of the dominant preparation reflects a problem inherent in approaching the recapitulation in this work. Although the effect is less drastic than the opening of Haydn's Op. 33, No. 1, the main theme of Op. 12 almost begins "in the wrong key"; the harmonic play in its opening measures is not a sharply defined juxtaposition of conflicting elements as it is in the Haydn—rather, it is a gentle blurring within the lyric unfolding of a theme that is firmly settled in the tonic. Nonetheless, the opening measures of the theme do not represent a clear goal toward which the harmonic action of the

Example 84.   Mendelssohn, Quartet in E♭ major, Op. 12, I, mm. 97–151.

development section can be directed: the friction between tonal orientation and harmonic detail would seem to make a strong preparation for either E♭ major or C minor the wrong approach.

The development quickly expires to quiet murmurs on V of G minor, eventually reaching an almost complete cessation of motion in the ritardando beginning in m. 175. In the midst of this, the first violin takes up the opening theme at its original pitch as the cello settles onto E♭, effecting a return to the tonic with absolutely no harmonic preparation at all. And there is no hint of C minor in this unexpected reappearance of the opening of the theme—the tonic itself provides a submediant coloring in relation to the G minor out of which it emerges. Furthermore, all of this occurs during a gradual ritardando, so the materialization of the tonic and the main theme—a remarkable double return that is, paradoxically, more "tonic" than the opening of the exposition—sounds more like a transition than an arrival: tonic stability has, in fact, become a magically elusive goal. (There is a wonderful detail here—in the original version of the theme the return to the tonic takes place at the end of the first phrase; now the theme begins on the tonic, and the cadence at the end of the first phrase—and at the still-point of the ritardando—settles into a beautifully deceptive cadence to C minor.) As we should be now expect, this will have consequences later in the movement.

After a short outburst of "Harp-Quartet" agitation (mm. 212–17), the end of the recapitulation subsides into a new transitional passage (mm. 230–44—recalling, almost verbatim, the parallel place in the first movement of Op. 74, mm. 198–214). The harmony has slowly swung around to an augmented sixth of F minor, and the new theme from the development section returns in its original key—pointedly *not* in the tonic (mm. 245ff.). Paralleling the development, the continuation leads sequentially toward G minor, settling into a cadence that centers on the diminished seventh, A-C-E♭-F♯ (mm. 252–58). This is essentially the chord that had been shunted from V7 of B♭ major to V7 of G minor near the end of the development section, derailing

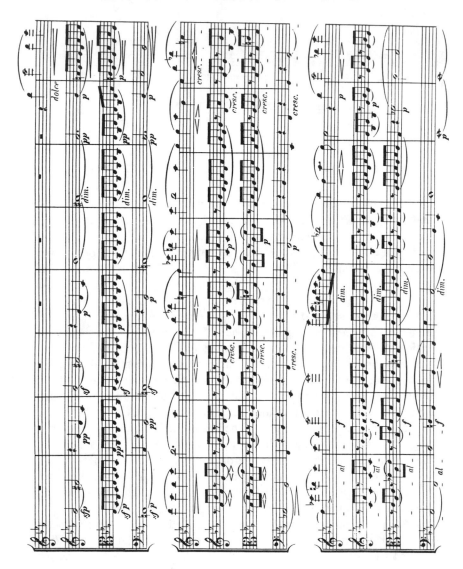

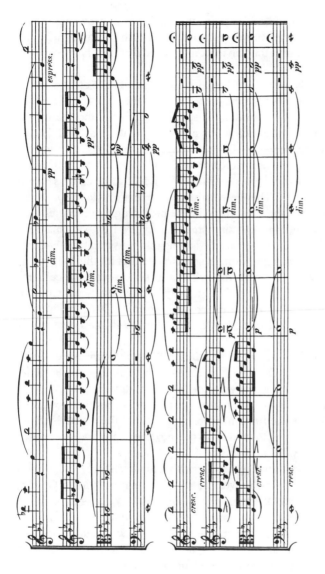

Example 85. Mendelssohn, Quartet in Eb major, Op. 12, I, mm. 252–92.

the drive toward the tonic that had spanned the middle of the movement. This time, the chord leads to a statement of the main theme in the tonic that pulls together many of the strands that have been threaded through the movement (Example 85).

The opening of the theme (m. 259) regains e♭''', linking back to the end of the recapitulation (m. 225) and to the pivotal e♭''' at the end of the development section (m. 151)—by extension, it seems to gather in the prominent d'''s that are laced through the exposition and recapitulation, as well. But as Example 85 shows, this downbeat E♭ is no longer the third of C minor, as it was at the beginning of the exposition, nor the doubled tonic root, as it was at the beginning of the recapitulation—it is the seventh of a dominant seventh chord on the supertonic, F. This new harmonic context explicitly pulls the supertonic step back into the tonic realm while providing a reinterpretation of the delicate ambiguity surrounding E♭—the tonic pitch—to initiate a tonic cadence of exquisite lyric grace. Reflecting this new stability, the cello remains in the lower register, providing a solid foundation for this long-with-held affirmation of the tonic. (Note that within this new context the cello re-tains the line that supported the first, tonally elusive, statement of the theme—B♭-C-B♭-A♭-G-F-B♭-E♭ (compare mm. 259-62 with mm. 18-21)—nothing seems to elude Mendelssohn's grasp in the finest of his works.)

This cadential impulse is spun out over the last thirty-three measures of the coda in a line that stretches from e♭''' (m. 259) to e♭'' (m. 279) to e♭' in the final measure (m. 292). Along the way, the first violin touches on g''''—the high point of the movement—as the harmony turns for the last time toward C minor (mm. 269-70). In the final measures, the head of the theme is trans-formed one last time, turning toward IV as the movement gradually comes to rest, oscillating gently within the tonic.

The first movement is shaped by a lyricism that is surprisingly uncommon in these early works—the first movement of the A-major Quintet, Op. 18, and, perhaps, the *Hebrides* Overture, are its only equals. What is remarkable in this work is that the lyric impulse provides the basis for the formal organi-zation of the movement. The fundamental stages of the formal process—marking the beginning of the exposition, development, recapitulation, and coda—are articulated by progressive transformations of the main theme—transformations hinging on new interpretations of the tonic-submediant rela-tion posited in the opening measures and reflecting the functional role of the gesture within the form as beginning, continuation, or conclusion. Over the course of the work as a whole, every level of structure—from the harmonic organization of themes to the largest structural processes of entire move-ments—are shaped by this same tonic-submediant relation.

The inner movements reveal the flexibility with which Mendelssohn could manipulate the intertwined harmonic and thematic motives of the work, molding them into more personally characteristic shapes than he achieved in Op. 13. The opening of the second movement, the Canzonetta, picks up the G minor toward which the first movement occasionally drifted, but the theme traces a delicately ephemeral version of the main theme of the first movement at its original pitch level—pivoting around g', bb' and eb'' and playing out a new interpretation of the harmonic and melodic relations of its constituent elements—in particular, Eb and D—the leading tone and tonic in the first movement, the flatted sixth degree and dominant in the second (Example 86). This method of reinterpretation and obscured recollection is much closer to Beethoven's thematic procedures in, for example, the first movement of Op. 132—or, for that matter, in Mendelssohn's finest works—than the stiffly baroque technique of motivic spinning-out that characterized Op. 13.

The third movement—one of Mendelssohn's finest serious slow movements—explores, on many levels, an expressive interplay between Bb major and G minor—another tonic-submediant relation embedded in the opening gesture of the theme (Example 87, mm. 1–2).

The closing measures of the movement are strongly colored by the local subdominant, which is, of course, Eb major. The final cadence just manages to retain its equilibrium on Bb, but it cannot completely dispel the sense that it is really only a half cadence that is going to fall back to Eb. In terms of the larger structure of the work, the slow movement would seem to be serving as a dominant preparation for a return to the tonic at the beginning of the finale, supplying the conclusive V–I cadential resolution so pointedly avoided at important junctures in the first movement. (The effect would be similar to the cadential displacement in Beethoven's A-major Piano Sonata, Op. 101. The opening of the first movement of that work never quite establishes the tonic, and the opening of the recapitulation carefully avoids a V–I cadence; when the opening phrase of the main theme returns at the end of the slow movement, it is woven into an elaborate passage of dominant preparation that introduces a tonic expanse—the opening of the fugue in the finale—that is laid out with broader strokes than can be found anywhere else in Beethoven's entire output: Rosen observes that the "unclassical looseness" of the harmonic structure in this movement "brings it close to many works of Mendelssohn."[42] When Mendelssohn wrote his elaborate—and often beautiful—parody of this work, the E-major Sonata, Op. 6, (1826), he carefully inserted quotations from the first movement to frame the finale, but he missed the point of Beethoven's design: the opening of Mendelssohn's first

Example 86. Mendelssohn, Quartet in E♭ major, Op. 12, II, mm. 1–10.

Example 87. Mendelssohn, Quartet in E♭ major, Op. 12, III, mm. 1–10.

movement is already squarely settled in the tonic, so there is no problematic tonal ambiguity to be rectified by the rather garish E major of this finale.)

But the *attacca* at the end of the third movement of Op. 12 does not lead to Eb major. The finale opens with a vigorous fanfare on the dominant of C minor, reestablishing the confused relation between the tonic and its submediant with remarkable force. In fact, it turns out that the submediant is not simply a momentary tint within a firmly established tonic; the main theme of the finale is entrenched in C minor, and there is, at first, absolutely no hint of Eb major at all. The exposition moves off almost immediately through its own submediant, Ab major, however, and soon reaches Eb major—the tonic (or is it?)—for a second theme. As Example 88 shows, both the C-minor and Eb-major themes outline the general profile of the F-minor theme from the development section of the first movement.

This Eb-major theme proves to be a temporary outpost within the first group and quickly leads back to C minor (m. 35). A brief transition leads to G minor (the minor dominant of C minor), and the arrival is marked by yet another new theme fashioned from the intervallic materials of the F-minor theme from the first movement (mm. 44ff.). This agitated material seems to lead with surprising abruptness to a final cadence, but at the last moment another new theme—once again outlining the ascending sixth and descending scale figure that are the fundamental elements of all these themes—slips in— in Bb major (Example 89).

Like the Eb-major theme in the first group, this turn to the mediant proves to be a temporary diversion; the exposition eventually storms to a conclusion in G minor. On the highest structural level, the entire finale seems to be in the wrong key; instead of providing a concluding area of tonic stability, the movement, so far, has acted as an enormous deceptive cadence, playing out, on the largest possible scale, the tonic-submediant blur first elaborated in the opening measures of the first movement. At the same time, the pull toward the tonic—toward the Eb major so strongly implied at the end of the third movement—is continually reinforced within the exposition by the elaborate detours to Eb in the first group and Bb in the second group. It seems that Mendelssohn has, in fact, written a double exposition, establishing both C minor and Eb major in the first group, and both G minor (the dominant key of C minor) and Bb major (the dominant of Eb major) in the second group: he has transformed the delicate harmonic coloring of his—subthematic—motive into a tonal structure that shapes the largest outlines of the movement.

The relation of all this to the first movement is made explicit in the opening measures of the development section, when a sudden harmonic shift leads into F minor and the theme—and accompaniment—from the development section of the first movement reappears verbatim (Example 90, mm.

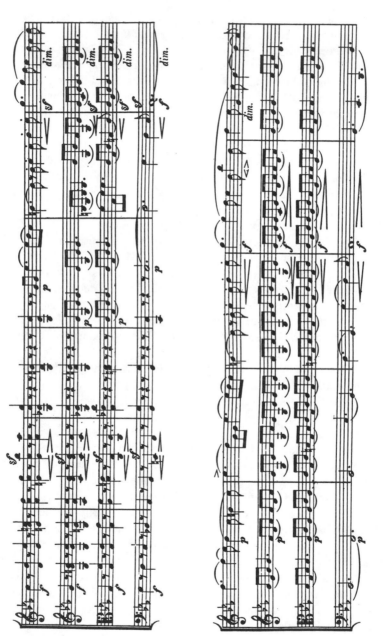

Example 88a. Mm. 11–21.

Example 88b.   Mm. 22–33.

Example 88.   Mendelssohn, Quartet in E♭ major, Op. 12, IV.

Example 89. Mendelssohn, Quartet in E♭ major, Op. 12, IV, mm. 56–77.

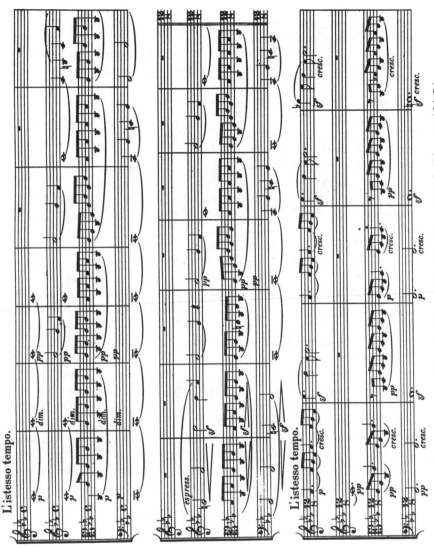

Example 90.   Mendelssohn, Quartet in Eb major, Op. 12, IV, mm. 106–24.

106ff., which are identical to mm. 105ff. of the first movement). The theme itself quickly evaporates, leaving behind only the characteristic Ab–G–F figure; this proves, of course, to be a close relative of the minor thirds that have run through every theme of the finale. With the accomplishment of this motivic linkage, the development section, which lasts only twenty measures, is over: like the exposition, its function is determined more by the role of the finale within the larger structure of the work rather than by the internally generated processes of the movement, for which a more expansive development section, exploring the wealth of thematic material and harmonic interrelations from the exposition, might seem to be more appropriate.

The recapitulation stays essentially within the framework of the movement's own business, seemingly unaffected by the precarious tonal basis on which the entire structure is built. Indeed, the only important deviations from the design of the exposition tend to intensify the harmonic problems of that structure.

The most striking of these is the return of the lyric second theme (the theme which had originally appeared in Bb major in the exposition) in F minor instead of Eb major (mm. 181ff.). On one level, this could be seen as a reflection of the role—or rather, of the uncertain status of the role—Eb major plays in the strategies of the movement: Mendelssohn seems intent on avoiding even the hint of a stable reference to this strangely elusive tonic. On a more immediate level, this F-minor version of the theme re-echoes both the key of the development section and the Ab–G–F figure that has proved to be one of the common links in the thematic web drawn from the F-minor theme. In fact, this figure is given a delicate prominence throughout the recapitulation (see the new inner voice, second violin, mm. 151–53, and the first violin, mm. 165–66): the relation of the finale to the rest of the Quartet appears to be shaping the events of the movement more and more firmly. But there has been no substantial move toward resolving the overriding tonal problem that has been posed by the finale: the integration of an essentially self-contained sonata movement in C minor—a movement that certainly shows no signs of being an introduction to a "real" last movement—into a work ostensibly in Eb major. This ambiguous situation throws all of the resolutions within the framework of the C-minor structure into the background, and the longer the large-scale tonal problem remains unresolved, the more pointedly the overall issue of closure—on both the local and the largest scale—remains unaddressed.

The issue comes to a head in the coda. The final cadence of the recapitulation is expanded slightly and leads into a rather grandiose new theme (mm. 299ff.) that seems intent, at first, on a ponderously stable confirmation of C minor (Example 91). But the expansion of the melodic line from C–Eb to

C–Ab(–G–F) in mm. 233–34 brings another echo of the development section theme that suddenly accomplishes the work's long overdue tonal resolution. The timorous F minor with which this theme has invariably been associated now erupts, *fortissimo*, in a particularly resonant disposition. And this F minor, which has been played upon with increasing prominence since the development section, proves to be the harmonic pivot between the precariously juxtaposed tonal centers of the finale: C minor simply evaporates, subsumed in an instant within a vi–ii–V–I cadence that finally settles onto Eb major in m. 237.

Of course, this reversal is too sudden to counterbalance the tonal bias of the finale, and the remainder of the coda supplies an expansive confirmation of Eb major.

A new theme winds through a two-octave descent from eb''', but the final step to eb' is never accomplished. Instead, the line turns back on itself, settling onto f' in mm. 247 and 251, and the second degree is then prolonged in an elaborate recitative passage that recalls once again the F-minor theme from the first movement. (The use of recitative at this crucial juncture is striking. Even in a work with no overtly dramatic or programmatic content, the rupture of internal formal consistency engendered by explicit cyclic procedures points—however obscurely—to expressive forces that lie beyond the specifically musical processes that shape the work; the rupture, which places the autonomy of the work in question, must be explained. Schumann's quotations of *An die ferne Geliebte* are relatively obvious examples of the procedure. The expressive power of instrumental recitative is precisely that it presses hard at the threshold of articulation; that it conveys a message—a program—lurking just below the level of explicit expression. Beethoven exploited this technique in a number of the late works—most obviously, of course, in the Ninth Symphony; the expressive core of the A-minor Quartet, to take another example, is, after all, the "Heiliger Dankgesang," and the throbbing F–E motive in the finale is set off by a turbulent passage of instrumental recitative.)

In the finale of Op. 12, the programmatic significance of the recitative is, perhaps, particularly elusive—it seems a little overwrought for its circumstances. As a signpost indicating an important event, its meaning is clear, however: this emotionally charged passage, with its web of motivic associations, leads naturally enough into a restatement of the entire F-minor theme, and—echoing the analogous place at the end of the first movement—this in turn leads into a restatement of the coda from that earlier movement, which originally grew out of a restatement of the F-minor theme.

The function of this return is beautifully calculated. The gradual cadential descent from eb''' (mm. 273ff.) that unfolds over the course of the coda

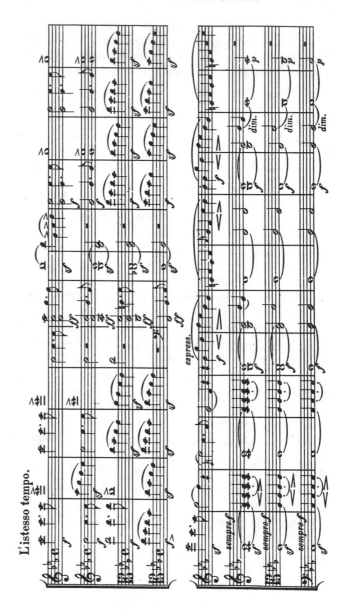

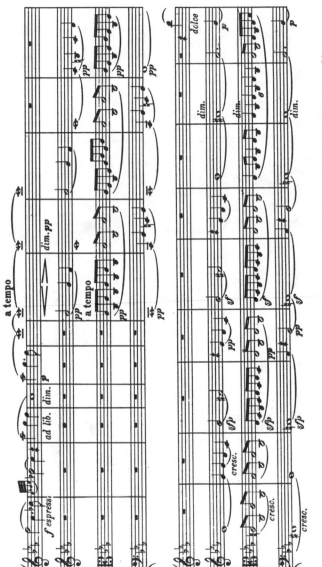

Example 91. Mendelssohn, Quartet in Eb major, Op. 12, IV, mm. 229–313. (Continued.)

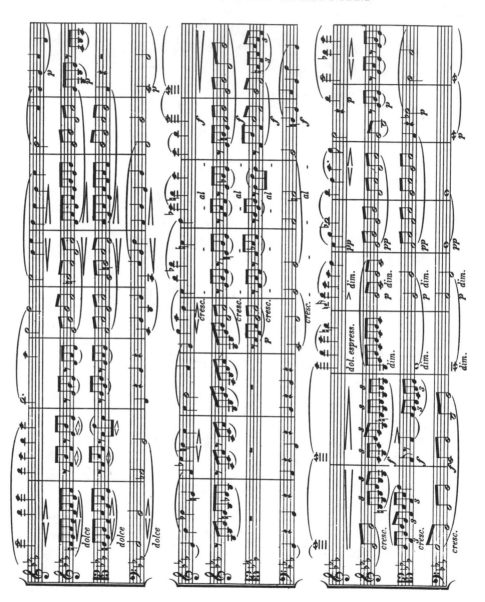

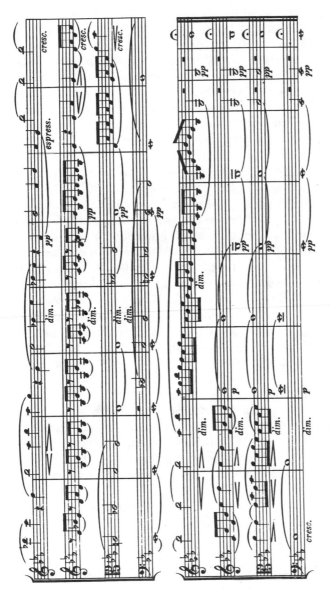

Example 91. (Continued.)   Mendelssohn, Quartet in Eb major, Op. 12, IV, mm. 229–313.

reaches back and fills in the cadence sketched out in mm. 241–47, completing the drive to the tonic begun there. And, of course, this material was originally concerned with the assimilation of the C minor–Eb major ambiguity that controlled the structure of the first movement. In the finale, following interior movements that have continued to explore this fundamental relation in ways that avoid both overt reference and explicit resolution—that ambiguity has been magnified into a structural problem that underlies every formal issue within the movement, and the resolution provided by the coda is even more impressively persuasive, embracing harmonic and thematic processes elaborated at every level and at every stage of the work. It would seem that Mendelssohn had recognized—and solved—the formal problems that undermined the more flamboyant cyclic design unfurled in Op. 13.

Indeed, if the logic of organizational principles was the only criterion for success, Op. 12 would seem to be almost flawless: its "secret," the gentle tonic-submediant blur first heard in the opening measures of the first movement, effects every element of the work, and its resolution reverberates in the final cadence of the last movement. And the music itself is, for the most part, of the highest quality; the first three movements achieve almost the same level of characteristic individuality that marks Mendelssohn's finest works of this remarkable period. But the emotional tone of the work wavers unsteadily between the lyric grace of the first three movements and the bustling—and not entirely convincing—passion of the finale. This, I think, is the one significant weakness of the work, and it stems from the cyclic design itself.

Mendelssohn's solution to the finale problem—and to the problem of the relation between independent movements and the larger cyclic design—is impressive: the integrity of the finale is itself the central structural issue concerning the role of the movement within the larger design. But there has been no hint in the course of the first three movements that anything like the agitation of the finale might be encountered within the expressive universe of the work. The sudden eruption of Mendelssohnian passion can be understood, of course, as a massive elaboration of the Eb major–C minor relation, but the resulting expressive design simply is not fully comprehensible; there is a sense that the passion erupts in response to the harmony instead of the harmony erupting in response to the passion; a sense that, as Tovey observed, Mendelssohn "seemed able to play chess with symphonies, oratorios, and songs with and without words, while other composers were grappling in their music with real life."[43]

Lurking behind this problem, of course, is the fact that the generative issue of the cyclic design, the confrontation between Eb major and C minor on which the structure of the finale is based—the gentle ambiguity first unfolded in the opening measures of the main theme of the first movement—was resolved so beautifully over the course of that movement, each stage of the process marked by a new reinterpretation of the theme and culminating in the calm serenity of the coda. For all the clarity—and often great beauty—with which Mendelssohn accomplishes his design over the four movements of Op. 12—and with much greater sophistication than in the seemingly more advanced procedures of Op. 13—there is no compelling processive structure to support the expressive implications of the cyclic elements he has deployed.

Mendelssohn's most thoroughgoing attempt to solve this problem is found in the A-minor Symphony, Op. 56, the "Scottish," where the composer attempted a remarkable synthesis of overt cyclic procedures, a functionally defined process of thematic transformations, and a network of motivic and inflectional interrelations carried out within the framework of a dialectic confrontation of sharply contrasting thematic material that spans all four movements. The resulting design offers an illuminating measure of the strengths and weaknesses of the composer's mature style.

The work has a complicated history. In a letter to his family, Mendelssohn explained that the initial ideas for the work came to him in the ruins of the chapel at Holyrood during his tour of Scotland in the summer of 1829—little more than a week later he announced, in this next letter (in almost identical terms), the inception of the *Hebrides* Overture.[44] Work on the Overture proceeded slowly enough, as we have seen, but the Symphony was not completed until the first months of 1842; it is both an early work and a late one, and it represents both the most persuasive and the most grievously miscalculated of Mendelssohn's cyclic designs.

The thematic structure of the Symphony has been considered in some detail in the literature; the network of relations is elaborate but relatively straightforward.[45] There are two primary thematic elements. The ascending figure outlined in the opening measures of the introduction to the first movement provides the frame upon which most of the melodic material for the entire work is built (Example 92a). A descending scale figure first appears later in the introduction as a countermelody to the main theme; it becomes more prominent over the course of the work, first as the second theme of the second movement and later as the main theme of the finale (Example 92b). The confrontation of these contrasting thematic groups, and the transfer of structural weight from one to the other—a typical formal premise for a romantic sonata-form movement—emerges as the basis of the cyclic process that shapes the entire work.

In addition to these explicit thematic interconnections, the four movements, which are played without pause, are linked through manipulations of

Example 92a. Themes derived from motive A.

an inflectionally sensitized half-step figure—the by now familiar ♭6-5 figure in A minor, F♮–E—which is threaded prominently through the thematic
fabric of the first movement, controls important aspects of the tonal relationship between adjacent movements, and on which the turn to A major in the
coda of the finale is hinged.

All of the primary thematic material in the first movement is derived from
motive A, and is all, therefore, related to the elegiac theme stated in the opening measures of the introduction (Example 92a); a particularly beautiful
transformation yields the closing theme of the exposition (mm. 181ff.), in
which the gestures that frame the first two phrases of the introduction—the

Example 92b.   Themes derived from motive B.

Example 92.   Mendelssohn, Symphony in A minor, "Scottish," Op. 56.

rising fourth leap (m. 1) and descending stepwise third (mm. 7–8)—are inverted and played in reverse order.

Even the most prominent thematic formations derived from motive B are clearly subordinate to the motive-A themes: the countermelody to the main theme of the introduction (mm. 32ff.) and, later, the agitated figure that initiates the transition away from the tonic in the exposition of the main body of the movement (mm. 99ff.). This latter, in particular, is clearly an intrusion, marked by a sharp break in thematic content, dynamic level, texture, rhythm, and even tempo. In the final pages of the movement, the delayed restatement of this transitional material sweeps in on the climax of the "storm music" of the coda, but the passage dies away abruptly, leading, with magical calm, to a restatement of the opening measures of the introduction (the original form of motive A), which now close into the chain of hushed cadences at the end of the movement.

Linking back to a last upper-voice resolution of F♮ to E in those cadences, the *pianissimo* staccato F♮s that open the second movement seem to quiver with echoes of the inflectional energies that coursed through much of the thematic material of the first movement. The opening seems to emerge, as if through haze and distance, from delicate reverberations that linger in the silence that separates the movements.

The main theme of the second movement is organized around the ascending triadic figure of motive A (see Example 92a). The clarinet rushes up and down over this triadic framework, spinning out an almost-purely pentatonic melody centered on F that restricts the pitch collection to the white-note scale elements common to F major and the A minor of the first movement. (Much of the "bardic" quality of the first movement, especially in the lyric second theme, arises from a continual alternation between the raised and lowered leading tone—between a diatonic A minor, with its G♯, and a folk-modal white-note scale, with G♮. The pentatonic scale of the Scherzo tune, on the other hand, avoids both B♭ and B♮, setting the tonic key, F major, slightly off kilter; there are B♭s in the accompaniment, however.) Given this shared pitch collection, the shift to F in the opening measures of the Scherzo represents less a change of key in the normal sense than a readjustment of referential centricity in which the inflectional relations within the pitch collection are realigned around a transformation of the subsidiary F♮–E relation of the first movement, in which F♮ continually falls back to E, into a leading-tone—tonic relation in the second, in which E resolves naturally, to F. The slight ambiguity concerning the "F–majorness" of this new orientation of the pitch collection in turn smooths the transition to the secondary key area, C major, which, of course, shares this same white-note collection: to at least a certain extent, the emergence of the second theme in the exposition registers as a resolution, providing the most stable context for this seemingly innocent collection of inflectionally unpredictable white notes. This unusual tonal design will obviously have significant ramifications in the later stages of the movement.

The development section eventually settles into a statement of the second theme in F minor over a dominant pedal—presumably serving as an expressively intensified tonic $^6_4$ that will lead into the opening of the recapitulation (mm. 153ff.). Naturally enough, the passage soon lands on a diminished seventh chord, B♮–D–F–A♭, that seems to push strongly toward V7 of V. But at the last moment, B♮ falls to B♭; the harmony swings around to V7 of E♭ major, and the flute nonchalantly takes up the main theme in this unlikely key (mm. 176ff.). Abrupt shifts in instrumentation and register reinforce the sense that this "return" has been precipitously disengaged from its preparation, and things only get as far as the end of the first phrase of the tune, with its distinctly articulated minor third, which happens, now, to be b♭''-g'' (m. 179). This is immediately taken up by the violins, and tweaked slightly to yield the major third, b♮''-g'', which is in turn echoed back by the flute while the lower voice (bassoon) drops to D♭, producing an augmented sixth that presses back toward F (mm. 179-82). The outer voices expand to a dominant pedal—the lower voice finally completing its motion to C (in register)—that supports the consequent phrase of the main theme, forming a large-scale cadential $^6_4$ that will undoubtedly lead—finally—to a stable reestablishment of the tonic; part of the main theme, in the tonic at the opening of the recapitulation, functions as the retransition *to* the tonic.

Under the best of circumstances, the quasi-pentatonic opening theme might not provide a completely persuasive reaffirmation of the tonic key, but the bizarre turn of events that has emerged at this critical juncture in the formal process seems to have completely overwhelmed the delicate harmonic balance of that theme. In particular, the point seems to be that these events have hinged on the fourth scale degree of F major—precisely the area that was so carefully avoided in the pentatonic scale of the main theme: B♭, the seventh of the home dominant seventh chord, apparently cannot be accommodated within the return of the main theme, but neither can B♮, which, as b♮'', is left hanging, conspicuously unresolved, in the passage following mm. 181-82. The suddenly urgent issue of establishing a satisfactory articulation of tonic stability will clearly require a conclusive resolution of the tangled relations of B♮ and B♭ to each other and to the tonic.

That resolution is quickly accomplished: the continuation of the consequent phrase dissolves into a brief transition that presses on—in only four measures—to the diatonic clarity of the second theme, now firmly settled in the tonic (mm. 193ff.): the lower voice finally reaches F; the b♮'' of mm. 181-82 is linked to the first note of the theme, c'''; and B♮ is then explicitly neutralized, replaced by a B♭ that is no longer a troublesome intruder but a perfectly normal element of this perfectly normal F-major tune; in fact, the two flutes present both of the resolutions of b♮'' required to clarify the inflectional issues raised in the preceding music—to c''' and to b♭''—simultaneously in the upbeat V⁷ that begins the second theme.

This double return (of the tonic and the *second* theme) is marked by a *fortissimo* tutti eruption (in the exposition, the entire second group had rushed by *pianissimo*), initiated by the root-position tonic chord on the downbeat of m. 193 (in the exposition, the first root-position tonic in the secondary key was the *last* chord of the second group). This tonic arrival—in a very real sense the first one of the movement—has been carefully prepared by every gesture in this delightfully bustling Scherzo to serve as the climax of the design, and Mendelssohn's seemingly textbook-schematic sonata form proves

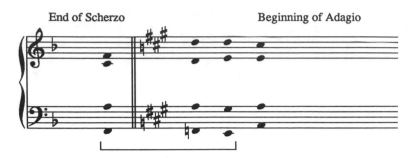

Example 93. Mendelssohn, Symphony in A minor, "Scottish," Op. 56, transition from II to III.

to be a colorful, sweeping journey toward tonic stability that begins in the silence preceding the first staccato Fs at the beginning of the movement and is completed only in the recapitulation of the second theme in the tonic. Form and content are, as perfectly as in any of the early works, realizations of the same functional process—a process accomplished with a lightness of touch and delicacy of color that the composer rarely equaled, and a process that will prove in turn to be a central element in the larger structural design of the work as a whole.

As Example 93 shows, the transition from the second and third movements is accomplished through a re-transformation of the relation between F♮ and E, leading F♮ back down to E, and then calming the inflectional tensions inherent in this pairing by replacing F♮ with F♯ as the main theme of the slow movement emerges in A major.

In spite of this clearly marked transitional path, the third movement seems to stand slightly apart from the larger structural issues of the work as a whole. On the one hand, for example, only a fleeting reference—in a subsidiary phrase of the main theme—is made to the ascending fourth of motive A (mm. 18ff.), while motive B seems to play no part in the movement at all. On the other hand, the themes themselves are characterized by extraordinarily sharply drawn expressive contrasts—the uncertain lyricism of the first theme, the ponderously faceless fanfares of the second, and the renewed, but still uneasy lyricism of the third—and these expressive contrasts are juxtaposed with absolutely no connective material, creating a distinctly episodic sequence that suggests a programmatically conceived confrontation; the fanfares, in particular, sound like an intrusion that momentarily disrupts the lyric flow of the first theme, which is then taken up again in mid-gesture by the third theme (mm. 50–51), drifting gently to a cadence in the secondary key, E major. Perhaps this design—a confrontation in which restrained lyricism somehow holds its own in the face of oppressive formality—reverberates with the impressions that so moved the composer as he stood within the ruined chapel at Holyrood. A suitably romantic image of Mary Stuart might come more readily to mind if the movement were not cast in a rigid sonata-form mold that necessitates the dutiful restatement of this thematic sequence with no discernible intensification of dramatic—or musical—significance.

The finale opens with a vigorous theme derived from motive B, to which a theme derived from motive A functions as a contrasting middle section (mm. 15-22). Details of the joints of its various phrases put a persistent emphasis on the half-step pair, F♮-E, and on an uneasy wavering between F♮ and F♯ that fleetingly recalls the troubled A major of the preceding movement and foreshadows the triumphant return to that key in the coda.

A bustling transition soon begins making dominant preparations for an arrival in the mediant—a persistent shifting between E♮ and E♭ makes it momentarily unclear whether this will be C major or C minor (mm. 54-64). The passage dies away to a quivering b♮ in the violins (m. 66), but, magically, this leading tone is taken as a dominant pedal, supporting a hauntingly wistful motive-A theme in E minor that vanishes almost instantly into C major (Example 94, mm. 67ff.—these elements alternate once more before the exposition closes noisily in C major).

The distinctive scoring of the E-minor passage, for oboe and clarinets with only a thin string accompaniment, fosters a sense of recollection, distinctly, but as if from a distance, of the opening measures of the introduction to the first movement, where a similar theme has been played by a slightly larger group of winds over a light string accompaniment.

This is a remarkable moment: harmonically, thematically, timbrally, and expressively this new theme is clearly an intrusion—an explicit reference to events outside the movement itself—that disrupts the formal processes of the finale, and which must be swept aside before those processes can be resumed. But, at the same time, it is by far the most strikingly individual event in the movement, and, although it cannot seem to establish itself against the weight of those formal processes, it is, in fact, the new theme which sweeps the rather stilted impetuosity of its surroundings into the expressive background. The precarious harmonic situation of the theme—perched on a tonal mirage—is a brilliant formal realization of this double character.

Mendelssohn's exploitation of harmonic, registral, and dynamic juxtapositions to set off this peculiarly elusive cyclic return is in some ways reminiscent of the techniques used by Berlioz in the second movement of the *Symphonie fantastique* discussed earlier in this chapter. In contrast to the essentially narrative significance of Berlioz's scheme, however, Men-

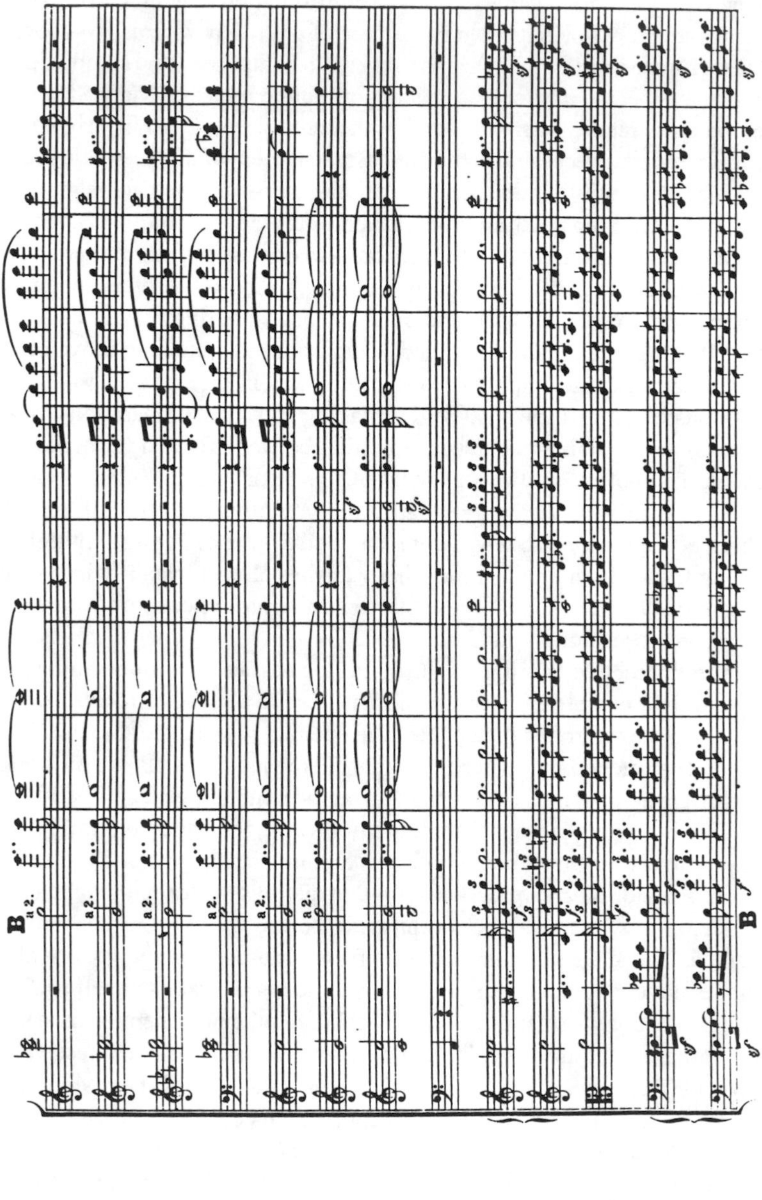
B
a 2.

Example 94. Mendelssohn, Symphony in A minor, "Scottish," Op. 56, IV, mm. 53–73.

delssohn's procedure reflects the convergence of intertwined formal functions that span various levels of the formal design of the work. Within the processes of the finale, the return represents a cadential prolongation of a preparatory dominant, dramatically delaying the establishment of the secondary key—the sudden shifts of harmony, pace, and dynamic level at the appearance of the new theme are well suited to the task of intensifying the dramatic character of this event. At the same time, these disjunctions clearly segregate this passage from the principal action of the movement, and it is this resistance to assimilation that points to a larger functional design in which the return is taking part.

In the most persuasive of Mendelssohn's cyclic designs—the Octet or the "Italian" Symphony, for example—thematic recall in the finale (generally rather later in the course of the finale than is the case here) has served to indicate that the closing tonic expanse of the movement was to be understood as a final cadence for the entire work. The themes themselves are only signs of that larger significance—the cyclic return does not engender any specific process of transformation or resolution, either within the movement or across the larger design of the work. In contrast, the cyclic return in the finale of the "Scottish" Symphony marks the crucial moment in a thematic process that has been woven through the entire course of the work.

As we have seen, the first movement of the Symphony focused almost exclusively on thematic material derived from motive A. The rollicking energy of the main theme of the second movement seems, at first, to reaffirm the priority of motive-A material, but the delicate pentatonic coloring of that theme carries with it ambiguities concerning tonal stability that tilt the structural weight of the movement onto the second theme—a strongly individualized motive-B theme which emerges in the recapitulation as the goal toward which the entire movement has been leading. The third movement, for the most part, seems to explore thematic material unrelated to either motive A or motive B, but the opening of the finale reaffirms the new priority of thematic material derived from motive B, relegating motive-A material to a clearly subsidiary position.

The palpable sense of distance—both physical and temporal—that surrounds the intrusion of the cyclic motive-A theme in the finale provides a striking measure of "how far we have come" from the opening measures of the work while posing a structural problem—the assimilation of this riveting moment into the formal design of the movement—that integrates the finale within the larger design of the work as a whole in a completely new way. Bringing this striking material within the functional processes of the finale will—unavoidably, it would seem—transfer the expressive and structural weight of the movement back to motive A, and this, quite explicitly, will lead the larger thematic process that has been carried out over the course of the work back to its starting point. Or, rather, to somewhere very near that starting point; one of the most impressive aspects about Mendelssohn's strategy is that the final element of the design is not a literal return to the beginning, but a recollection of that opening gesture; the cyclic process—and it is clearly a *process* in this work—has been endowed with a richly romantic aura of nostalgia. The thematic process has, in turn, been elevated to a functional status analogous to that of tonality itself, with motive A serving as a thematic "tonic realm" to which motive B functions as an explicitly polar opposite; resolution is marked by the reestablishment of the work's "thematic tonic."

The process of drawing the cyclic intrusion into the formal design of the finale, and conversely, of opening the design of the finale to accommodate its function as the conclusion of the entire work, is impressively worked out. The cyclic theme returns at the end of the development section, *fortissimo*, tutti, and in the tonic, but over a carefully prepared dominant pedal, serving to mark the climax of the retransition to the tonic for the opening of the recapitulation (mm. 226ff.). It returns again at the expected point within the recapitulation, but this time it is not set off as an intrusion: the dominant pedal, again on E, is embedded in a larger cadential drive that is clearly focused on the tonic, A minor. In each instance, then, the cyclic theme (and texture) prepares an important formal articulation of the tonic, but in each instance the theme itself remains standing only at the threshold of the tonic.

The final stages of the recapitulation are expanded, reaching a *fortissimo* climax that collapses into a sudden hush that leaves only octave Es echoing in the violins and winds (Example 95). This disintegration recalls the corresponding point at the end of the first movement, where the "storm" music of the coda died away to the e'''-e'' octaves in the winds, leading into the quiet postlude—a restatement of the opening of the introduction. Here, at the end of the finale, after the lower strings add the tonic root beneath the octave Es, the clarinet takes up the cyclic theme, now, for the first time settled firmly in the tonic but wrapped in a texture as ephemeral as the Highland mist. This remarkable moment—one of the most delicately beautiful effects in the symphonic literature—is both the goal of the cadential drive that spans the final section of the movement and the culmination of the thematic design that spans the entire Symphony—a distillation of the work's fundamental motivic elements which, as those motivic elements are gradually liquidated as the passage continues, seems literally to evaporate into that mist.

These intertwined threads—the reference to the opening of the first movement at the end of the finale, the stabilization of the cyclic theme in the tonic, rounding off both the cadential processes of the finale and the thematic design of the entire work, the disintegration of the motivic substance into improvisatory arabesques, and an instrumental setting that is an extreme refinement of the texture of the opening measures of the work—combine to form a complex of closural gestures that encompass both the finale and the Symphony as a whole. After this gentle elegy, the first violins once again take up the E-F♮-E figure, leading it through a final cadential descent toward the e′ with which the work opened. The last f′-e′ step (mm. 394-95) seems about to close the circle, and there appears to be nothing left to add, either emotionally or structurally. Indeed, if the music had simply evaporated into silence—as it seems to be doing in these measures—the extraordinary poetry and structural logic of this work would place it among Mendelssohn's finest achievements.

Unfortunately, the Symphony does not dissolve into the mists. Instead, it closes on a swelling tide of A-major solemnity, sounding the fatal touch of Victorian profundity that stalks through so much of Mendelssohn's later music; as Shaw observed, the Symphony "would be great if it were not so confoundedly genteel."[46] But the coda is not, in itself, quite as dreadful as it seems in its context. The writing is richly sonorous—"strong, like a men's choir" is Mendelssohn's own description of the effect he desired[47]—and the logic of the harmonic shift, which focuses on a transformation of the principal cyclic theme and hinges on the replacement of the ever-present inflectionally charged F♮ of the tonic minor with the diatonic clarity of F♯, is perfectly clear. The problem lies in the relation of this massive gesture to the larger design.

The turn to A major simply comes too late. The close to A minor in m. 361, where the lower strings add the tonic root to the octave Es floating in the violins and winds, and the clarinet takes up the cyclic theme, has provided a decisive "clinch" of extraordinary poetic beauty for both the internal processes of the finale and for the larger cyclic design of the entire work. In the wake of this convergence of closural elements from both within the movement and the entire course of the work, the A major of the conclusion is less a resolution than a contradiction, and one that lacks the intensity that might make it persuasive.

Perhaps the composer felt that a "Scottish" Symphony dedicated to Queen Victoria could not end in an atmosphere of ineffable romantic ambiguity; or perhaps, as Martin Witte suggests, the "Männerchor" music represents "a song of thanks after a victorious battle"[48]—the tempo indication for the main body of the movement, Allegro guerriero, is a suggestive, if characteristically understated clue, although the warring armies seem at times to be stalking with catlike tread through a Gilbert and Sullivan production rather than battling across the wilds of the Scottish border country. But neither the

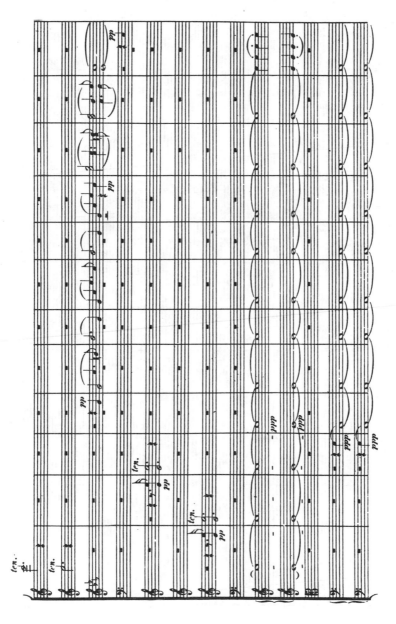

Example 95. Mendelssohn, Symphony in A minor, "Scottish," Op. 56, IV, mm. 358–95. (Continued.)

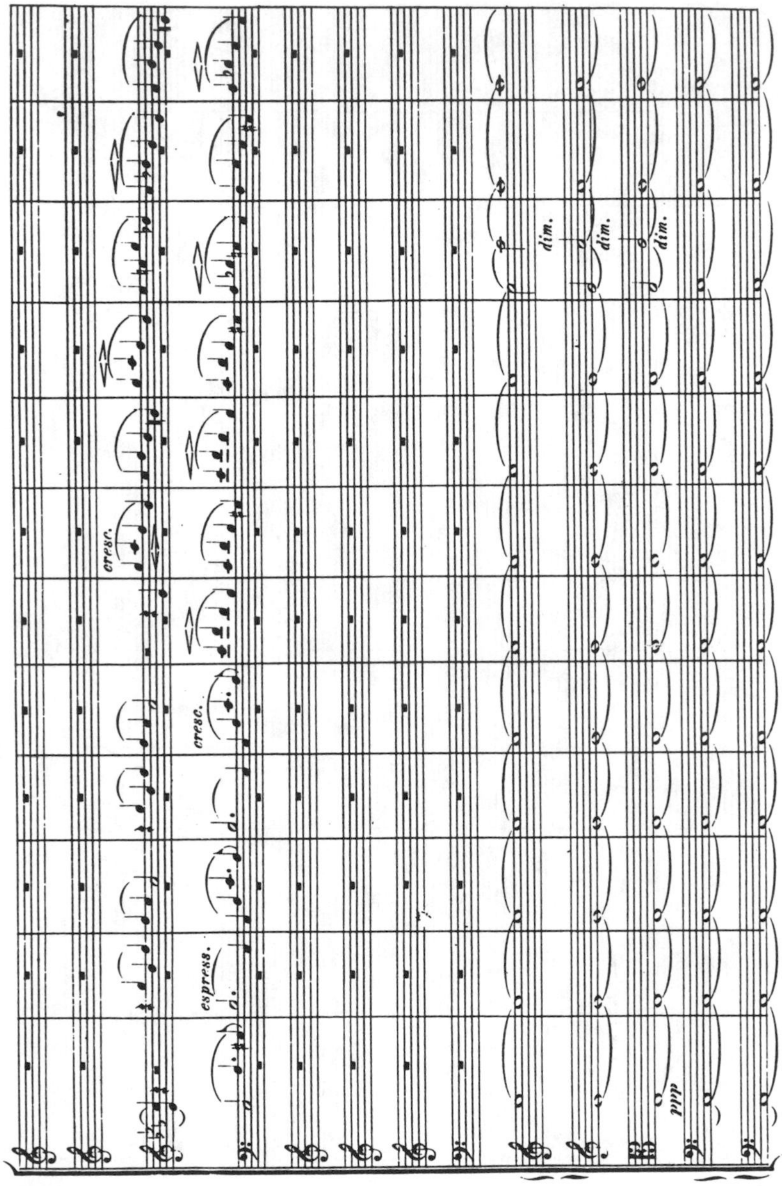
espress.
cresc.
cresc.
dim.
dim.
dim.

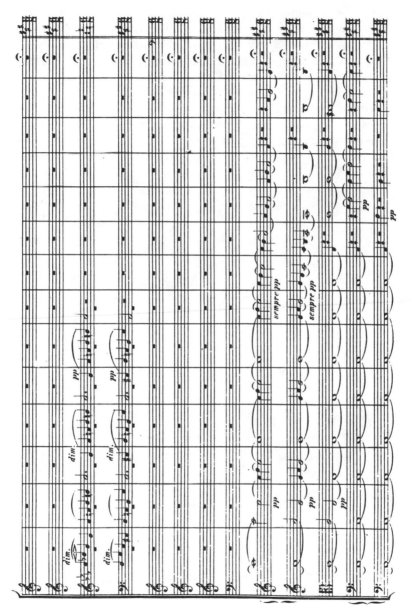

Example 95. (Continued.)   Mendelssohn, Symphony in A minor, "Scottish," Op. 56, IV, mm. 358–95.

obligations of civic-mindedness nor a program can rebalance the structural weight of the work. The A–major coda, unfortunately, is a dismally perfect realization of Schoenberg's definition of the coda as an "extrinsic addition," and in this case—in contrast to the designs worked out in the codas of the *Hebrides* Overture, the *Midsummer Night's Dream* Overture, every movement of the Octet, or the first and third movements of the A–major Quintet—"it would be difficult to give any other reason for the addition of a coda than that the composer wants to say something more."[49] Mendelssohn, usually so reticent, simply did not know when to stop, and he buried one of his most impressively romantic cyclic designs under a mass of Victorian bouquets.

CHAPTER 6

THE LATER MENDELSSOHN

Over the course of this study I have tried to show how Mendelssohn achieved, in his early works at least, a synthesis of the formal principles of the classical sonata style and the harmonic, thematic, and organizational characteristics of the romantic language. It would be appropriate, then, to close with a brief reconsideration of one of the most vexing aspects of the "Mendelssohn Problem"—the relation of that achievement to the music of the later nineteenth century, including Mendelssohn's own later works.

Certain aspects of Mendelssohn's influence are obvious—notorious, in fact: the pious sentimentality of Gounod's music, for example, can be traced back without difficulty to those eminent Victorians, Elijah, St. Paul, and Athalie, or to the lurid propriety of the chorale theme in the finale of the C-minor Piano Trio, while the earnest vapidity of so much of the nineteenth-century symphonic literature—of which, for example, Sullivan's "serious" works are a typical, though particularly distressing realization—merely carry forward expressive tendencies first propounded in the Piano Trios, the Cello Sonatas, and even, as we have seen, the "Scottish" Symphony.

But in the central body of the nineteenth-century repertoire, that influence is not easy to detect. James Webster, for example, categorically states that "of Mendelssohn's influence on Brahms's large-scale instrumental music there is hardly a trace."[1] Tovey, on the other hand, occasionally did discover echoes of Mendelssohn's procedures in Brahms's works—in the finale of the A-major Serenade, Op. 16, or the passage leading into the recapitulation in the first movement of the First Symphony, for example.[2] Those echoes are equally clear, I think, in the first and third movements of the Second Symphony, where the manipulation and interrelation of thematic profiles recalls the elusive thematic processes of the *Hebrides* Overture and the orchestral writing approaches the transparency of the *Midsummer Night's Dream* Over-ture. And I would suggest that the unsettling Neapolitan in the cadences of the Scherzo of the F-minor Piano Quintet, Op. 34, is at least as closely related to the final measures of the Andante of Mendelssohn's Octet as to the closing cadence of Schubert's C-major String Quintet, the work Tovey puts forward as Brahms's model.[3] As we come to recognize the truly characteristic ele-ments of Mendelssohn's style—rather than the empty facility our preconcep-tions have led us to expect in his music—further examples of his influence on central issues of compositional technique will surely come to light. It is not really very far, after all, from the process of thematic generation through the abstraction and rearrangement of intervals worked out in Mendelssohn's A-minor Quartet to the feverishly intense motivic transformations Schoenberg traced through his own Op. 22.[4]

Nevertheless, it is obvious that Mendelssohn's achievements in the early works did not provide the groundwork for a fully developed romantic sonata style; the mainstream of the nineteenth-century sonata traces back to the more impassioned, but less coherently integrated forms of Schumann and Schubert—forms about which Tovey observed that

> when we find (as, for instance, in the first movement of the great C-major Symphony) that some of the most obviously wrong digressions contain the profoundest, most beautiful, and most inevitable passages, then it is time to suspect that Schubert, like other great classics, is pressing his way towards new forms.[5]

An example will help illustrate the situation. In the other of Schubert's great C-major works, the Quintet, Op. 163, the emergence of Eb major over the first part of the exposition and its gradual evaporation into the G major of the second group is surely one of the most profoundly inevitable things in all of music; but Schubert simply cannot assimilate his remarkable modulatory scheme into a recapitulation that begins and ends in the tonic. Instead of re-creating the delicate balance of pitch relations that controlled the harmonic design of the exposition, Schubert simply inserts a turn to the subdominant early in the recapitulation of the first group. This assures that everything will come out right at the closing cadence, but the magically inevitable path traced through the exposition has been transformed into a "rigid repetition" that is, at best, picturesquely redundant.[6] This is, of course, exactly the strat-egy Schumann employed in fashioning a recapitulation for his F#-minor Pi-ano Sonata, Op. 14: the stiff symmetries into which these superbly romantic works are forced provide an accurate gauge of the distance they stand from the new forms toward which they point.

In contrast, the suppleness with which Mendelssohn treated formal proc-esses in his early works is almost unique in music after Beethoven; indeed, it is unique even in Mendelssohn's own output. His later works often exhibit that wearisome regularity of form that has come to be considered quintessentially Mendelssohnian: he does not even seem to have had a strong influence on himself. Of course there are exceptions to this, most often in the less pretentious of the later works—the Violin Concerto, the incidental music to *A Midsummer Night's Dream,* and the quicker inner movements of the chamber and orchestral works of the thirties and forties. Even the Scherzo of the *Lobgesang* has an undeniable charm—at least until a version of "that abominable platitude for the trombones" shows up in the middle of the movement.

Friedhelm Krummacher cites the first movement of the String Quartet in E minor, Op. 44, No. 2, as a paradigm for Mendelssohn's later sonata style. I believe he is correct in this, and his impressively detailed analyses of the movement provides important insights into the fundamental principles of that style.[7]

The most important of these concern the nature of the thematic material from which Mendelssohn fashions his movement. Krummacher uses a comparison of the opening theme of the Quartet and the first theme from the finale of Mozart's G-minor Symphony, K. 550,—to which Mendelssohn's theme bears on obvious resemblance—to set the scale of distance between Mendelssohn's procedures and some of the normal thematic functions of the classical sonata style.[8]

Mozart's theme is a sentence-form constructed from groups of four—later two—measures that are themselves each made up of two sharply contrasting elements. The initial two-measure group is an ascending arpeggio in quarter notes that is opposed and balanced by the narrowly circling chromatic figure in eighth notes in mm. 3–4. This synthesis of balance and contrast reflects the structural basis of the classical style on the smallest possible scale: it is the initial confrontation of forces that will eventually provide the impetus for a clearly articulated move away from the tonic and the establishment of a polarized secondary key area.[9]

Of course, the sharp juxtaposition of elements in Mozart's theme is an exceptionally vivid realization of this principle, but some embodiment of the dynamic underlying it animates the opening of any classical sonata-form movement—exceptions tend to sound exceptional. When Beethoven, particularly in middle period works, does indulge in a more smoothly contoured lyric theme at the beginning of a movement, he is always careful to undermine the straightforward regularity on which it appears to be based. In the opening of his F-major Quartet, Op. 59, No. 1, for example, an important element of the dynamic impulse of the exposition is generated through the cadential energy built up within what seems to be a square cut lyric theme—

energy generated through a continual expansion of phrases and a corresponding delay of the expected cadence. (Tovey suggests the illuminating exercise
of holding one's breath until the dominant in m. 8 closes back to the tonic in
the second phrase of this melody.)[10] This energy is further reinforced by the
harmonic uncertainties inherent in the ambiguous role of the lower voice as
both accompanied melody and bass line. On the other hand, the lyric elaboration at the beginning of the "Eroica," which in some ways resembles the leisurely expansiveness of Mendelssohn's designs, is gently ruffled at the
outset by the mysterious excursion to C♯, and the opening theme itself eventually proves to be only the initial stage of an enormous first group that encompasses sharply defined oppositions on a correspondingly enormous
scale.[11]

In contrast, at the beginning of the E-minor Quartet, Mendelssohn establishes a unified, twenty-four measure field in which a single lyric gesture is
unfolded; as Krummacher notes, internal contrast is simply non-existent.
The introduction of continuous eighth notes in the latter stages of the passage
merely spins out the cadential quarter-note figure of the theme itself rather
than establishing a dynamic contrast of fundamental structural elements; this
essentially baroque procedure bears no relation to either the dynamic juxtaposition of elements in Mozart's theme or the subtle disruptions that animate
the opening of the "Eroica." For all the pulsing agitation of the accompaniment, the opening gesture in Mendelssohn's Quartet implies nothing beyond
its own cadence. Krummacher's description of the principal themes of this
movement as functioning "like self-contained lyric episodes"[12] helps identify the disjunction between the dramatic pretensions of the theme, marked
Allegro assai appassionato, and the distinctly uneventful regularity of its
structure—a disjunction that reveals the fundamental weakness of Mendelssohn's expressive vocabulary in these later works.

The lyric second theme can offer little contrast to the opening. Indeed, as
Krummacher points out, the principal themes are almost identical in phrase
structure and rhythm.[13] The only discernible difference between them is that
the second theme proceeds by step, while the most striking gesture of the first
theme is its graceful opening arpeggio—a Mannheim rocket in slow motion.

The principal contrast in this movement resides in the transitional material—a strongly marked passage that separates (rather than connects) these
"lyric episodes." The first theme comes to a dead stop on the downbeat of m.
25, and all four voices begin a rushing sixteenth-note figure that eventually
whips itself into a modulation leading toward V of v.

For Krummacher, this is a satisfactory—even brilliant—fulfillment of the
necessity for contrast on which his conception of sonata form is based.[14]But
it is a contrast that has absolutely no motivation in the bland lyricism of the

main theme: the suspicion is unavoidable that the transition bustles along because that is what a transition is supposed to do. It is the definition of the form rather than the implications of the material that governs the events in this work; the admirable fluidity that marked Mendelssohn's earlier works seems to have congealed once again into the paratactic succession of themes and transitions that characterizes the classicist romantic sonata style. This hardening of the forms is particularly striking because the structural designs of these movements often hinge on subtle harmonic relations like those found in the early works; but in contrast to the close coordination of surface detail and underlying structure that was so impressive in those early works, the loose, sectionalized forms of the later works tend to weaken the form-determining force of these harmonic details, reducing them to rather feeble effects of harmonic "color."

The transition in the first-movement exposition of the Quartet eventually settles onto V of v and subsides to a quiet murmur on a G-F♯ (♭6–5) alternation in the cello. But at the last moment, F♯ is taken as the leading tone to G, and the second theme begins in G major, the submediant of the dominant key (mm. 52–53). A move to the submediant within the second group, hinging on a reinterpretation of the ♭6–5 half step, is, of course, a common enough element in the classical style, particularly in Mozart's more lyrically expansive works. The submediant passage functions as an appoggiatura to the dominant and is usually elaborated by a distinctive thematic articulation: the brief excursion to F major in the second group of the D-major String Quartet, K. 499 (mm. 65–73) is a particularly beautiful example of this effect. The strong inflectional pull back toward the dominant is suspended temporarily by the lyric prolongation of the submediant, giving the passage an extraordinary motionlessness, and the return to the local tonic acquires an almost spatially defined quality of return; Tovey captured the sense of lyric warmth on which this effect depends in referring to these subdominant turns as "purple passages."

In Op. 44, No. 2, though, these tensions are never brought into play. B minor is never actually established as the center from which G major can register as a deviation—the drive toward B-minor is simply dropped at the last cadence of the transition, and the second group sits firmly in G major from its first note to the final cadence of the exposition: the softness of the second theme derives in large part from the immediate perception that G major does *not* function in relation to B minor. There is no carefully articulated frame against which the G♮—and secondarily, C♮—of the submediant can register as inflectional disruptions that press toward resolution. As a result, the tonal shift lacks any sense of the chromatic pressure that animates Mozart's procedure: instead of a purple passage, Mendelssohn has created a sticky-sweet concoction more aptly described by Tovey's technical term, "giant thematic gooseberry."

But, if anything is to be learned from the exploration of Mendelssohn's earlier works, it is that the compositional strategies in even the most straightforwardly regular of his designs are usually far more complex than they appear—or, rather, than we have come to expect them to be. What is frustrating—and makes the Mendelssohn Problem a particularly vexing problem—is that even in a seemingly schematicized form like the first movement of the E-minor Quartet, Mendelssohn has not simply wilted into easygoing classicism; even pseudo-Mendelssohn never merely fills in the formal outlines the way Schumann and Schubert often seem to do.

Instead of simply repeating—in appropriately transposed keys—the harmonic deflection associated with the opening of the second theme every time this material reappears, Mendelssohn reworks the harmonic perspective at each restatement, not simply for variety, but to reflect the functional role this material fulfills at crucial hinges of the form. At the end of the development section, the retransition, using the cadential figure of the bridge passage, settles onto V of E minor, and the second theme duly reappears in C major. This harmonic relation is exactly parallel to the B minor-G major of the exposition, of course, but this time the submediant *does* function as an appoggiatura that presses back toward V of the tonic; the gradual emergence of E minor from the expiring C major at the end of the development is the most impressive moment in the entire movement—even the ambling lyricism of the main theme, floating quietly over the gentle oscillation between C major and E minor, contributes to the remarkable effect of this passage. Later, in the course of the recapitulation itself, a shortened transition presses toward E minor, but the second group enters in E major. This realigns the cadential disjunction that has colored every previous appearance of this material while retaining a larger drive back toward the tonic minor over the final stages of the movement. This final drive is set off by a restatement of the beginning of the transition passage from the exposition—the sixteenth-note bustle that had seemed so unmotivated when it first appeared. Here it grows naturally from the harmonic flux of the recapitulation, and its agitation reflects the urgency of the cadential process.

Every element of form seems to acquire its true significance only in the latter stages of the movement: the expansively unfolded arpeggio of the main theme at the beginning of the recapitulation; the tonal organization of the second group in the retransition at the end of the development section; and the transitional material at the end of the recapitulation. It is as though the basic functional elements of the exposition—the establishment of opposing key areas and the transition from one stable area to the other (or, rather, the disjunction between these functional elements and their surface articulations)—have themselves become the problems to be investigated over the course of the movement—problematic relations posited in the exposition and resolved through the closural processes of the recapitulation.

The conception is remarkable, and I would suggest that it represents an attempt to integrate specifically lyric thematic material within the processive structure of sonata form. In other words, the organizational principle that governs this movement does not, in itself, represent a decline from the achievements of the earlier works. If the result seems nonetheless "weak," or "nicht selten frostig"—terms Krummacher has collected from the critical literature on Op. 44[15]—I would suggest that the fault lies in the thematic material rather than in the conception.

It is useful to remember that Mendelssohn's themes were never particularly striking, even in the finest of his earlier works: the opening of the Octet is as notable for its conventionality as for its impetuosity, and as Krummacher rightly observed, the Scherzo of that work has hardly any thematic material at all. This does not register as a defect because the themes are perfectly well suited to their articulative function within the formal design; in the first movement of the Octet, in fact, the absolutely conventional harmonic design that underlies the opening is itself the fundamental structural generating element of the form. (If the second theme of the *Hebrides* Overture is an obvious exception to this generalization, the extraordinary beauty of that theme is one of the principal reasons that the Overture is an exceptional work. In this context, it is revealing that in the recapitulation, Mendelssohn is willing to sacrifice most of the restatement of this theme to the requirement of the larger closural process: the role of the thematic material is still determined by its articulative function within the structure of the form.)

Dahlhaus stated the issue this way:

> Classical form could survive banality in some (not all) of its parts: the banal did not become intolerable until the idea of a balance of parts distinguished by their functions was replaced by the principle of developing ideas, the concept of musical form as something which presented the history of a musical theme.[16]

The most vexing problem in Mendelssohn's later works arises precisely from the way his later sonata-form movements straddle the line between these two organizational principles. In the first movement of Op. 44, No. 2, the relation of the themes to the underlying structure is not the stylistic given on which a complex of unique formal processes is constructed: that relation is itself the problem that is to be worked out over the course of the movement. But to put it bluntly, Mendelssohn's themes simply are not interesting enough to make that problem a compelling one. It is because Schumann,

Schubert, and Chopin wrote better themes, not because they handled the processive character of the form more persuasively, that we are more inclined to accept their sonata-form works—with all their obvious defects and (often heavenly) longeurs—than we are Mendelssohn's brilliant, but in the end less gripping, attempts to reconcile lyricism and processive design in these late works.

The Quartet in F minor, Op. 80 (1847, published posthumously in 1849), is often cited as the signpost of a "new way" in Mendelssohn's output. And indeed, there are remarkable effects—primarily textural—in the outer movements; in fact the part-writing is often so stark that the work looks (and to a certain extent sounds) more like a sketch for a quartet than a finished work.[17] The thematic material in this curious work does begin to show traces of a greater tightness than can be found in the typical works of the late thirties and early forties, but the evidence for a new style is not entirely clear. The second movement, Allegro assai, is the most impressive in the Quartet—it is the only late work (aside from the *Midsummer Night's Dream* music) that Tovey could place on the level of the early works.[18] What Tovey does not mention is that the pulsing theme of this movement is an almost literal quotation— reharmonized from major to minor—of the middle section of the second movement of Beethoven's F-major Piano Sonata, Op. 10, No. 2: even the remarkable disintegration of the theme at the end of the movement has its origins in the fragmented dialogue that rustles through the Beethoven.

It is difficult, then, to speak confidently about what truly late Mendelssohn might have been like—assuming that he could have found a melodic voice suitable for works on a larger scale than the *Songs Without Words*. But the Mendelssohn Problem is not—as it often seems—one of an inexplicable, or at least unanalyzable, quantum leap from youthful spontaneity to withered formalism. Even pseudo-Mendelssohn continued to explore the possibilities of an accommodation between the lyricism of the romantic style and the processive energy of sonata style. Whether he had exhausted his capacity to integrate these conflicting tendencies in his earlier works is a question that obviously cannot be answered; Tovey has made an intriguing point, however:

> Gluck, Handel, Haydn, Wagner, and Verdi—none of these would have been particularly great names to us if we possessed only the works they had written before they reached the age at which Mendelssohn died.[19]

This is an imposing list, and the quality of so many of the works of Mendelssohn we do possess is almost miraculous. He still remains one of the strangest problems in music history.

NOTES

CHAPTER 1.   THE MENDELSSOHN PROBLEM

1. Tovey, *Essays* 4:90.
2. Shaw, "A Dismal Saturday," *The World*, 19 November 1890, repr. in *Shaw's Music* 2:203.
3. Letter from Beethoven to Breitkopf & Härtel, 9 October 1811; cited in Tyson, "Beethoven's *Christus am Oelberge*," 553.
4. "der Mozart des 19ten Jahrhunderts, der hellste Musiker, der die Widersprüche der Zeit am klarsten durchschaut, und zuerst versöhnt." Schumann, "Trios," 198 (my translation).
5. Tovey, *Essays* 2:145–46.
6. Tovey, Ibid. 4:102.
7. Ibid., 91.
8. Rosen, *Sonata Forms*, 366.
9. Corder, *A Dictionary of Music and Musicians (A.D. 1450–1883)*, s.v. "scherzo."
10. Sontag, *Against Interpretation*, 13.
11. Musical examples from the scores of works by Beethoven, Mendelssohn, and Schumann are taken, respectively, from: *Ludwig van Beethovens Werke: Vollständige kritisch durchgesehene überall berechtigte Ausgabe* (Leipzig, 1864–90); *Felix Mendelssohn-Bartholdys Werke: Kritisch durchgesehene Ausgabe*, ed. Julius Rietz (Leipzig, 1874–77); and *Robert Schumann's Werke*, ed. Clara Schumann (Leipzig, 1881–93).

CHAPTER 2.   THE CLASSICIST HERITAGE

1. Smith, *Poetic Closure*, 2.
2. See, for example, Tovey, *Musical Textures*, 52–65.
3. Smith, *Poetic Closure*, 99–100.
4. Tovey, *Essays* 3:14.
5. Smith, *Poetic Closure*, 53ff.
6. Ibid., 36.
7. Ibid., 27.
8. Cherubini, *Cours de contrepoint et de fugue*, 112. The work is actually a compilation by his pupil, Jacques-François-Fromental Halévy.
9. See, for example, Rosen, *Sonata Forms*, 22–27.

10. Easily accessible examples would include the Allemande and Courante from Bach's "French" Suite in G Major, and the Allemandes from his "English" Suites in A Minor and G Minor.
11. Tovey, *Main Stream*, 91.
12. Rosen, *Sonata Forms*, 98–100 and passim.
13. Tovey, *Musical Textures*, 58.
14. Ibid.
15. Rosen, *The Classical Style*, 26–27; also see his *Sonata Forms*, 229–61.
16. Rosen, *Sonata Forms*, 241.
17. Dahlhaus, *Die Musik des 19. Jahrhunderts*, 220–23.
18. Tovey, *Essays* 1:9.
19. Smith, *Poetic Closure*, 66.
20. Rosen, *The Classical Style*, 51.
21. Smith, *Poetic Closure*, 2.
22. Urbantschitsch, "Brahms," 265–85.
23. "die starre Wiederholung des bereits einmal Gesagten." Ibid., 282 (my translation).
24. "die obligate symmetrische Analogie mit dem ersten Teil." Ibid. (my translation).
25. Ibid.
26. See the analytical sketches in Schenker, "Beethovens Dritte Sinfonie"; cited by Milton Babbitt in his Foreword to Epstein, *Beyond Orpheus*, xi.
27. Tovey, *Main Stream*, 287.
28. Chorley, *Modern German Music* 2:414.
29. Rosen, *The Classical Style*, 115–18.
30. Ibid.
31. "Er löst es in der Ouvertüre zu 'Coriolan', indem er die 'Auseinandersetzung' und hie[r]mit den Höhepunkt des Werkes aus der Durchführung in die Koda verlegt; die Durchführung bleibt ein Intermezzo und die Reprise wirkt fast als Repetition." Urbantschitsch, "Brahms," 282 (my translation).
32. The analysis that follows owes much to the illuminating discussion of this work in Morgan, "The Delayed Structural Downbeat and its Effects on the Tonal and Rhythmic Structure of Sonata Form Recapitulations," 64–69, 138. Where Morgan is concerned primarily with the larger tonal design, however, my analysis focuses more on the interrelation of surface and structural elements.
33. Morgan, "Delayed Structural Downbeat," 67.
34. Ibid., 66–67.
35. Ibid., 65–66, 138.
36. Mies, "Zur Coriolan-Overtüre op. 62," 267.
37. *The New Grove*, s.v. "sonata form."
38. *New Harvard Dictionary of Music*, s.v. "coda."
39. Schoenberg, *Fundamentals of Musical Composition*, 185.
40. More recently, the functional role of the coda has been addressed with notable insight and sophistication. One of the most significant changes in the revised edition of Rosen's *Sonata Forms* is the addition of a chapter on codas; this, and Kerman's study, "Notes on Beethoven's Codas," have helped to put many fundamental issues in clearer focus.
41. Smith, *Poetic Closure*, 33ff.

42. Lewis Lockwood has provided a particularly illuminating study of this work, including various elements of its closural processes, in "'Eroica' Perspectives," 85–105.
43. Tovey, *Essays* 1:29–34.
44. Rosen, *Sonata Forms*, 290–93; Tovey, *Essays* 1:30–31.
45. Kerman, "Theme and Variations," 52.
46. Kerman, "Notes on Beethoven's Codas," 143.
47. Todd, "Instrumental Music," 259.
48. "sechs Symphonien nach Art der alten, ohne Blaseinstrumente [sic]." Lea Mendelssohn-Bartholdy to Henriette von Pereira-Arnstein, Berlin, letter of 19 October 1821; cited in *Neue Leipziger Ausgabe der Werke Felix Mendelssohn-Bartholdys*, Foreword to vol. 1, *Sinfonien*, n. p. (my translation).
49. "Er hat eine grosse Anzahl von 'Kammersinfonien'geschrieben, in der er zur weitern Entwicklung des Sonatensatzes beiträgt, eine reichere, volle Instrumentation mit mehr realen Stimmen entwickelt, namentlich auch wirkungsvoll mehrchörig schreibt und Fugen- und Kanontechnik in die bisher leichtgefügte Form einführt. . . . Im Gegensatz zu den Mannheimern bevorzugen die Berliner die alte dreisätzige Form, unter den Sinfonien J. G. Grauns findet sich eine einzige viersätzige mit Menuett. Es gibt unter ihnen auch solche, die nur für Streichinstrumente geschrieben sind und dabei nur auf einfache Besetzung zählen, also Stücke, die wir heute als Quartette bezeichnen würden." Nef, *Geschichte der Sinfonie und Suite*,134–35 (my translation).
50. Wagner, *My Life*, 50–53, 139–57.
51. Cosima Wagner, Sunday, 13 February 1870, *Cosima Wagner's Diaries, 1869–1877* 1:189.
52. "die neusten Arbeiten des Wunderknaben, zumeist Sinfoniesätze für Streichquintet mit Klavierbegleitung." Dorn, *Aus Meinem Leben* 3:49 (my translation).
53. Finscher, *Studien zur Geschichte des Streichquartetts* 1:106–16.
54. Mendelssohn to his family, London, letter of 26 May 1829; in Hensel, *Die Familie Mendelssohn* 1:236–37.
55. Todd, *Mendelssohn's Musical Education*, 33–35, 124–48.
56. Fugue can be assimilated within sonata forms under certain carefully controlled circumstances; some of these will be considered in chapter 4.
57. Tovey, *Essays* 2:145.
58. Dahlhaus, *Between Romanticism and Modernism*, 44.
59. Rosen, *Sonata Forms*, 394.

CHAPTER 3.   THE OCTET

1. A facsimile of the manuscript has been published as *Octet for Strings, Opus 20: A Facsimile of the Holograph in the Whittall Foundation Collection*.
2. For discussions of various aspects of Mendelssohn's revisions, see, among others, Abraham, "The Scores of Mendelssohn's 'Hebrides',"172–76; Gerlach, "Mendelssohns Kompositionsweise," 119–33, and "Mendelssohns Kompositionsweise (II), 149–67; Krummacher, *Mendelssohn—der Komponist*, 99–132 and passim, "Mendelssohn's Late Chamber Music," 71–84, and "Zur Kompositionsart Mendelssohns," 169–84; Mintz, "'Melusine': A Men-

delssohn Draft," 480-99, and "Sketches and Drafts"; Seaton, "Mendelssohn's 'Scotch' Symphony," 129-35, "Mendelssohn's Sketches," and "The Romantic Mendelssohn," 398-410; Thomas, *Instrumentalwerk*, and "Zur Kompositionsweise in Mendelssohns Ouvertüren," 129-48; Todd, "An Unfinished Piano Concerto by Mendelssohn," 80-101, "An Unfinished Symphony by Mendelssohn," 293-309, "Of Sea Gulls and Counterpoint," 197-213, and "Instrumental Music"; and Walker, "Mendelssohn's 'Die einsame Insel'," 148-50.

3. For a discussion of Goethe's conception of botanical morphology, see Magnus, *Goethe as a Scientist*, 39-68.

4. Of course, the influence of Goethe's notions of organicism becomes an explicit element in the music of Schoenberg and his school; see, for example, Webern's series of talks collected as "The Path to Twelve-Note Composition," in *The Path to the New Music*, 42-56.

5. Landon, *The Symphonies of Joseph Haydn*, 319, 413; Todd, *Instrumental Music*, 264, 281.

6. Rosen, *Sonata Forms*, 71ff.; Tovey, *Essays* 3:14-24.

7. Krummacher, *Mendelssohn—der Komponist*, 156; Todd, "Instrumental Music," 266-67.

8. Tovey, *Essays* 2:145.

9. Krummacher, for example, states categorically that there is no relation between the two themes, and suggests that this represents a weakness in the formal design; *Mendelssohn—der Komponist*, 404.

10. Ibid., 405.

11. On the three-key exposition in general, see Rosen, *Sonata Forms*, 234-49.

12. Tovey, *Musical Textures*, 58.

13. Krummacher, *Mendelssohn—der Komponist*, 373-74; Thomas, *Instrumentalwerk*, 42.

14. Rosen, *The Classical Style*, 213.

15. Tovey, *Essays* 3:24-25 and passim.

16. Todd, "Instrumental Music," 225-26.

17. Cone, *Musical Form and Musical Performance*, 76-77.

CHAPTER 4.   THE THEMATIC SHAPE

1. The tritone figure is borrowed from Clara's Op. 5; see Solomon, "Solo Piano Music," 47. This same A-D# pairing will be elaborated on an extraordinary scale in the finale; see Rosen, *Sonata Forms*, 369-83.

2. Rosen, *Sonata Forms*, 369.

3. G. A. Macfarren, Philharmonic program-book, 30 April 1877; cited in *A Dictionary of Music and Musicians (A.D. 1450–1883)*, s.v. "Mendelssohn."

4. Tovey, *Essays* 4:100.

5. Ibid., 4:101-2.

6. Young, *Something of Great Constancy*, 91.

7. Tovey, *Essays* 4:102.

8. The Overture was written in 1828, but this original version was subjected to extensive revisions before its publication in 1834; various aspects of these revisions will be considered below.

9. Fanny Hensel to Karl Klingemann, letter of 18 June 1828; in Hensel, *Die Familie Mendelssohn* 1:210.

10. Rosen, *Sonata Forms*, 223.

11. Todd, "Instrumental Music," 442–43.

12. Ibid., 459–60.

13. For valuable information on the sketches and publishing history of this work and analytical commentary, see Todd, "Instrumental Music," 293–328.

14. Krummacher, *Mendelssohn—der Komponist*, 249–50.

15. See Levy, "Texture as a Sign," 482–531.

16. Rosen discusses the matter of displaced second themes, primarily with reference to the first movement of Haydn's "Farewell" Symphony, in *Sonata Forms*, 156–60.

17. See for example, Warren Kirkendale, *Fugue and Fugato*, 329; Thomas, *Instrumentalwerk*, 39; and Krummacher, *Mendelssohn—der Komponist*, 454–55.

18. For a summary of the tangled compositional history of this work, see Todd, "Of Sea Gulls and Counterpoint," 197–213.

19. "Kompositionstechnisch beruht die musikalische Darstellung von Natur in den hervorstechendsten Beispielen—im Waldweben aus *Siegfried*, in der Nilszene aus *Aida* oder in der Szene am Fluss aus Gounods *Mireille*—fast immer auf einem Prinzip, das in der Neuen Musik des 20. Jahrhunderts ins Extrem getrieben und zur Formidee ganzer Werke erhoben wurde: dem Prinzip der gleichsam stehenden, aber in sich bewegten Klangfläche. Gleichgültig, ob es sich um eine Idylle oder um eine Gewitterszene (wie im Vorspiel zum ersten Akt der *Walküre*) handelt: Die Musik verharrt—unabhängig davon, wie heftig oder schwach die rhythmische Bewegung ist—motivisch und harmonisch auf der Stelle." Dahlhaus, *Die Musik des 19. Jahrhunderts*, 257 (my translation).

20. Ibid., 257–59.

21. "Die Stelle, wo die Oboen allein durch die anderen Instrumenten hindurch klagend wie der Wind über die Wellen des Meeres zur Höhe steigen, ist von ausserordentlicher Schönheit." von Wolzogen, *Erinnerungen an Richard Wagner*, 36.

22. Tovey, *Essays* 4:92–93.

23. "Siehst Du das ist eine[r] von meinen Puncten! Die Beziehung aller 4 oder 3 oder 2 oder 1 Stücken einer Sonata auf dieandere [n] und die Theile, so dass man durch das blosse Anfangen durch die ganze Existens so eines Stückes schon das Geheimniss weiss (denn wenn das blosse d-dur wieder anfängt, die 2 Noten, so ist es mir weich um das Herz) das muss in die Musik." Mendelssohn to Adolf Fredrik Lindblad, cited in Krummacher, *Mendelssohn—der Komponist*, 72 (my translation).

24. A facsimile of the 1830 version has been published as *Die Hebriden. First Version of the Concert Overture.*

25. Tovey, *Beethoven*, 30.

26. Thomas, *Instrumentalwerk*, 243. Mendelssohn's interest in early vocal music is well documented in his letters—this was undoubtedly a natural outgrowth of his work with Zelter at the *Singakademie*.

CHAPTER 5. THEMATIC PROCESS AND CYCLIC FORM

1. Rosen, *The Classical Style*, 36–42.
2. Rosen, *Sonata Forms*, 393–94.
3. "die Geschlossenheit der Form ist das Korrelat zur Autonomie des Werkes." Dahlhaus, *Die Idee der absoluten Musik*, 109 (my translation).
4. See Treitler, "Beethoven's Ninth," 196–98.
5. Rosen, *Sonata Forms*, 124–25.
6. For alternate readings of this movement, see Jonas, *Einführung in die Lehre Heinrich Schenkers*, 102–3; and Beach, "A Schenkerian Analysis," 204–16. Neither of these place the movement within the context of the work as a whole.
7. Rosen, *The Classical Style*, 396–99.
8. Rosen, *Sonata Forms*, 123–32; Tovey, *The Forms of Music*, 229.
9. For a detailed study of this movement and the sketches see Mintz, "Sketches," 392–458.
10. See Treitler, "Beethoven's Ninth," 193–98, and Ernest Sanders, "Form and Content," 59–76.
11. Tovey, *Essays* 1:42–44.
12. "le theme de la *Symphonie fantastique*, 'l'idée fixe,' s'interpose obstinément comme une idée passionnée épisodique au milieu des scènes qui lui sont étrangères et leur fait diversion, tandis que le chant d'Harold se superpose aux autres chants de l'orchestre, avec lesquels il contraste par son mouvement et son caractère, sans en interrompre le développement." Berlioz, *Mémoires* 1:298 (my translation).
13. On this, and many other matters, see the illuminating discussion in Ruston, *The Musical Language of Berlioz*, in particular, Part III.
14. Review, "A Symphony by Berlioz," trans. Edward T. Cone in his edition of Hector Berlioz, *Fantastic Symphony*, 246.
15. "Schumanns Gedanke, die Sätze des Zyklus durch Zitate und Reminiszenzen miteinander zu verknüpfen, ist ein "poetisches" Moment, das andererseits als Ausgleich einer formalen Schwäche erscheint: Der Reichtum an assoziativen Verklammerungen ersetzt die tektonische Festigkeit, die dem Werk mangelt." Dahlhaus, "Studien zu Romantischen Symphonien," 115 (my translation). For another view of this work, and stimulating views on Schumann's formal procedures in general, see Newcomb, "Schumann's Second Symphony," 233–50, and "Narrative Strategies," 164–74.
16. See Rosen, *The Classical Style*, 451–53.
17. Godwin, "Early Mendelssohn and Late Beethoven," 272–74.
18. There is an obvious problem of chronology surrounding the idea that Mendelssohn modeled his quartet on Beethoven's work: Op. 132 was not published until September of 1827, several months after Mendelssohn had begun work on Op. 13. Friedhelm Krummacher's suggestion that Mendelssohn might have come into contact with the work before its publication through Schlesinger, the publisher of Op. 132 and of many of Mendelssohn's early works, is undoubtedly correct: Krummacher, "Synthesis des Disparaten," 112 n. 44. On the publication history of Op. 132, see Thayer, *Life of Beethoven*, 959–63, 1009; and Tyson, "Maurice Schlesinger as a Publisher of Beethoven," 187–90; on Mendelssohn's relations with Schlesinger, which were not always particularly cor-

dial, see Elvers, "Acht Briefe von Lea Mendelssohn," 47–53; and *Briefe an deutsche Verleger*, 277–84.

19. Dahlhaus, "Cantabile und thematischer Prozess," 82–84.
20. Kerman, *The Beethoven Quartets*, 245.
21. Carl Schachter has examined a similar play on an unchanging intervallic motive in his illuminating article, "Beethoven's Sketches for the First Movement of Op. 14, No. 1," 1–21.
22. Kerman, *The Beethoven Quartets*, 250–51.
23. See, for example, Schenker, *Harmony*, 59–69; Mason, *The Quartets of Beethoven*, 192–99; and Kerman, *The Beethoven Quartets*, 253–61.
24. Brandenburg, "Historical Background," 163–67.
25. In fact, this cadential ploy proves to be so orthodox that Kerman detects in it "the old familiar smell of the classroom" that occasionally seems to threaten his enjoyment of the quartets. Kerman, *The Beethoven Quartets*, 257.
26. Brandenburg, "Historical Background," 182.
27. Ibid., 164, 166.
28. Kerman, *The Beethoven Quartets*, 262.
29. Mason, *The Quartets of Beethoven*, 205.
30. Kerman, *The Beethoven Quartets*, 264.
31. "Das Lied was ich dem Quartette beifüge ist das Thema desselben. Du wirst es im ersten und letzten Stücke mit seinen Noten, in allen vier Stücken mit seiner Empfindung sprechen hören. Wenn es Dir das erstemal missfällt—was kommen kann, so spiele es zum zweiten Male und wenn Du etwas menuettartiges darin findest, so denke an Deinen steifen und formellen Felix mit der Halsbinde und dem Diener. Ich dächte ich spräche aus dem Liede wohl, und es klingt mir wie Musik." Mendelssohn to Adolf Lindblad, undated letter, *Bref till Adolf Fredrik Lindblad*, ed. Dahlgren, 20 (my translation). Krummacher suggests a date during the first half of 1828, *Mendelssohn—der Komponist*, 513 n. 85.
32. Tovey, *Essays* 4:95.
33. For a stimulating examination of these discontinuities, see Agawu, "The First Movement of Beethoven's Opus 132," 30–45.
34. See Mies, *Beethoven's Sketches*, 5–9; the useful term "curtain" is Riemann's.
35. Tovey, *Essays* 1:44.
36. "unsere Lieblingsidee vom 'sich in den Schwanz beissen'." Mendelssohn to Karl Klingemann, letter of 23 June 1834; in *Briefwechsel mit Legationsrat Karl Klingemann*, ed. Klingemann, 135 (my translation).
37. "Viele Leute haben es noch schon gehört, aber ist es schon einem einzigen (meine Schwester nehme ich aus und Rietz und Marx auch) sonst eingefallen ein ganzes darin zu sehen? Der Eine lobt das Intermezzo, der Andere das, der Dritte jenes. Pfui über Alle!" *Bref till Adolf Fredrik Lindblad*, 20ff. (my translation).
38. Smith, *Poetic Closure*, 188.
39. Ibid., 189.
40. See, for example, Kohlhase, "Studien zur Form," 77–80.
41. "Du scheinst Dich aber etwas über mein A-moll-Quartett zu moquieren, wenn Du von einer andern Instrumentalmusik sagst, sie koste Kopfzerbrechen, um herauszukriegen, was der Verfasser gedacht habe, der aber nichts dabei gedacht habe. Das Stück müsste ich denn vertheidigen, denn es ist mir auch lieb; aber es kommt nur gar zu viel auf die Ausführung an." Letter from Men-

delssohn to his father, Paris, 31 March 1832; in *Reisebriefe*, ed. Paul Mendelssohn, 52 (my translation).
42. Rosen, *The Classical Style*, 403.
43. Tovey, *The Forms of Music*, 127.
44. Letters from Mendelssohn to his family, 30 July and 7 August 1829; in Hensel, *Die Familie Mendelssohn* 1:252–53, 258.
45. See, for example, Longyear, "Mendelssohn's 'Scottish' Symphony," 38–48. My analysis of the thematic organization of the work is somewhat different from Longyear's, reflecting a fundamentally different view of the nature of cyclic process.
46. Shaw, "Knighthood and Dancing," *The Star*, 21 February 1890, repr. in *Shaw's Music* 1:927.
47. "stark wie ein Männerchor." Letter to Ferdinand David, who was preparing the premiere, 12 March 1842; in *Reisebriefe*, 119 (my translation).
48. "ein Art 'Danklied nach gewonnener Schlacht'." Witte, "Zur Programmgebundenheit der Sinfonien Mendelssohns," 125 (my translation).
49. Schoenberg, *Fundamentals of Musical Composition*, 185.

CHAPTER 6. THE LATER MENDELSSOHN

1. Webster, "Schubert's Sonata Form," [Part II], 56.
2. Tovey, *Essays* 1:137, 221.
3. Tovey, *Main Stream*, 244.
4. Schoenberg, "Analysis," 25–45.
5. Tovey, *Main Stream*, 122.
6. On the processive relation between the exposition and recapitulation in this movement, see Allen, "Schubert's C Major String Quintet," 11–13.
7. Krummacher, *Mendelssohn—der Komponist*; "Zur Kompositionsart Mendelssohns," 149–67; and "Mendelssohn's Late Chamber Music," 71–84.
8. Krummacher, *Mendelssohn—der Komponist*, 136–38.
9. See, for example, Rosen, *The Classical Style*, 80–95,185– 89, 199–210; and Dahlhaus, "Zur Theorie der musikalischen Form," 29–32.
10. Tovey, *Beethoven*, 82.
11. See Kerman, *The Beethoven Quartets*, 89–103, for a discussion of these two works, and Dahlhaus, "Cantabile und thematischer Prozess," 81–98, for a broader analysis of Beethoven's use of lyric material in sonata-form movements.
12. "wie geschlossene lyrische Situationen." Krummacher, *Mendelssohn—der Komponist*, 140 (my translation).
13. Ibid., 138–39.
14. Ibid., 140–41, 277–91.
15. Krummacher, *Mendelssohn—der Komponist*, 25, 34.
16. Dahlhaus, *Between Romanticism and Modernism*, 43–44.
17. Krummacher, in fact, suggests that the published score does not represent a finished work—that it is, in a real sense, a sketch that the composer did not live to complete; *Mendelssohn—der Komponist*, 325–33.
18. Tovey, *Essays* 4:90.
19. Ibid.

BIBLIOGRAPHY

Abraham, Gerald. "The Scores of Mendelssohn's 'Hebrides'." *Monthly Musical Record* 78 (1948): 172–76.

Agawu, V. Kofi. "The First Movement of Beethoven's Opus 132 and the Classical Style." *College Music Symposium* 27 (1987): 30–45.

Allen, Judith Shatin. "Schubert's C Major String Quintet, Opus 163/I: The Evolving Dominant." *In Theory Only* 6, no. 5 (July 1982): 3–16.

Babbitt, Milton. Foreword to *Beyond Orpheus: Studies in Musical Structure*, by David Epstein. Cambridge: MIT Press, 1979.

Beach, David. "A Schenkerian Analysis [of the *Introduzione* to Beethoven's Piano Sonata Op. 53/II]." In *Readings in Schenker Analysis and Other Approaches*, edited by Maury Yeston. New Haven: Yale University Press, 1977. (First Published in "Analysis Symposium." *Journal of Music Theory* 13 (1969): 188–203.)

Beethoven, Ludwig van. *Ludwig van Beethovens Werke: Vollständige kritisch durchgesehene überall berechtigte Ausgabe.* 24 vols. and suppl. Leipzig: Breitkopf & Härtel, 1864–90.

Berlioz, Hector. *Mémoires.* 2 vols. Edited by Pierre Citron. Paris: Garnier-Flammarion, 1969.

Brandenburg, Sieghard. "The Historical Background to the 'Heiliger Dankgesang' in Beethoven's A-minor Quartet Op. 132." In *Beethoven Studies*, vol. 3, edited by Alan Tyson. Cambridge: Cambridge University Press, 1982.

Cherubini, Luigi. *Cours de contrepoint et de fugue.* Paris: Schlesinger, 1835.

Chorley, Henry F. *Modern German Music.* 2 vols. London, 1854. Reprint. New York: Da Capo Press, 1973.

Cone, Edward T. *Musical Form and Musical Performance.* New York: W.W. Norton, 1968.

___, ed. *Fantastic Symphony*, by Hector Berlioz. New York: W.W. Norton, 1971.

Corder, Fredrick. Article, "Rondo." In *A Dictionary of Music and Musicians (A. D. 1450–1883)*, 1st ed. Edited by George Grove. London: Macmillan, 1883.

Dahlhaus, Carl. *Between Romanticism and Modernism: Four Studies in the Music of the Later Nineteenth Century.* Translated by Mary Whittall. Berkeley and Los Angeles: University of California Press, 1980.

___. "Cantabile und thematischer Prozess." *Archiv für Musikwissenschaft* 37 (1980): 81–98.

___. *Die Idee der absoluten Musik.* Kassel: Bärenreiter Verlag, 1978.

___. "Mendelssohn und die Musikalische Gattungstraditionen." In *Das Problem Mendelssohn*, edited by Carl Dahlhaus.

___. *Die Musik des 19. Jahrhunderts.* Neues Handbuch der Musikwissenschaft, vol. 6. Wiesbaden: Akademische Verlagsgesellschaft Athenaion, 1980.

___. "Studien zu Romantischen Symphonien." *Jahrbuch des Staatlichen Instituts für Musikforschung Preussischer Kulturbesitz Berlin,* 1972: 104–19.

___. "Zur Theorie der musikalischen Form." *Archiv für Musikwissenschaft* 34 (1977): 20–37.

___, ed. *Das Problem Mendelssohn.* Studien zur Musikgeschichte des 19. Jahrhunderts, vol. 11. Regensburg: Gustav Bosse Verlag, 1974.

Dorn, Heinrich. *Aus meinem Leben.* Vol. 3, *Erinnerungen.* Berlin: E. Graetz, 1872.

Droysen, Gustave. "Johann Gustave Droysen und Felix Mendelssohn-Bartholdy." *Deutsche Rundschau* 111 (1902): 107–26, 193–215, 386–408.

Elvers, Rudolf. "Acht Briefe von Lea Mendelssohn an den Verleger Schlesinger in Berlin." In *Das Problem Mendelssohn,* edited by Carl Dahlhaus.

___, ed. *Briefe an deutsche Verleger.* Berlin: Walter de Gruyter, 1968.

Finscher, Ludwig. *Studien zur Geschichte des Streichquartetts.* Vol. I, *Die Enstehung des klassischen Streichquartetts. Von den Vorformen zur Grundlegung durch Joseph Haydn.* Saarbrücker Studien zur Musikwissenschaft, vol. 3. Kassel: Bärenreiter, 1974.

Gerlach, Reinhard. "Mendelssohns Kompositionsweise: Vergleich zwischen Skizzen und Letztfassung des Violinkonzerts opus 64." *Archiv für Musikwissenschaft* 28 (1971): 119–33.

___. "Mendelssohns Kompositionsweise (II). Weitere Vergleiche zwischen den Skizzen und Letztfassung des Violinkonzerts op. 64." In *Das Problem Mendelssohn,* edited by Carl Dahlhaus.

Godwin, Joscelyn. "Early Mendelssohn and Late Beethoven." *Music & Letters* 55 (1974): 272–85.

Goethe, Johann Wolfgang von. *Goethes Werke.* 14 vols. Edited by Erich Trunz, et al. Hamburg: C. Wegner, 1958.

Hensel, Sebastian. *Die Familie Mendelssohn 1729–1847: Nach Briefern und Tagebüchern.* 18th ed. 2 vols. Leipzig: Insel Verlag, 1924.

Jonas, Oswald. *Einführung in die Lehre Heinrich Schenkers: Das Wesen des musikalischen Kunstwerkes.* 2nd ed. Vienna: Universal Edition, 1972.

Keller, Hans. "The Classical Romantics." In *Of German Music: A Symposium,* edited by H. H. Schonzeler. London: Wolff, 1976.

Kerman, Joseph. *The Beethoven Quartets.* New York: Alfred A. Knopf, 1967.

___. "Notes on Beethoven's Codas." In *Beethoven Studies,* edited by Alan Tyson, vol. 3.

___. "Theme and Variations." Review of *Sonata Forms,* by Charles Rosen. *New York Review of Books* 27, no. 16 (23 October 1980): 50–52.

Kirkendale, Warren. *Fugue and Fugato in Rococo and Classical Chamber Music.* 2nd ed. Translated by Margaret Bent and the author. Durham, N.C. : Duke University Press, 1979.

Klingemann, Karl. *Felix Mendelssohn-Bartholdys Briefwechsel* mit Legationsrat Karl Klingemann in London. Edited by Karl Klingemann, Jr. Essen: G. D. Baedeker, 1909.

Köhler, Karl-Heinz. "Das Jugendwerk Felix Mendelssohns: Die vergessene Kindheitsentwicklung eines Genies." *Deutsche Jahrbuch der Musikwissenschaft* 7 (1963): 18–35.

___. Article, "Mendelssohn (-Bartholdy), (Jakob Ludwig) Felix." In *The New Grove Dictionary of Music and Musicians*, 20 vol., edited by Stanley Sadie. London: Macmillan, 1980.

Kohlhase, Hans. "Studien zur Form in den Streichquartetten von Felix Mendelssohn Bartholdy." *Hamburger Jahrbuch für Musikwissenschaft* 2 (1977): 75-104.

Krummacher, Friedhelm. *Mendelssohn—der Komponist: Studien zur Kammermusik für Streicher.* Munich: Wilhelm Fink Verlag, 1978.

___. "Mendelssohn's Late Chamber Music: Some Autograph Sources Recovered." In *Mendelssohn and Schumann: Essays on Their Music and Its Context*, edited by Jon W. Finson and R. Larry Todd. Durham, N.C.: Duke University Press, 1984.

___. "Synthesis des Disparaten: Zu Beethovens späten Quartetten und ihrer frühen Rezeption." *Archiv für Musikwissenschaft* 37 (1980): 99-134.

___. "Zur Kompositionsart Mendelssohns: Thesen am Beispiel der Streichquartette." In *Das Problem Mendelssohn*, edited by Carl Dahlhaus.

Landon, H. C. Robbins. *The Symphonies of Joseph Haydn.* London: Universal Edition, 1955.

Levy, Janet M. "Texture as a Sign in Classic and Early Romantic Music." *Journal of the American Musicological Society* 35 (1982): 482-531.

Lindblad, Adolf Fredrik. *Bref till Adolf Fredrik Lindblad från Mendelssohn, Dohrn, Almqvist, Atterbom, Geijer, Fredrika Bremer, C. W. Böttiger och andra.* Edited by L. Dahlgren. Stockholm: A. Bonnier, 1913.

Lockwood, Lewis. "'Eroica' Perspective: Strategy and Design in the First Movement." In *Beethoven Studies*, edited by Alan Tyson, vol. 3.

Longyear, Rey M. "Cyclic Form and Tonal Relationships in Mendelssohn's 'Scottish' Symphony." *In Theory Only* 4, no. 7 (January 1979): 38-48.

Macfarren, G. A. Philharmonic program-book for 30 April 1877. Cited in the article, "Mendelssohn," in *A Dictionary of Music and Musicians (A.D. 1450–1883)*, 1st ed., edited by George Grove, London: Macmillan, 1883.

Magnus, Rudolf. *Goethe as a Scientist.* Translated by Heinz Norden. New York: Collier, 1961. Originally published as *Goethe als Naturforscher*. Leipzig: Barth, 1906.

Mason, Daniel Gregory. *The Quartets of Beethoven.* New York: Oxford University Press, 1947.

Mendelssohn, Felix. *Felix Mendelssohn-Bartholdys Werke: Kritisch durchgesehene Ausgabe.* 19 vols. Edited by Julius Rietz. Leipzig: Breitkopf & Härtel, 1874-77.

___. *Die Hebriden. First Version of the Concert Overture.* Edited by Max Schneider. Basle: Amerbach, 1947.

___. *Neue Leipziger Ausgabe der Werke Felix Mendelssohn Bartholdy.* Series I, *Orchestral Works.* Edited by the International Felix Mendelssohn Society. Vols. 1-3, *Sinfonien*, Edited by Helmuth Christian Wolff. Leipzig: Deutscher Verlag für Musik, 1972.

___. *Octet for Strings, Opus 20: A Facsimile of the Holograph in the Whittall Foundation Collection.* Introduction by Jon Newsom. Washington, D. C.: Library of Congress, 1976.

___. *Reisebriefe von Felix Mendelssohn Bartholdy aus den Jahren 1830 bis 1832.* 4th ed., edited by Paul Mendelssohn Bartholdy. Leipzig: H. Mendelsohn, 1862.

Mies, Paul. *Beethoven's Sketches: An Analysis of His Style Based on a Study of his Sketch-Books.* Translated by Doris L. Mackinnon. London: Oxford University Press, 1929. Reprint. New York: Dover Books, 1979.

___. "Zur Coriolan-Overtüre op. 62." *Beethoven Jahrbuch* 11 (1965-68): 260-68.

Mintz, Donald. "'Melusine': A Mendelssohn Draft." *The Musical Quarterly* 43 (1957): 480-99.

___. "The Sketches and Drafts of Three of Felix Mendelssohn's Major Works." 2 vols. Ph.D. diss., Cornell University, 1960.

Morgan, Robert P. "The Delayed Structural Downbeat and its Effects on the Tonal and Rhythmic Structure of Sonata Form Recapitulations." Ph.D. diss., Princeton University, 1969.

___. "The Theory and Analysis of Tonal Rhythm." *The Musical Quarterly* 64 (1978): 435-73.

Nef, Karl. *Geschichte der Sinfonie und Suite.* Leipzig: Breitkopf & Härtel, 1921.

Oster, Ernst. "Register and Large-Scale Connection." In *Readings in Schenkerian Analysis and Other Approaches,* edited by Maury Yeston. New Haven: Yale University Press, 1977.

Radcliffe, Philip. *Mendelssohn.* London: J. M. Dent & Sons, 1954.

Randel, Don Michael, ed. *The New Harvard Dictionary of Music.* Cambridge: Harvard University Press, 1986.

Ratner, Leonard G. *Classic Music: Expression, Form, and Style.* New York: Schirmer Books, 1980.

___. "Eighteenth-Century Theories of Musical Period Structure." *The Musical Quarterly* 62 (1956): 439-54.

___. "Harmonic Aspects of Classic Form." *Journal of the American Musicological Society* 2 (1949): 159-68.

___. "Key Definition: A Structural Issue in Beethoven's Music." *Journal of the American Musicological Society* 23 (1970): 472-83.

Rosen, Charles. *The Classical Style: Haydn, Mozart, Beethoven.* New York: W. W. Norton, 1972.

___. *Sonata Forms.* Rev. ed. New York: W. W. Norton, 1988.

Rushton, Julian. *The Musical Language of Berlioz.* Cambridge: Cambridge University Press, 1983.

Salzer, Felix. "Die Sonatenform bei Franz Schubert.: *Studien zur Musikwissenschaft* 15 (1928): 86-125.

Sanders, Ernest. "Form and Content in the Finale of Beethoven's Ninth Symphony." *The Musical Quarterly* 50 (1964): 59-76.

Schacter, Carl. "Beethoven's Sketches for the First Movement of Op. 14, No. 1." *Journal of Music Theory* 26 (1982): 1-21.

Schenker, Heinrich. "Beethoven's Dritte Sinfonie zum erstenmal in ihrem wahren Inhalt dargestellt." *Das Meisterwerk in der Musik: ein Jahrbuch von Heinrich Schenker,* vol. 3. Munich: Drei Masken Verlag, 1930. Reprint (3 vols. in 1). Hildesheim: Georg Olms Verlag, 1974.

___. *Free Composition (Der freie Satz).* Vol. 3 of *New Musical Theories and Fantasies.* Edited and translated by Ernst Oster. New York: Longman, 1979.

___. *Harmony.* Edited by Oswald Jonas, translated by Elisabeth Mann Borgese. Cambridge: MIT Press, 1973.

___. "Organic Structure in Sonata Form." Translated by Orin Grossman. In *Readings in Schenker Analysis and Other Approaches*, edited by Maury Yeston. New Haven: Yale University Press, 1977.

Schoenberg, Arnold. "Analysis of the Four Orchestral Songs Op. 22." Translated by Claudio Spies. In *Perspectives of New Music* 3 (1965): 1-21. (Reprinted in *Perspectives on Schoenberg and Stravinsky*, rev. ed., edited by Benjamin Boretz and Edward T. Cone. New York: W. W. Norton, 1972.)

___. *Fundamentals of Musical Composition*. Edited by Gerald Strang and Leonard Stein. New York: St. Martin's Press, 1967.

Schumann, Robert. Review, "A Symphony by Berlioz." Translated by Edward T. Cone in his edition of *Fantastic Symphony* by Hector Berlioz. New York: W. W. Norton, 1971.

___. *Robert Schumann's Werke*. 14 vols. Edited by Clara Schumann. Leipzig: Breitkopf & Härtel, 1881-93.

___. "Trio's für Pianoforte, Violine und Violoncello." *Neue Zeitschrift für Musik* 13 (1840): 197-98.

Seaton, Stuart Douglass. "A Draft for the Exposition of the First Movement of Mendelssohn's 'Scotch' Symphony." *Journal of the American Musicological Society* 30 (1977): 129-35.

___. Review of *Mendelssohn--der Komponist*, by Friedhelm Krummacher. *Journal of the American Musicological Society* 32 (1979): 356-60.

___. "The Romantic Mendelssohn: The Composition of *Die erste Walpurgisnacht*." *The Musical Quarterly* 68 (1982): 398-410.

___. "A Study of a Collection of Mendelssohn's Sketches and Other Autograph Material, Deutsche Staatsbibliothek Berlin 'Mus. mss. autogr. Mendelssohn 19'." Ph.D. diss., Columbia University, 1977.

Shaw, George Bernard. *Shaw's Music*. Edited by Dan H. Laurence. 3 vols. New York: Dodd, Mead, 1981:

Smith, Alexander Brent. "The Workmanship of Mendelssohn." *Music & Letters* 4 (1923): 18-25.

Smith, Barbara Herrnstein. *Poetic Closure: A Study of How Poems End*. Chicago: University of Chicago Press, 1968.

Solomon, Yonty. "Solo Piano Music (I) The Sonatas and Fantasie." *In Robert Schumann: The Man and His Music*, edited by Alan Walker. New York: Barnes and Noble, 1974.

Sontag, Susan. *Against Interpretation*. New York: Farrar, Straus & Giroux, 1966.

Thayer, Alexander Wheelock. *Life of Beethoven*. Revised and edited by Elliot Forbes. Princeton: Princeton University Press, 1967; one-volume paperback edition, 1970.

Thomas, Mathias. *Das Instrumentalwerk Felix Mendelssohn-Bartholdys: Eine Systematisch-theoretische Untersuchung unter besonderer Berücksichtigung der zeitgenössischen Musiktheorie*. Göttinger musikwissenschaftliche Arbeiten, vol. 4. Göttingen, 1972.

___. "Zur Kompositionsweise in Mendelssohns Ouvertüren." In *Das Problem Mendelssohn*, edited by Carl Dahlhaus.

Todd, R. Larry. "The Instrumental Music of Felix Mendelssohn-Bartholdy: Selected Studies Based on Primary Sources." Ph.D. diss., Yale University, 1979.

___. *Mendelssohn's Musical Education: A Study and Edition of his Exercises in Composition—Oxford, Bodleian MS Margaret Deneke Mendelssohn C. 43.* Cambridge: Cambridge University Press, 1983.

___. "Of Sea Gulls and Counterpoint: the Early Versions of Mendelssohn's *Hebrides* Overture." *19th-Century Music* 2 (1979): 197-213.

___. "An Unfinished Piano Concerto by Mendelssohn." *The Musical Quarterly* 68 (1982): 80-101.

___. "An Unfinished Symphony by Mendelssohn." *Music & Letters* 61 (1980): 293-309.

Tovey, Donald Francis. *Beethoven.* London: Oxford University Press, 1944.

___. *Essays in Musical Analysis.* 6 vols. and suppl. London: Oxford University Press, 1935-44.

___. *The Forms of Music.* London: Oxford University Press, 1957. Originally published as *Musical Articles from the Encyclopedia Britannica.* London: Oxford University Press, 1944.

___. *The Main Stream of Music and Other Essays.* London: Oxford University Press, 1949.

___. *A Musician Talks.* Vol. 1 *The Integrity of Music.* London: Oxford University Press, 1941.

___. *A Musician Talks.* Vol. 2 *Musical Textures.* London: Oxford University Press, 1941.

Treitler, Leo. "History, Criticism, and Beethoven's Ninth Symphony." *19th-Century Music* 3 (1980): 193-211.

Tyson, Alan. "The 1803 Version of Beethoven's *Christus am Oelberge.*" *The Musical Quarterly* 56 (1970): 551-84. (Reprinted in *The Creative World of Beethoven,* edited by Paul Henry Lang. New York: W. W. Norton, 1970.)

___. "Maurice Schlesinger as a Publisher of Beethoven." *Acta Musicologica* 35 (1963): 182-91.

___, ed. *Beethoven Studies.* Vol. 3. Cambridge: Cambridge University Press, 1982.

Urbantschitsch, Viktor. "Die Entwicklung der Sonatenform bei Brahms." *Studien zur Musikwissenschaft* 14 (1927): 264-85.

Wagner, Cosima. *Cosima Wagner's Diaries, 1869-1877.* Edited by Martin Gregor-Dellin and Dietrich Mack, translated by Geoffrey Skelton. New York: Harcourt Brace Jovanovich, 1978.

Wagner, Richard. *My Life.* Edited by Mary Whittall, translated by Andrew Gray. Cambridge: Cambridge University Press, 1983.

Walker, Ernest. "Mendelssohn's 'Die einsame Insel'." *Music & Letters* 26 (1945): 148-50.

Webern, Anton. *The Path to the New Music.* Edited by Willi Reich, translated by "L. B." Bryn Mawr: Theodore Presser, 1963.

Webster, James. "Schubert's Sonata Form and Brahms's First Maturity." *19th-Century Music* 2 (1978): 18-35, and 3 (1979): 52-71.

___. Article, "Sonata Form." In *The New Grove Dictionary of Music and Musicians,* 20 vol., edited by Stanely Sadie. London: Macmillan, 1980.

Werner, Eric. *Mendelssohn: A New Image of the Composer and His Age.* Translated by Dika Newlin. New York: Free Press of Glencoe, 1963.

Wimsatt, William K. "Organic Form: Some Questions About a Metaphor." In *Organic Form: The Life of an Idea*, edited by G. S. Rouseau. London: Routledge & Keagan Paul, 1972.

Witte, Martin. "Zur Programmgebundenheit der Sinfonien Mendelssohns." In *Das Problem Mendelssohn*, edited by Carl Dahlhaus.

Wolff, Hellmuth Christian. "Zur Erstausgabe von Mendelssohns Jugendsinfonien." *Deutsches Jahrbuch der Musikwissenschaft* 12 (1967): 96–113.

Wolzogen, Hans von. *Erinnerungen an Richard Wagner*. Leipzig, n. d.

Young, David P. *Something of Great Constancy: The Art of "A Midsummer Night's Dream."* Yale Studies in English, vol. 164. New Haven and London: Yale University Press, 1966.

INDEX

*Page numbers in boldface type indicate the inclusion of musical examples.